D0873936

Thomas Randolph
B. A. 1627-8.

Thomas Randolph
M. A. 1631-2.

BIRTHPLACE OF THOMAS RANDOLPH

POETICAL AND DRAMATIC WORKS

OF

THOMAS RANDOLPH

OF TRINITY COLLEGE, CAMBRIDGE

*Now First Collected and Edited from the early Copies and
from MSS. with some Account of the Author
and Occasional Notes*

BY

W. CAREW HAZLITT

Sæculi sui Ovidius dici meruit
JAMES DUPORT

VOL. I.

BENJAMIN BLOM   New York / London

First Published 1875
Reissued 1968 by
Benjamin Blom, Inc., Bronx, New York 10452
and 56 Doughty Street, London, W.C. 1
Library of Congress Catalog Card Number 68-57192

PRINTED IN THE USA
BY
HALLMARK LITHOGRAPHERS, INC.

PREFATORY NOTICE.

—o—

S O long ago as 1833, the late Mr Dyce, who cannot
be suspected of an undiscriminating enthusiasm
for our old writers, remarked "that Randolph's works
deserve to be reprinted ;"[1] the Rev. Joseph Hunter
("New Illustrations of Shakespeare," 1845) speaks
of this poet as "less known than he deserves to be ;"
and that such a republication has not hitherto been
attempted, while a crowd of obscurer and less valuable
authors have found editors, appears to be one of
those anomalies and caprices of fortune which it is
impossible to account for. Of all the minor English
poets of his century, Randolph may perhaps be
considered as standing at the head. He was distinguished by his wealth and happiness of fancy, a
fertile and racy wit, and a vein of thought the fresh-
ness of which always charms, while its mellowness
and propriety in one so young cannot fail to take us
agreeably by surprise. Possibly if he had lived to
publish his works, he would have pruned some of the
luxuriances of his too libertine muse. In the early
development of his powers, and the precocity of his
genius, he excelled even Browne, Suckling, and Carew;
and on the whole, his writings must be allowed to

---

[1] Shirley's Works, 1833, i. lxxvii.

hold a far higher place in our literature than those of the three poets just named.

The present edition embraces everything which is known to be extant from the poet's pen, both in prose and verse. All the early printed copies from 1638 to 1668 are more or less imperfect and inaccurate, and the following pages contain, with the fullest account of Randolph's life, much that has not hitherto been collected, and several pieces believed to be now printed for the first time. The portrait which faces the title has been carefully re-engraved from the original print attached to the edition of 1640.

I am indebted to the kindness of Mr Henry Huth and Mr F. W. Cosens for the loan of several MSS. referred to in the course of the book; to Mr A. G. Greenhill, of St John's College, Cambridge, for his help in getting me the dates of Randolph's admission, &c., at Trinity; and to Mr H. R. Luard for a tracing of the autograph signatures of the poet from the College Register.

Colonel Chester obligingly informs me that he has made repeated search for the will of the poet at Doctors' Commons without success; but it is more than probable that Randolph died intestate.

W. C. H.

KENSINGTON, LONDON
March 1875.

SOME ACCOUNT OF THOMAS RANDOLPH.

—— o ——

THOMAS RANDOLPH, one of the most delightful lyric and dramatic poets of his age, was the second son of William Randolph, gentleman, of Hammes (now Hamsey), in the hundred of Barcombe, and rape of Lewes, county of Sussex, by his first wife, Elizabeth, daughter of Thomas Smith, of Newnham-cum-Badley, near Daventry, Co. Northampton. The poet's father was steward to Edward Lord Zouch.

The poet was born in 1605 at the house of his maternal grandfather, in whose descendants the place remained down to the early years of the present century.[1] Its state, in Baker the Northamptonshire historian's day, is shown by an illustration which he gives. "It stands," says he, "on a bank at the end of the lane leading to Dodford." Of the other members of Randolph's family we know nothing, except that he had a younger brother Robert who, according to Baker, took holy orders, and whose name will occur again.

Randolph was baptized on the 15th June 1605, received his education at Westminster as a King's Scholar, and was thence chosen into Trinity College,

---

[1] Baker's "Northamptonshire," i. 261.

Cambridge.   He was matriculated a pensioner of
Trinity College July 8, 1624, and graduated B.A. in
January 1627–8, his name appearing eighth on the list
of bachelors.   He was admitted a minor fellow 22d
of September 1629, and major fellow 23d March
1631–2, when he proceeded M.A.   In 1631–2 he was
incorporated M.A. at Oxford, but the precise date
seems to be wanting.

He very early began to exercise his poetical talents,
if it be true, as it has been said, that a " History of the
Incarnation of our Saviour," in verse, extant in Wood's
time (it seems)[1] in the juvenile author's own hand-
writing, was composed at the age of nine or ten years.
As he grew up, the ingenuity of his literary perform-
ances procured him the esteem, as we shall see by
numerous testimonies, of all who had any pretensions
to wit, among the rest of Ben. Jonson,[2] who adopted
him as one of his sons, Thomas Bancroft, Sir Aston
Cokain, and Shirley the dramatist, but particularly of
those private and attached acquaintances, the Hattons
of Kirby and the Staffords of Blatherwick, in Northamptonshire, both of whom afforded him substantial
tokens of their regard and affectionate friendship.

Among Randolph's works are three poetical effusions
addressed to Jonson, of which one purports to have
been composed on the occasion of his literary adoption, and another at the time when the veteran
dramatist was out of humour with the public in consequence of the failure of the " New Inn."   The
third is entitled " An Eclogue to Mr Jonson," and is

---

[1] " Athenæ," edit. Bliss, i. 564-6, and see " Fasti," under
1631.
[2] Among the verses which accompany the " Jealous Lovers,"
1632, is a copy addressed to Randolph's master, Master
Osboston.   They are couched in grateful and respectful terms,
and the young poet gives his tutor the merit of everything which
he has written worthy of preservation.   An amiable hyperbole !

the most interesting of all, since it portrays Randolph's early life and studies at Cambridge, before he came to the metropolis.

His lively and agreeable conversation had the unfortunate effect of drawing him into the company of boisterous and quarrelsome spirits; and in one instance, at some festive gathering, a fray arose, in which the poet lost one of his fingers. Upon this accident he wrote two copies of verses,[1] inserted in the editions of his works.

It is to be concluded that an irregular and too free mode of living had the effect of shortening Randolph's valuable and busy life. After residing with his father for some time at Little Houghton, Northamptonshire, he went to stay with William Stafford of Blatherwick, where (under what precise circumstances is not known) he died in March 1634-5, in his thirtieth year.[2] On the 17th of the month he was buried in an aisle adjoining to Blathcrwick Church, among the Stafford family; and subsequently Sir Christopher (afterwards Lord) Hatton caused a monument of white marble, wreathed with laurel, to be erected to his friend's memory, with the following inscription, written by Peter Hausted, of Cambridge : [3]—

---

[1] Only one appears in the 4o of 1638, but both occur in the editions of 1640-3, '52, '64, '68. It also appears from a passage in one of his poems that latterly he was marked by the smallpox.

[2] Both Mr Dyce and Mr Collier point out the discrepancy between the date of Randolph's birth and death, as given in the biographies and the inscription upon Marshall's portrait, published in 1640, in which the poet is represented as having died in 1634, *an æt.* 27 ; but perhaps the wording of this statement may have been careless, and the meaning may be that Randolph was twenty-seven when the likeness engraved after his decease was taken.

[3] Hausted was the author of a play called "The Rival Friends," printed in 1632, after a good deal of difficulty,

Memoriæ Sacrum

THOMÆ RANDOLPHI (dum inter pauciores) Fœlicissimi et facillimi ingenii Juvenis necnon majora promittentis si fata virum non invidissent sæculo.

> Here sleepe thirteene
> Together in one tombe.
> And all these greate, yet quarrell not for rome :
> The Muses and yᵉ Graces teares did meete
> And grav'd these letters on yᵉ churlish sheete,
> Who having wept their fountaines drye
> Through the conduit of the eye,
> For their freind who here does lye,
> Crept into his grave and dyed,
> And soe the Riddle is untyed.
> For wᶜʰ this Church, proud that thè Fates bequeath
> Unto her ever-honour'd trust
> Soe much and that soe precious dust,
> Hath crown'd her temples with an Iuye wreath,
> Wᶜʰ should have Laurelle beene,
> But yᵗ the grieved plant to see him dead
> Tooke pet and withered.

Cujus cineres brevi hac (qua potuit) imortalitate donat Christopherus Hatton, Miles de Balneo et Musarū amator. Illius vero (quem deflemus) supplendâ carminibus quæ marmoris et æris scandalum manebunt perpetuum."

The two anecdotes,[1] which I subjoin here, of the poet may be presumed to rest on some traditional foundation, and are at any rate worth quoting as the only things of the sort which appear to have been handed down—

---

occasioned by some offence it gave when performed before the king and queen at Cambridge, 19th March 1631-2. Hausted did not contribute any of the laudatory poems prefixed to the early copies of Randolph's works. See Halliwell's "Dictionary of Old Plays," in *v.* A curious copy of verses upon Hausted's "Rival Friends" is inserted in Mr Huth's "Inedited Poetical Miscellanies," 1870. Hausted was also the author of a Latin drama called "Senile Odium," performed at Queen's College, Cambridge, and printed in 12°, 1633.

[1] Hazlitt's "New London Jest-Book," 1871, p. 338.

" Randolph, who was then a student in Cambridge, having stayed in London so long that he might truly be said to have had a parley with his empty purse, was resolved to see Ben Jonson with his associates who, as he heard, at a set time kept a club together at the Devil Tavern, near Temple Bar. Accordingly he went thither at the specified time ; but, being unknown to them, and wanting money, which, to a spirit like Tom's, was the most daunting thing in the world, he peeped into the room where they were, and was espied by Ben Jonson, who, seeing him in a scholar's threadbare habit, cried out, 'John Bo-peep, come in !' which accordingly he did. They immediately began to rhyme upon the meanness of his clothes, asking him if he could not make a verse, and withal to call for his quart of sack. There being but four of them, he immediately replied—

> 'I John Bo-peep,
> To you four sheep,
> With each one his good fleece ;
> If that you are willing,
> To give me five shilling,
> 'Tis fifteen pence a-piece.'

'Why,' exclaimed Ben Jonson, 'I believe this is my son Randolph ;' which being made known to them, he was kindly entertained in their company, and Ben Jonson ever after called him his son."

The other story is taken from the MS. common-place-book of Henry Oxinden of Barham, 1647, and is called "Randolph his answer to some merry companion"—

"Several wits being a drinking together, hearing that Randolph the poet was in the house, being desirous to make sport with him, sent for him into their company. Randolph came to them : they in their discourse propounded who was the best poet, so one said Virgil, another Horace, another Ovid, &c., and gave their reasons. Randolph being demanded his opinion, said he thought the sweet singer of Israel the best. They asked him why? He said because—

> 'From all the ills that I have done, Lord, quit me out of hand,
> And make me not a scorne to fools that nothing understand.'"

The following has been attributed to several poets, but Sir Aston Cokain, it will be presently seen, in his "Poems," 1658, gives it to Randolph ; and elsewhere the (no doubt apocryphal) story is still further im-

proved, and acclimatised by the introduction in it
of Henrietta Maria as the heroine—

> " Si verum hoc esset, *pauper ubique jacet,*
> In thalamis, regina, tuis hâc nocte jacerem "—

Englished.

> " Queen, in your chamber I should lie to-night,
> If *a poor man lies everywhere,* were right."

" *To Sir Robert Hilliard.*

> " Who made this distich, it is fit I tell,
> Which I have Englished but indiff'rent well—
> I think Tom Randolph. Pardon what's amiss
> In my translation for my gift of his.
> Whom you and I so well did love and know,
> When Cambridge (for his wit) extoll'd him so."

So far Cokain. The *jeu-d'esprit,* however, is far
older than Randolph's time, and is to be found in
Italian in Domenichi's "Facetie, Motti, e Burle," 1565,
p. 459, where the reply is attributed to the secretary
of the Queen of Poland.

Cokain speaks of his personal acquaintance with
Randolph—

> " Donne, Suckling, *Randolph,* Drayton, Massinger,
> Habington, Sandys, May, my acquaintance were ;
> Jonson, Chapman, and Holland I have seen."

And Thomas Bancroft, in his "Two Books of Epigrams and Epitaphs," 1639, has the following—

" *On Thomas Randall.*

> " Who knew not this brave spark of Phœbus ? whose
> Both life and learning might detraction pose,
> Save only that he drank too greedily
> Of the Muses' spring, and left the Sisters dry ?
> Who (smiling) therefore gave the Fates command
> His body to convert to pearly sand,
> And strew it in their fountain, there to shine
> Like his clear thoughts, and make this draught divine."

In the Address to the Reader attached to the
"Jealous Lovers," 1632, Randolph himself observes :
"I do not aim at the name of a poet. I have always
admired the free raptures of poetry ; but it is too
unthrifty a science for my fortunes."

As elsewhere noticed,[1] Randolph is commemo-
rated by George Daniel of Beswick among the choice
spirits of his age—

> "The noble Falkland, Digby, Carew, Mayne,
>   Beaumont, Sands, *Randolph*, Allen, Rutter, May."

The opinions and feelings of men of the period
who might have seen and known him, as some of
them no doubt did, had and have their illustrative
value. In some verses before Harding's "Sicily and
Naples, or the Fatal Union," 1640, the writer places
our poet on a sort of literary equality with Jonson—

> "Thus, friend, the bays still flourish. Jonson dead,
>   Randolph deceas'd, they fall to crown thy head."

And Rowland Watkyns, in his "Poems without
Fictions," 1662, has a piece entitled "The Poet's Con-
dition," where Jonson and Randolph are set side by
side, and both placed in very good company (p. 110)—

> "A poet, and rich? that seems to be
>   A paradox most strange to me.
>   A poet, and poor? that maxim's true,
>   If we observe the canting crue.
>   What lands had *Randolph*, or great *Ben*,
>   That plow'd much paper with his pen?
>   Wise *Chaucer*, as old records say,
>   Had never but his length of clay :
>   And by some men I have been told,
>   That *Cleaveland* had more brains than gold.
>   Show me a poet, and I'll show thee
>   An emblem of rich poverty :
>   An hundred verses, though divine,
>   Will never buy one pint of wine."

---

[1] Carew's Poems, by Hazlitt, p. xlv.

An anonymous contributor to "Witts Recreations" (edit. 1817, p. 11), adopts a highly complimentary strain—

> "*To Mr Thomas Randolph.*
>
> "Thou darling of the Muses, for we may
>   Be thought deserving; if, what was thy play
>   Our utmost labours can produce, we will
>   Freely allow thee heir unto the hill
>   The Muses did assign thee, and think't fit
>   Thy younger years should have the elder wit."

Winstanley says of Randolph: "He was one of such a pregnant wit, that the Muses may seem not only to have smiled, but to have been tickled at his nativity, such the festivity of his poems of all sorts."[1] Philips had, a few years before, given an equally favourable character of him: "Thomas Randolph, one of the most pregnant young wits of his time, flourishing in the University of Cambridge, the quiet conceit and clear poetic fancy discovered in his extant poems seemed to promise something extraordinary from him, had not his indulgence to the too liberal converse with the multitude of his applauders drawn him to such an immoderate way of living as, in all probability, shortened his days."[2]

Even if the memorials of the poet were more ample than they are, it would be improper to exclude the graceful and tender tribute offered to him, in the nature of an epitaph, by his early friend Dr James Duport. The lines have been transcribed from a volume by Duport little known to literary inquirers,

---

[1] "Lives of English Poets," 1687, p. 142. It is rather curious that Headley, in his "Select Beauties," 1787 and 1810, does not so much as name Randolph—an undoubted oversight. Ellis, however, gives some specimens of him.

[2] "Theatrum Poetarum," 1675, edit. 1824, p. 16.

yet containing a good deal of useful and curious bio-
graphical information.[1]

"In obitum THOMÆ RANDOLPHI, M.A. Collegii Trinitatis
Cantab. Socii, Poetæ Ingeniosissimi, et qui sæculi sui Ovidius
dici meruit.

"Alpha Poetarum, Musarum sola voluptas
Castaliique decus deliciumque Chori,
Quam, Randolphe, novem te deperiere sorores,
Et te certârunt æmula turba, frui ;
Zelotypæ tui Amatrices : ita scilicet olim
Me memini scenæ præcinuisse tuæ.
Cum nos Occidui eduxit Schola Regia Petri,
Ingenium dispar : anni, animique pares.
Quando puer jussus tecum componere versus,
Conjunctus toties anser olore fui.
Quam facilis tibi vena fuit ! quam mobile plectrum !
Quam leni et placido Musa tenore fluens !
Credo ego Peligni genium migrâsse Poetæ
In pectus, vates ingeniose, tuum.
Huic Ovidi et fatum tibi contigit : exul ab urbe
Qui nempe, et nobis, tam cito factus erat.
Nec tamen offensi rapuit te Cæsaris ira
Nec tua te fecit ficta Corinna reum.
Te sed amicorum nobis malus abstulit error
Ingeniique tui non moderatus amor.
Immodicis brevis est ætas, et rara senectus
Hæc tua culpa fuit, te placuisse nimis."

In the absence of material for the formation of a
definite or confident opinion as to Randolph's personal intimacies, it would be of course useless to
advance any vague theories on the subject. It is
sufficiently certain that Duport was one of the fore-
most of his early college friends, and that with
Anthony Stafford and Sir Christopher Hatton the
younger he was on the best and most affectionate
terms. We do not believe that of Jonson, and the
circle by which that poet was surrounded, Randolph
ever knew actually much ; and the very anecdote

---

[1] "Musæ Subsecivæ," 1696, pp. 469-70.

where the younger poet's adoption by Jonson is narrated seems to confirm such a view. Randolph probably, indeed, spent a good deal of his short time at the University or in Northamptonshire, and at the period to which the story referred to must belong—a period when our author had done quite enough to render his name celebrated—his appearance could not have been unfamiliar to Jonson and the rest, if Randolph had been at all in the habit of frequenting their society.

The sixth volume of the *Retrospective Review* has an excellent article, occupying twenty-seven pages, on Randolph, to whose high merits and qualities it does ample justice. As the *Review* now ranks among scarce books, it may be allowable to transcribe the more important parts of the article. " Thomas Randolph," observes the critic, " was one of those bright spirits which burn too fast, cast a vivid flash over their time, and then suddenly expire. He seems to have been so supplied with vigour, both mental and corporeal, as to have started, pursued, and ended his race by the time that the phlegmatic genius of other men is just ready for the course. He died before the age of twenty-nine, and yet can hardly be said to have lived a shorter time than other men, with such enjoyment did he consume his minutes, in such a state of excitement did he spend his days and nights, such a number of ideas flashed through his brain, so many kindred spirits doubled his gratifications by sharing his pleasures. He passed through the University, where the brilliancy of his wit and the liveliness of his manners made him a general favourite, and where his talents ensured him success, and his poetical productions brought him in a large harvest of fame which, on his removal from Cambridge to London, secured him a most cordial reception from the wits and poets of the metropolis. . . . .

" In the University he was a fellow in one of the most wealthy and considerable foundations : when he died, he had a brother at Christ Church, Oxford : his death took place at the house of an ancient family in Staffordshire [Northamptonshire], with the ancestors of which he was buried, and had a monument erected to his memory at the charge of his friend [Sir Christopher, afterwards] Lord Hatton. . . . .

" The qualifications of Randolph as a poet we fortunately need not rest on the word of a panegyrist. The poems speak for themselves. . . . . They bear evidence of a most varied and highly-endowed nature ; for they are full of lively sallies of wit and fancy, deep learning, shrewd observations on man, and eloquent descriptions of passions."

The "Aristippus" and "Conceited Peddler," printed together in 1630, were probably early pieces of drollery, partly arising out of the author's academical reading, and partly out of a shrewd observation of the abuses of the time.[1] When Allot, the publisher of the tract, procured a licence for it at Stationers' Hall, in April 1630, he entered it in the books as the work of *Robert Davenport ;* but an uncertainty, perhaps, as to the correctness of his ascription, or a disavowal on the part of the reputed writer, led subsequently to the issue of the small volume without any name attached. A MS. copy had probably found its way to London, and fell into the bookseller's hands without Randolph's knowledge or sanction.

In his " Jealous Lovers " the poet has adopted from

---

[1] Randolph's " Aristippus " differs from the character portrayed by Gower in his " Confessio Amantis," and by Edwards in his " Damon and Pithias " (Hazlitt's Dodsley, iv.) The original authority for him is Diogenes Laertius.

Jonson's "Cynthia's Revels," 1601, the name of Asotus, and there are one or two indications that the later drama owed a few of its touches to its author's recollection of the earlier one. But far heavier obligations would not have deprived Randolph's work of its claim to be regarded as an original composition. Randolph seems to have been struck by the name Asotus; for we meet with it again among the *dramatis personæ* of "The Muses' Looking-Glass."

To the present collected edition two poems have been first added (among several others): "The High and Mighty Commendation of a Pot of Good Ale," and "The Battle fought between the Norfolk Cock and the Wisbeach Cock." They were printed together, as by *Thomas Randall*, a very usual mode at that time of spelling the poet's name, in a 4° tract of four leaves, published in 1642; and their insertion appeared to be warranted, notwithstanding their exclusion from the editions after 1642, by the threefold consideration that all those editions were very negligently superintended, that we are without any ground for challenging the almost contemporary attribution, and that at the time of the publication of the first and second impressions, in 1638–40, the two pieces may have lain in MS. in the hands of some private acquaintance, to whom Randolph perhaps communicated them. At the same time, it would be improper to conceal the fact that, in an early MS. Miscellany in the library of Mr Huth, the "Combat of the Cocks" is (rightly or wrongly) said in the heading of the verses there to have taken place June 17, 1637, which would of course at once set Randolph's claim to them aside. These poetical commonplace-books are, however, not very trustworthy.

The only prose works known to be extant from Randolph's pen is the address prepared, and probably delivered, by him in 1632 as Cambridge "Prevaricator." It is couched in the facetious and satirical vein custom-

ary on such occasions, and introduces a notice of Peter
Hausted's "Rival Friends" and "Senile Odium,"
the former of which the author met with some difficulty
in publishing. Randolph also alludes to the suspension
and incarceration of certain Oxford *Terræ Filii;* but
the whole allocution is jocular and inconsequent. The
"Oratio" is preserved in a small octavo MS. in Mr
Huth's library, distinguished elsewhere as the "Scatter-
good MS." It has not been found in print.

Besides the works printed in the present volume,
Randolph wrote a play entitled "The Prodigal
Scholar," which was extant in MS. so late as 1660,
on the 29th of June of which year it was licensed for
the press. It seems to have perished. On the 8th
April 1630, Robert Allot entered at Stationers' Hall a
piece called the "Peddler," ascribing it to Robert
Davenport, but doubtless this was an error on Allot's
part, and the "Peddler" was no other than Randolph's
production, printed at the end of his "Aristippus,"
1630, of which Allot was the publisher.

From Randolph's "Conceited Peddler" Dodsley
took the hint of his dramatic performance called "The
Toy-shop."

Manuscript copies of many of Randolph's poems
are preserved in public and private libraries, namely,
for instance, in Ashmole MS. 38, Harl. MSS. 3357 and
6918, Addit. MS. 11,811, three or four MSS. Miscellanies in the library of Mr Henry Huth, and in one or
two in that of Mr F. W. Cosens. But, as a general rule,
the manuscript work of the seventeenth century is of
very inferior importance to that of the preceding cen-
turies, and presents, to a large extent in fact, a de-
based and corrupt text of the printed books of the
period. Of course there are such matters as autograph originals, and other occasional exceptions; and
there are, again, cases where the MSS. form our only
resource. But where an author has been thought

worth paper and print by his own generation, the published volume contains, in nine instances out of ten, superior and purer readings, the MSS. being often derived merely from the printed text, with the accession of such blunders of every kind as an illiterate and slovenly scribe might be expected to perpetrate. With original prints it is otherwise, for the copy of a detached poem, contributed to a collection of University verses, or some other temporary demand, will be found more frequently or not freer from errors than the text inserted in a subsequent collected edition of the writer's works ; and again, with singularly few reservations, the *editio princeps* of a poet is more correct than its successors, though the latter undoubtedly were set up from the parent volume. The earliest impression of Randolph, as Mr Heber (I believe) first pointed out, is also the best and most exempt from errors of the press.

TABLE OF CONTENTS.

———o———

PAGE

PAGE

ARISTIPPUS,

OR

THE JOVIAL PHILOSOPHER.

EDITIONS.

Aristippvs, Or, The Ioviall Philosopher. Presented in a priuate Shew. To which is added, The Conceited Pedler. Omnis Aristippum decuit color et status et res. Semel insaniuimus. London. Printed for Robert Allot. MDCXXX. 4°.

Aristippvs . . . . London, Printed for Robert Allot. M.DC.XXXI. 4°.

Aristippvs . . . . London, Printed for Robert Allot. MDCXXXV. 4°.

Aristippus is also included in the collected editions of Randolph, 1652-68.

Mr Halliwell remarks (*Dict. of Old Plays*, 1860, in *v.*)— "*Aristippus* would appear, from the quaintness of the title, to have been written humorously, to excuse those excesses to which the author was too fatally attached. . . . . Its curiosity, in a literary point of view, we do not remember to have seen noticed. In addition to allusions to Muld Sack, Robin Goodfellow, Taylor the Water-Poet, Banks's horse, Scoggin's fleas, Skelton, Fennor, &c., there is a ridicule of the prologue of Shakespeare's *Troilus and Cressida;* and at p. 21 is a line which Milton has nearly verbally copied in his poem of *L'Allegro.* There is a copy of this play in the British Museum, MS. Sloane, 2531."

Randolph's *Aristippus,* slight as it is in conception and structure, must be admitted to be a masterpiece of wit and pleasantry. It was probably an early production, yet it exhibits traces of tolerably wide reading, and possesses an abundant store of humorous and popular allusions. The same is to be said of the *Conceited Peddler,* which is a shrewd satire on the follies and vices of the age, as pungent as it is sparkling. Neither of these dramatic efforts was intended, it is to be presumed, for representation.

THE PRÆLUDIUM.

Shews having been long intermitted, and forbidden by authority for their abuses, could not be raised but by conjuring.[1]

Enter PROLOGUE, *in a Circle.*

BE not deceiv'd, I have no bended knees,
   No supple tongue, no speeches steep'd in oil ;
No candied flattery, nor honied words.
I come, an armed Prologue : arm'd with Arts ;
Who, by my sacred charms and my stick-skill,
By virtue of this all-commanding wand,
Stoln from the sleepy Mercury, will raise
From black abyss and sooty hell that mirth
Which fits their learned round.   Thou long-dead Shew,
Break from thy marble prison ; sleep no more
In miry darkness ; henceforth I forbid thee
To bathe in Lethe's muddy waves : ascend
As bright as morning from her Tithon's bed,
And red with kisses that have stain'd thy cheek,
Grow fresh again.   What ! is my power contemn'd ?

---

[1] Interludes, common shows, &c., were forbidden on Sundays, by a statute of Charles I., June 8, 1625. See it printed in "The English Drama and Stage," 1869, p. 59, and compare Collier, ii. 1, 2. I suppose this to be the authoritative prohibition referred to.

Dost thou not hear my call, whose power extends
To blast the bosom of our mother Earth?
To remove heaven's whole frame from off her hinges,
And to reverse all Nature's laws?   Ascend,
Or I will call a band of Furies forth,
And all the torments wit of hell can frame,
Shall force thee up.

Enter SHOW, *whipt by two Furies.*

Show. O, spare your too officious whips awhile,
Give some small respite to my panting limbs.
Let me have leave to speak, and truce to parley.
Whose powerful voice hath forc'd me to salute
This hated air.   Are not my pains sufficient,
But you must torture me with sad remembrance
Of my deserts, the causes of my exile?
Pro. 'Tis thy release I seek; I come to file
Those heavy shackles from thy wearied limbs,
And give thee leave to walk the stage again,
As free as Virtue.   Burn thy wither'd bays,
And with fresh laurel crown thy sacred temples;
Cast off thy mask of darkness, and appear
As glorious as thy sister Comedy.
But first with tears wash off thy guilty sin:
Purge out those ill-digested dregs of wit,
That use their ink to blot a spotless fame.
Let's have no one particular man traduc'd:
But, like a noble eagle, seize on vice,
As she flies, bold and open—spare the persons.
Let us have simple mirth and innocent laughter,
Sweet smiling lips, and such as hide no fangs,
No venomous biting teeth, or forked tongues.
Then shall thy freedom be restor'd again,
And full applause be wages of thy pain.
Show. Then from the depth of truth I here protest,
I do disclaim all petulant hate and malice;

I will not touch such men as I know vicious,
Much less the good.   I will not dare to say,
That such a one paid for his fellowship,
And had no learning but in's purse ; no officer
Need fear the sting of my detraction.
I'll give all leave to fill their guts in quiet.
I'll make no dangerous almanacks, no gulls,
No posts with envious news and biting packets,
You need not fear this show, you that are bad—
It is no Parliament.   You that nothing have,
Like scholars, but a beard and gown, for me
May pass for good, grand Sophies ; all my skill
Shall beg but honest laughter, and such smiles
As might become a Cato : I shall give
No cause to grieve that once more yet I live.

   Pro. Go, then ; and you, beagles of hell, avant,
Return to your eternal plagues.   [*Exeunt* FURIES.

   Pro. Here take these purer robes and, clad in these,
Be thou all glorious, and instruct thy mirth
With thy sweet temper ; while I entreat
Thy friends, that long lamented thy sad fates,
To sit and taste, and to accept thy cates.

                    [*Exit* SHOW.

   Pro. Sit, see, and hear, and censure, he that will ;
I come to have my mirth approv'd, not skill :
Your laughter['s] all I beg, and where you see
No jest worth laughing at, faith, laugh at me.

Aristippus.

Enter SIMPLICIUS.

*SECUNDUM gradum compossibilitatis, et non
secundùm gradum incompossibilitatis.* What
should this Scotus [1] mean by his possibilities and in-
compossibilities? my Cooper, Rider, Thomas, and
Minsheu, are as far to seek as myself: not a word
of *compossibilitas* or *incompossibilitas* is there. Well,
I know what I'll do. I have heard of a great philosopher; I'll try what he can do. They call him
Aristippus, Aristippus, Aristippus. Sure, a philosopher's name. But they say he lies at the Dolphin,
and that, methinks, is an ill sign : yet they say, too,
the best philosophers of the town never lie from
thence. They say 'tis a tavern, too. For my part I
cannot tell; I know no part of the town, but the
Schools and Aristotle's well; but since I am come
thus far, I will inquire ; for this same *compossibilitas*
or *incompossibilitas* sticks in my stomach.   [*Knocks.*

Boy within. Anon, anon, sir.

Sim. What philosophy is this?   [*Knocks.*

Boy. Anon, anon, sir.

Enter BOY.

Boy. Please you see a room, sir? what would you
have, sir?

Sim. Nothing but Aristippus.

Boy. You shall, sir.

Sim. What is this? the Dolphin? now verily it

---

[1] Duns Scotus.

looks like a green fish. What's yonder? Greek, too? now surely it is the Philosopher's motto: *Hippathi, hippathi, aut disce, aut discede incontinenter*—a very good disjunction.

Boy. A pint of Aristippus to the bar.

Enter BOY *again.*

Boy. Here, sir.

Sim. Ha, what's this?

Boy. Did not you ask for Aristippus, sir?

Sim. The great Philosopher lately come hither.

Boy. Why, this is Aristippus.

Sim. Verily, then, Aristippus is duplex, *Nominalis et Realis;* or else the Philosopher lives like Diogenes in dolio, the President of Hogs-head College. But I mean one Aristippus κατ' ἐξιχὴν, the great Philosopher.

Boy. I know not what you mean by losopher, but here be scholars in the house—I'll send them to you. Anon, anon, sir; I cannot be here and there, too. Anon, anon, sir.   [*Exit.*

Sim. This boy would have put a fallacy upon me *in interrogatione plurium:* this boy is a mere animal; ha, ha, he! he has not a jot of language more than *Anon, anon, sir.* O Giggleswick, thou happy place of education! This poor wretch knows not what a philosopher means. To see the simpleness of these people! They do everything ἀπλῶς, and have not a jot, nor an inch of κατὰ τί in them. O, what had become of me, if I had not gone barefoot to my preceptor with a satchel at my back?

Enter two SCHOLARS.

Slaves are they that heap up mountains,
Still desiring more and more:

Still let's carouse in Bacchus' fountains,
Never dreaming to be poor.
Give us then a cup of liquor,
Fill it up unto the brim;
For then (methinks) my wits grow quicker,
When my brains in liquor swim.

Ha! brave Aristippus,
Pox of Aristotle and Plato, a company of dry rascals!
But hey, brave Aristippus!

Sim. Certainly these are Aristippus his scholars!
Sir, pray can you resolve me what is *gradus compossibilitatis?*

   1st Schol. *What ails thee, thou musing man?*
       Diddle diddle doo.

   2d Schol. *Quench thy sorrows in a can,*
       Diddle diddle doo.

Compossibilitas? why, that's nothing, man; when
you ne'er drink beyond your *poculum necessitatis,* you
are *in gradu incompossibili* to all good fellowship.
Come, hang Scotus, we'll lead you to Aristippus. One
epitome of his in quarto is worth a whole volume of
these Dunces.

Sim. O gentlemen, you will bind me to thank you
in *poculo gratiarum.* But what philosophy doth he
read, and what hours doth he keep?

1st Schol. None at all precisely, but indistinctly all;
night and day he pours forth his instructions, and fills
you out of measure.

2d Schol. He'll make the eyes of your understanding
see double, and teach you to speak fluently, and utter
your mind in abundance.

Sim. Hath he many scholars, sir?

1st Schol. More than all the philosophers in the town
besides. He never rests but is still called for. Aris-

tippus, says one; Aristippus, says another. He is generally asked for; yea, and by doctors sometimes.

2d Schol. And as merry a man. There can be no feast but he is sent for; and all the company are the merrier for him.

1st Schol. Did you but once hear him, you would so love his company, you would never after endure to stand alone.

Sim. O, pray help me to the sight of him.

2d Schol. We will, brave boy; and when you have seen him, you'll think yourself in another world, and scorn to be your own man any longer.

Sim. But, I pray you, at what price reads he?

1st Schol. Why, truly his price hath been raised of late, and his very name makes him the dearer.

2d Schol. A diligent lecturer deserves eightpence a pint tuition. Nay, if you will learn anything, scholarship must be paid for. Academical simony is lawful: nay, did you ever hear of a good preacher in a fat benefice, unless his purse were the leaner for it? Make much of him; for we shall have no more such in haste.

Enter WILD-MAN.

Sim. But who is this?

1st Schol. The University Ramist, a malt heretic, *alias* the Wild-man, that is grown mad to see the daily resort to Aristippus—but let us leave him to his frenzies.

> *But comè, you lads that love Canary,*
> *Let us have a mad fegary :*
> *Hither, hither, hither, hither,*
> *All good fellows flock together.* [*Exeunt.*

Wild-m. Brains, wits, senses, all fly hence. Let fools live limed in cages; I am the Wild-man, and I will be wild. Is this an age to be in a man's right wits, when the lawful use of the throat is so much

neglected, and strong drink lies sick on his death-bed?
'Tis above the patience of a malt-house to see the
contempt of barley, and not run mad upon't.   This
is Aristippus, Aristippus!   Now a devil or two take
his red-nosed philosophy!   'Tis he, my beer, that has
vowed thee to the vinegar bottle; but I'll be revenged.   When next I meet him, I'll twist and twitch
his bush-beard from his tavern face; 'tis not his
Hipathie hapathie can carry him out.   Let him look
to be soundlier dashed by me, than ever he was by
Drawer, for his impudence.   I'll teach my Spanish
Don a French trick; I'll either plague him with a
pox, or have some claret-whore burn him for an
heretic, and make him challenge acquaintance of
mulled sack.   If he was not either sent hither from the
British Politic, or be not employed by Spinola to
seduce the king's lawful subjects from their allegiance
to strong beer, let me hold up my hand at the bar,
and be hanged at my sign-post if he had not a hand
in the powder treason!   Well, I say nothing; but he
has blown up good store of men in his days, houses,
and lands, and all.   If they take no order with him
here in the University, the poor country were as
good have the man in the moon for their pastor as a
scholar.   They are all so infected with Aristippus
his Arminianism, they can preach no doctrine but
sack and red noses.   As for the Wild-man, they have
made him horn-mad already.

Enter a Fellow crying wine-pots.

Heyday, there goes the Hunts up! this is the mandrake's voice that undoes me: you may hear him, in
faith.   This is the devil of his that goes up and down
like a roaring sheepshead to gather his Pewter Library.
I'll fit him, i' faith.   [*Beats him.*]   Now you calves'-
skin impudence, I'll thresh your jacket.   [*Beats him
out.*]

Enter ARISTIPPUS *and his two* SCHOLARS.

Arist. What a coil's here ! what fellow's that ? he looks like a mad hogshead of March-beer that had run out, and threatened a deluge. What's he ?

1st Schol. O, 'tis the Wild-man ! a zealous brother, that stands up against the persecution of barley-broth, and will maintain a degree above the reputation of *aqua vitæ.*

2d Schol. I have heard him swear by his *hora octava,* that sack and *Rosa solis* is but water-gruel to it.

Wild-m. O, art thou there, Saint Dunstan ? thou hast undone me, thou cursed Friar Bacon, thou hellish Merlin. But I'll be revenged upon thee ! 'Tis not your Mephistopheles, nor any other spirits of ruby or carbuncle, that you can raise, nor your good father-in-law Doctor Faustus, that conjures so many of us into your wives' circle, that with all their magic shall secure you from my rage. You have set a spell for any man's coming into my house now.

Arist. Why, none of my credit hath choked up your doors !

Wild-m. But thou hast bewitched my threshold, disturbed my house, and I'll have thee hanged in gibbets for murthering my beer ! I'll have thee tried by a jury of tapsters, and hanged in anon, anon, sir, thou dismal and disastrous conjuror.

Arist. Why dost thou call me conjuror ? I send no fairies to pinch you, or elves to molest you : has Robin Goodfellow troubled you so much of late ? I scarce believe it ; for I am sure, since sack and I came to town, your house hath not been so much haunted.

Wild-m. I'll put out thine eyes, Don Canarios : I'll scratch thee to atoms, thou Spanish Guzman.

Arist. If he and his beer will not be quiet, draw 'um both out.

Wild-m. Yet I'll be revenged, you rascal. I do not fear the Spanish Inquisition : I'll run to the Council, and bewray thy villany. I'll carry thee bound for a traitor. But for you, sir, we had taken Cales, and might afterwards have conquered Lisbon and Seville. You notorious villain, I knew thee for a rogue at first, thy ruff looked so like the moon crescent in '88—thy very breath is invincible, and stinks of an Armada.

Arist. Kick him out of the presence : his company will metamorphose us to balderdash.

Wild-m. Well, Diogenes, you were best keep close in your tub ; I'll be revenged on you ; I'll complain on you for keeping ill hours ; I suffer none after eight, by St John, not I.

1st Schol. Well, domine, though the *hora octava* be not come, yet you may be gone. [*Kicks him. Exit.*

Arist. Come, pupil, have you any mind to study my philosophy?

Sim. Yes, *me Hercule*, sir, for I have always accounted philosophy to be *omnibus rebus ordine, naturâ, tempore, honore prius;* and these schoolmen have so puzzled me and my dictionaries, that I despair of understanding them either *in summo gradu* or *remisso;* I lay sick of an *Hæcceitas* a fortnight, and could not sleep a wink for't. Therefore, good sir, teach me as ἐπιτόμως as you can, and pray let it be *conceptis verbis*, and *ex mente philosophi.*

Arist. I warrant thee, a good proficiency ; but, ere you can be admitted to my lectures, you must be matriculated, and have your name recorded in *Albo Academiæ.*

Sim. With all my heart, sir, and *totaliter;* for I have as great a mind as *materia prima* to be informed with your instructions.

Arist. Give him the oath.

2d Schol. Lay your hand on the book.

Sim. Will *tactus virtualis* serve the turn, sir?

2d Schol. No, it must be *reale quid, et extra intellectum.*

Sim. Well, sir, I will do it *quoad potentiam obedientialem.*

1st Schol. First, you must swear to defend the honour of Aristippus, to the disgrace of brewers, ale-wives, and tapsters, and profess yourself a foe, *nominalis*, to maltmen, tapsters, and red lattices.

2d Schol. Kiss the book.   [*He drinks.*

1st Schol. Next, you shall swear to observe the customs and ordinances instituted and ordained by Act of Parliament in the reign of King Sigebert, for the establishing of good government in the ancient foundation of Mitre College.

2d Schol. Kiss the book.   [*Drinks again.*

Sim. Ay, sir, *Secundùm veritatem intrinsecam, et non æquivoce.*

1st Schol. That you keep all acts and meetings, *tam privatim,* in private houses, *quam publicè,* in the Dolphin schools ; that you dispute *in tenebris*, yet be not asleep at reckonings : but always and everywhere show yourself so diligent in drinking, that the proctor may have no just cause to suspend you for negligence.

2d Schol. Kiss the book.   [*Drinks.*

1st Schol. Lastly, that you never walk into the town without your habit of drinking, the fuddling cap and casting hood ; especially when there is a convocation ; and of all things, take heed of running to the assizes.

Sim. Is this the end, I pray you, sir ? is this the *finis,* τοῦ ἕνεκα ?

1st Schol. It is *ultimum*, sir.

Sim. How, pray you, sir ? *intentione* or *extentione ?*

1st Schol. *Executione*, that follows the assizes.

Sim. But (methinks) there is one *scrupulum ;* it seems to be *actus illicitus*, that we should drink so much, it being lately forbidden, and therefore *contra formam statuti.*

2d Schol. Ay ; but therefore you are sworn to keep customs—*non omnino secundùm formam statuti.*

Arist. What, have you enrolled him *in Albo?* have you fully admitted him into the society, to be a member of the Body Academic ?

Sim. Yes, sir ; I am one of your pupils now, *unitate numerica,* we have made an end of it, *Secundùm ultimum complementum et actualitatem.*

Arist. Well, then, give the attendance.—Most grave audience, considering how they thirst after my philosophy, I am induced to let you taste the benefit of my knowledge, which cannot but please a judicious palate ; for the rest, I expel them, my scholars, as fitter to hear Thales and drink water.

Sim. We will attend, sir, and that *bibulis auribus.*

Arist. The many errors that have crept into the science, to distract the curious reader, are sprung from no other causes than small beer and sober sleeps ; whereas, were the laudible custom of sack-drinking better studied, we should have fewer gowns and more scholars.

1st Schol. A good note ; for we cannot see wood for trees, nor scholars for gowns.

Arist. Now the whole University is full of your honest fellows that, breaking loose from a Yorkshire belfry, have walked to Cambridge with satchels on their shoulders : there you shall have them study hard for four or five years, to return home more fools than they came : the reason whereof is drinking college tap-lash, that will let them have no more learning than they size, nor a drop of wit more than the butler sets on their heads.

2d Schol. 'Twere charity in him to sconce 'em soundly : they would have but a poor *quantum* else.

Arist. Others there be that spend their whole lives in Athens, to die as wise as they were born ; who, as they brought no wit into the world, so in honesty they will carry none out on't. 'Tis beer that drowns their souls in their bodies. Hewson's cakes and Paix his ale hath frothed their brains. Hence is the whole tribe contemned, every prentice can jeer at their brave cassocks, and laugh the velvet-caps out of countenance.

1st Schol. And would it not anger a man of art to be the scorn of a *What lack you, sir ?*

Arist. 'Tis beer that makes you so ridiculous in all your behaviour : hence comes the bridelike simpering at a Justice of Peace his table, and the not eating methodically, when, being laughed at, you show your teeth, blush, and excuse it with a rhetorical *hysteron proteron.*

Sim. 'Tis very true, I have done the like myself, till I have had a disgrace for my *mittimus.*

Arist. 'Tis beer that hath putrified our horsemanship, for that you cannot ride to Ware or Barkway, but your hackney's sides must witness your journeys. A lawyer's clerk or an Inns-a-Court gentleman, that hath been fed with false Latin and pudding-pie, contemns you, as if you had not learning enough to confute a *noverint universi.*

Sim. Per præsentes me Simplicium.

Arist. If you discourse but a little while with a courtier, you presently betray your learned ignorance, answering him (he concludes) not syllogistically, and asking him in what mood and figure he speaks in, as if learning were not as much out of fashion at court, as clothes at Cambridge ? Nor can you entertain discourse with a lady without endangering the half of your buttons. All these, and a thousand such errors, are the friends of beer, that nurse of barbarism and foe to philosophy.

Sim. O, I am ravished with this admirable metaphysical lecture. If ever I drink beer again, let me turn civil lawyer, or be powdered up in one of Luther's

barrels. Pray lend me the book again, that I may
forswear it. Fie upon it. I. could love Sir Giles for
Aristippus, thou art equally divine τῇ δυνάμει καὶ [κατ']
ἐντελέχείαν, the only father of *Quodlibets,* the prince of
presenting those notorious ale-wives. O Aristippus,
formalities. I ask my stars, whose influence doth
govern this *orbem sublunarem,* that I may live with
thee, and die like the royal Duke of Clarence, who
was soused up to immortality in a butt of malmsey.

2d Schol. You interrupt him, sir, too much in his
lecture, and prevent your ears of their happiness.

Sim. O heavens! I could hear him *ad æternitatem,*
and that, *tam à parte ante, quàm à parte post.* O,
proceed, proceed! thy instructions are mere ortho-
dox[ic]al, thy philosophy canonical; I will study thy
scientiam both *speculativam et practicam.* Pray, let me
once more forswear the pollution of beer; for it is
an abominable heretic; I'll be his perfect enemy, till
I make him and bottle-ale fly the country.

Arist. But sack is the life, soul, and spirits of a
man—the fire which Prometheus stole, not from
Jove's kitchen, but his wine-cellar, to increase the
native heat and radical moisture, without which we
are but drowsy dust or dead clay. This is nectar,
the very nepenthe the gods were drunk with; 'tis
this that gave Ganymede beauty, Hebe youth, to Jove
his heaven and eternity. Do you think Aristotle
drank perrey, or Plato cider? Do you think Alexander
had ever conquered the world, if he had been sober?
He knew the force and valour of sack—that it was the
best armour, the best encouragement, and that none
could be a good commander that was not double-
drunk—with wine and ambition!

1st Schol. Only here's the difference: ambition
makes them rise, and wine makes them fall. [*Aside.*

Arist. Therefore the garrisons are all drinking-
schools, the soldiers trained up to the mustering of

pewter pots daily : learning to contemn death by accustoming to be dead-drunk. Scars do not so well become a captain as carbuncles ; a red nose is the grace of a serjeant-major ; and they unworthy the place of ensigns that have not good colours. The best shot to be discharged is the tavern bill ; the best alarm is the sounding of healths ; and the most absolute march is reeling.

2d Schol. And the best artillery-yard is the Dolphin.

Arist. Thus you may easily perceive the profit of sack in military discipline, for that it may justly seem to have taken the name of sack from sacking of cities.

Sim. O wonderful, wonderful philosopher ! If I be a coward any longer, let me swear a little to drink sack, for I will be as valiant as any of the knights-errant. I perceive it was only *culpa ignorantiæ*, not *pravæ dispositionis*, that made me a coward. But, O enthusiastic, rare, angelical philosophy, I will be a soldier, a scholar, and everything. I will hereafter *nec peccare in materiâ, nec in formâ.* Beer, rascally beer, was the first parent of sophisters and the fallacies. But proceed, my Pythagoras, my *ipse dixit* of philosophy.

Arist. Next is the only elixir of philosophy, the very philosopher's stone : able, if studied by a young heir, *mutare rerum species*, to change his house, lands, livings, tenements, and liveries into *aurum potabile.* So that, though his lordships be the fewer for't, his manners shall be the more. Whose lands, being dissolved into sack, must needs make his soul more capable of divine meditation, he being almost in the state of separation by being purged and freed from so much earth.

2d Schol. Therefore, why should a man trouble himself with so much earth ? He is the best philosopher that can *omnia sua secum portare.*

Arist. And since it is the nature of light things to ascend, what better way, or more agreeing to nature, can be invented, whereby we might ascend to the height of knowledge, than a light head? A light head, being (as it were) allied with heaven, first found out that the motion of the orbs was circular, like to its own; which motions, *teste Aristotele*, first found that intelligence: so that I conclude all intelligence, intellect, and understanding to be the invention of sack and a light head. What mists of error had clouded philosophy, till the never-sufficiently-praised Copernicus found out that the earth was moved; which he could never have done, had he not been instructed by sack and a light head?

Sim. Hang me, then, when I turn grave.

Arist. This is the philosophy the great Stagyrite read to his pupil Alexander, wherein how great a proficient he was I call the faith of history to witness.

Sim. 'Tis true, *per fidem historicam;* for I have read how, when he had vanquished the whole world in drink, that he wept there was no more to conquer.

Arist. Now to make our demonstration to prove, no wine, no philosophy, is that admirable axiom, *In vino veritas;* and you know that sack and truth are the only butts which philosophy aims at.

1st Schol. And the hogshead is that *puteus Democriti*, from whence they might both be drawn.

Arist. Sack, claret, malmsey, white-wine, and hypocras, are your five predicables, and tobacco your *individuum.* Your money is your substance, full cups your quantity, good wine your quality; your relation is in good company, your action is beating, which produceth another predicament in the drawers, called passion; your *quando* is midnight, your *ubi* the Dolphin, your *situs* leaning, your *habitus* carousing; after-claps are your post-predicaments; your *priorums* breaking of jests, your *posteriorums*, of glasses; false bills are your fallacies, the shot is *subtilis objectio*, and the discharging of it is *vera solutio*. Several humours are your moods and figures, where *quarta figura* or gallons must not be neglected ; your drinking is syllo-gism, where a pottle is the *major terminus*, and a pint the *minor*, a quart the *medium;* beginning of healths are the premises, and pledging the conclusion, for it must not be divided. Topics or common-places are the taverns, and Hamon, Wolf, and Farlows are the three best tutors in the University.

Sim. And if I be not entered, and have my name admitted into some of their books, let *forma misti* be beaten out of me.

Arist. To persuade the vintner to trust you, is good rhetoric, and the best figure is *synecdoche*, to pay part for the whole. To drink above measure is a science beyond geometry. Falling backward is star-gazing, and no Jacob's staff comparable to a tobacco-pipe. The sweet harmony of good fellowship, with now and then a discord, is your excellent music ; sack itself is your grammar, sobriety a mere solecism; and Latin, be it true or be it false, a very cudgel to your priscian's pates. The reckoning is arithmetic enough, a receipt of full cups are the best physic to procure vomit, and forgetting of debts an art of memory ; and here you have an encyclopædia of sciences, whose method being circular, can never be so well learned as when your head runs round.

Sim. If mine have any other motion, it shall be *præter naturam,* ay, and *contra* too, if I live : I like that art of music wondrous well; life is not life with-out it; for what is life but an harmonious lesson, played by the soul upon the organs of the body? O witty sentence ! I am mad already : I see the immortality. Ha, brave Aristippus ! But in poetry it is the sole predominant quality, the sap and juice of the verse : yea, the spring of the Muses is the fountain of sack ; for to think Helicon a barrel of beer is as great a sin as to call Pegasus a brewer's horse.

Arist. I know some of these halfpenny almanac-makers do not approve of this philosophy, but give you most abominable counsel in their beggars' rhymes, which you are bound to believe as faithfully as their predictions of foul and fair weather.   You shall hear some of Erra Pater's poetry—

> *I wish you all carefully*
> *Drink sack but sparingly :*
> *Spend your coin thriftily,*
> *Keep your health warily.*
> *Take heed of ebriety :*
> *Wine is an enemy :*
> *Good is sobriety,*
> *Fly baths and venery.*

> *For your often potations much crudities cause*
> *By hindering the course of Mother Nature's laws.*
> *Therefore, he that desireth to live till October,*
> *Ought to be drunk in July; but I hold it to be a great*
>   *deal better that he went to bed sober.*

And let him alone, thou man in the moon ; yet hadst thou but read a leaf in this admired author, this *aureum flumen,* this *torrens eloquentiæ,* thou wouldst have scorned to have been of the water-poet's tribe, or Shelton's family.   But thou hast never tasted better nectar than out of Fennor's wassail-bowl, which hath so transformed him, that his eyes look like two tunnels, his nose like a faucet with the spicket out, and there-fore continually dropping.   And the almanac-makers and physicians are alike grand enemies of sack.   As for physicians, being fools, I cannot blame them if they neglect wine and minister simples ; but if I meet with you, I'll teach you another receipt.

Sim. Why, meet him, tutor ?   You may easily meet him.   I know him, sir, *et cognitione distinctâ et confusa,*

I warrant you. Do you not smell him, tutor? I know who made this almanac against drinking sack. Ha, Stroffe! have I found thee, Stroffe? You will show yourself, I see, when all is done, to be but a brewer's clerk.

Arist. But far better speaks the divine Ennius against your ale and barley-broth, who knew, too, full well the virtue of sack, when *nunquam nisi potus ad arma prosiluit dicenda;* his verses are in Latin, but because the audience are scholars, I have translated them into English, that they may be understood. Here, read them :—

> 1st Schol. *There is a drink made of the Stygian Lake,*
> *Or else of the waters the Furies do make,*
> *No name there is bad enough by which it to call,*
> *But yet as I wist, it is ycleped ale;*
> *Men drink it thick, and piss it out thin :*
> *Mickle filth, by Saint Loy, that it leaves within.*
> *But I of complexion am wondrous sanguine,*
> *And will love by th' morrow a cup of wine :*
> *To live in delight was ever my wone,*
> *For I was Epicurus his own son,*
> *That held opinion, that plainly delight*
> *Was very felicity perfite.*
> *A bowl of wine is wondrous good cheer,*
> *To make one blithe, buxom, and debonair ;*
> *'Twill give me such valour and so much courage,*
> *As cannot be found 'twixt Hull and Carthage.*

Arist. But above the wit of humanity, the divine Virgil hath extoll'd the encomium of sack in these verses :—

> 2d Schol. *Fill me a bowl of sack with roses crown'd ;*
> *Fill't to the brim; I'll have my temples bound*
> *With flowery chaplets, and this day permit*
> *My genius to be free, and frolic it.*

Let me drink deep; then fully warm'd with wine
I'll chaunt Æneas' praise, that every line
Shall prove immortal, till my moistened quill
Melt into verse, and nectar-like distil:
I'm sad or dull, till bowls brim-fill'd infuse
New life in me, new spirit in my muse;
But once reviv'd with sack, pleasing desires,
As in my childhood, kindle such active fires,
That my grey hairs seem fled, my wrinkled face
Grown smooth as Hebe's: youth and beauty's grace:
To my shrunk veins fresh blood and spirits bring,
Warm as the summer, sprightful as the spring.
Then all the world is mine: Crœsus is poor,
Compar'd with me; he's rich that asks no more.
And I in sack have all, which is to me
My home, my life: health, wealth, and liberty.
Then I have conquer'd all; I boldly dare
My trophies with the Pelean youth compare,
Him I will equal.   As his sword, my pen:
My conquer'd world of cares, his world of men.
Do not, Atrides, Nestors ten desire,
But ten such drinkers as that aged sire;
His stream of honeyed words flow'd from the wine,
And sack his counsel was, as he was thine,
Whoever purchas'd a rich Indian mine,
But Bacchus first, and next the Spanish wine?
Then fill my bowl, that, if I die to-morrow,
Killing cares to-day, I have out-liv'd my sorrow.

Arist. Thus, resting in the opinion of that admirable
poet, I make this draught of sack this lecture's period.
Dixi.

Sim. Dixi, dost thou say? Ay, and I'll warrant
thee the best *Dixi* in Cambridge. Who would sit
poring on the learned barbarism of the schoolmen,
that by one of thy lectures might confute them all,
pro and *con?* I begin to hate distinction *et actu-*

aliter et habitualiter; yet (a pox!) to see I cannot leave them *nec principaliter nec formaliter:* yet I begin to love the fox better than subtleness. O tutor, tutor, well might Fox be a college porter, that he might open the gates to none but thy pupils. Come, fellow-pupils, if I did not love you, I were ἁμάρτημα της φύσεως, and an absurdity in the abstract. Let's practise, let's practise; for I'll follow the steps of my tutor night and day. By this sack, I shall love this philosophy. Before I heard this lecture, Banks his horse was an Aristotle in comparison of me: I can laugh to think what a foolish Simplicius I was this morning, and how learnedly I shall sleep this night.

2d Schol. Sleep to-night! why, that's no point of your philosophy; we must sit up late, and roar till we rattle the welkin. Sleep! what have we to do with Death's cater-cousin? Do you think Nature gave stars to sleep by? Have you not day enough to sleep in, but you must sleep in the night too? 'Tis an arrant paradox!

Sim. A paradox? Let me be cramped if I sleep, then. But what, must we sleep in the day, then?

1st Schol. Yes, in the morning.

Sim. And why in the morning?

2d Schol. Why, a pox of the morning, what have we to do with the sober time of the day?

Sim. 'Tis true; I see we may learn something of our fellow-pupils. And what must we do now, fellow-pupils, what must we do now?

1st Schol. Why, confer our notes.

Sim. What is that?

2d Schol. Why, conferring of notes is drinking of cups; half-pots are saying of parts; and the singing of catches is our repetition.

Sim. Fellow-pupil, I'll confer a note with you.

1st Schol. Gramercy, brave lad, and it's a good one—excellent criticism; I would not have lost it for

Eustathius and his bishopric : it's a general rule, and true without exception.

Sim. Fellow-pupil, I'll confer a note with you too.

1st Schol. Faith, let me have it; let's share and share, like boon rascals.

Sim. I'll say my part to you both.

2d Schol. By my troth, and you have a good memory; you have conned it quickly, sir.

Sim. But what shall we have for repetitions now ?

2d Schol. Ay, what for repetitions ?

1st Schol. Why, the catch against the schoolmen, in praise of our tutor Aristippus.   Can you sing, Simplicius ?

Sim. How begins it, pray you ?

1st Schol. Aristippus is better.

Sim. O God, sir, when I was in the state of ignorance, I conned it without book, thinking it had been a proposition :—

> *Aristippus is better in every letter*
>   *Than Faber Parisiensis;*
> *Than Scotus, Socinus, and Thomas Aquinas,*
>   *Or Gregory Gandavensis :*
> *Than Cardan and Ramus: than old Paludanus,*
>   *Albertus and Gabriella :*
> *Than Pico Mercatus, or Scaliger Natus,*
>   *Than Nyphus or Zabarella.*
> *Hortado, Tromberus, were fools, with Tolerus,*
>   *Zanardus, and Will de Hales :*
> *With Occam, Javellus, and mad Argazellus,*
>   *Philoponus and Natalis.*
> *The Conciliator was but a mere prater,*
>   *And so was Apollinaris :*
> *Tandunus, Plotinus, the Dunce Eugubinus ;*
>   *With Masius, Savil and Suarez :*
> *Fonseca, Durandus, Baconus, Holandus,*
>   *Pererius, Avienture ;*

Old Trismegistus (whose volumes have miss'd us)
  Ammonius, Bonaventure,
Mirandula comes, with Proclus and Somes,
  And Guido the Carmelit-a ;
The nominal schools and the college of fools,
  No longer is my delight-a.
Hang Brerewood and Carter in Crackenthorp's garter :
  Let Keckerman, too, bemoan us :
I'll be no more beaten for greasy Jack Seaton,
  Or conning of Sandersonus.
The censure of Catos shall never amate us,
  Their frosty beards cannot nip us.
Your ale is too muddy : good sack is our study :
  Our tutor is Aristippus.

Enter the WILD-MAN, *with two* BREWERS.

Wild-m. There they be ; now, for the valour of
brewers ! knock 'um soundly. The old rogue ; that's
he. Do you not see him there ? soundly, soundly ;
let him know what companions good beer has.
  [*They beat out* ARISTIPPUS *and the* SCHOLARS.

WILD-MAN *solus.*

Now let them know that beer is too strong for
them ; and let me be hanged if ever I be milder to
such rascals. They shall find these but stale cour-
tesies. How now ? what's here ? [*He finds pots*] the
learned library, the philosophical volumes ? These
are the books of the black art ; I hate them worse
than Bellarmine, the Golden Legend, or the Turkish
Alcoran. I wonder what virtue is in this pewter-faced
author, that it should make every one fall in love with
it so deeply ? I'll try if I can find any *philtrum*,
any love-potion in it : by my *Domine*, not a drop !
[*He finds empty papers.*] *O stultum ingenium hominum*,
to delight in such vanities ! Sure, these are com-

ments upon tobacco, dry and juiceless vanities! I'll
try again. By my *bonâ fide*, but this doth relish
some learning. Still better, an admirable witty rogue,
a very flash! I'll turn another leaf : still better!
Has he any more authors like this? What's here?
Aristippus? a most incomparable author. O Bodley,
Bodley, thou hast not such a book in all thy library!
Here's one line worth the whole Vatican. O Aristippus, would my brains had been broken out when I
broached thy hogshead! O curst brewers! and most
accursed am I, to wrong so learned a philosopher as
Aristippus! What penance is enough to clear me
from this unpardonable offence? twenty purgations
are too little. I'll suck up all my beer in toasts to
appease him, and afterwards live by my wife and
hackneys. O, that I had never undertook this selling of beer! I might have kept my house with
fellows' commons, and never have come to this ; but
now I am a wild man, and my house a bedlam!
Aristippus, Aristippus, Aristippus!

Enter Medico de Campo.

Med. How now, neighbour Wild-man!

Wild-m. O Aristippus, Aristippus! what shall I
do for thee, Aristippus?

Med. What is this?

Wild-m. O Aristippus, Aristippus! what shall I
do for thee, Aristippus?

Med. Why, neighbour Wild-man? disclose your
griefs to me. I am a surgeon, and perchance may
cure 'em.

Wild-m. O, cry you mercy! you are the welcomest man on earth, Sir Signior Medico de Campo,
the welcomest man living, the only man I could have
wished for. O Aristippus, Aristippus!

Med. Why, what's the matter, neighbour? O, I

hear he has seduced away your parishioners; is this the cause of your lamentation?

Wild-m. O no, sir: a learned philosopher, one that I love with my soul: but in my rage I cannot tell you, sir; it is a dismal tale, the sharpest razor in your shop would turn edge at it.

Med. Never fear it; I have one was sent from a —— faith, I cannot think on's name, a great emperor—he that I did the great cure on; you have heard on't, I am sure? I fetched his head from China, after it had been there a fortnight buried, and set it on his shoulders again, and made him as lively as ever I saw him in my life; and yet to see I should not think on's name! O, I have it now!—Prester John, a pox on't! Prester John, 'twas he, i' faith; 'twas Prester John. I might have had his daughter, if I had not been a fool, and have lived like a prince all the days of my life; nay, and perchance have inherited the crown after his death; but, a pox on't, her lips were too thick for me; and that I should not think on Prester John!

Wild-m. O Aristippus, Aristippus! pox on your Prester John! sir, will you think on Aristippus?

Med. What should I do with him?

Wild-m. Why, in my rage, sir, I have almost killed him, and now would have you cure him in sober sadness.

Med. Why, call him out, sir.

Enter SIMPLICIUS.

Wild-m. Sir, yonder comes one of his pupils.

Med. Salve, Magister Simplicius.

Sim. Salve me! 'tis but a surgeon's compliment, Signior Medico de Campo; but you are welcome, sir; my tutor wants help. Are you there, you usquebaugh rascal, with your metheglin juice? I'll teach you, sir, to break a philosopher's pate; I'll make you leave your distinctions as well as I have done.

Wild-m. O, pardon, pardon me; I repent, sir, heartily. O Aristippus, Aristippus, I have broken thy head, Aristippus, but I'll give thee a plaister, Aristippus, Aristippus.

Med. I pray, sir, bring him out in his chair, and if the house can furnish you with barber's provision, let all be in readiness. [*Exit* SIMPLICIUS.

Wild-m. Pray, sir, do you think you can cure him?

Med. Him? why, neighbour, do you not remember the thumb?

Wild-m. What of the thumb? I have not heard of it as yet, sir.

Med. Why, the thumb—the thumb; do you not know the cure of the thumb?

Wild-m. No, sir; but, I pray, tell the cure of the thumb : do you still remember't, sir?

Med. Remember't? ay, and perfectly. I have it at my fingers' ends, and thus it is. Two gentlemen were fighting; one lost his thumb; I, by chance coming by, took it up, put it in my pocket; some two months after, meeting the gentleman, I set on his thumb again, and if he were now in Cambridge, I could have his hand to show for't. Why, did you ne'er hear of the thumb, sir? 'tis strange you never heard me speak of the thumb, sir.

Enter three SCHOLARS, *bringing forth* ARISTIPPUS
in his chair.

1st Schol. Signior de Medico Campo, if you have any art or skill, show it now; you never had a more deserving patient.

Med. Yet I have had many, and royal ones, too; I have done many cures beyond seas, that will not be believed in England.

2d Schol. Very likely so; and cures in England,

that will not be believed beyond seas, nor here neither; for in this kind half the world are infidels.

Med. The great Turk can witness, I am sure, the eyes that he wears were of my making.

1st Schol. He was then an eye-witness; but I hope he wears spectacles, signior?

Med. Why, won't you believe it? why, I tell you I am able to say't; I saw it myself. I cured the King of Poland of a wart on's nose, and Bethlem Gabor of a ringworm.

1st Schol. The one with raw beef, and the other with ink-horns.

Med. Pox of your old wives' medicines! the worst of my ingredients is an unicorn's horn, and bezoar stone. Raw beef and ink-horns! Why, I cured Sherley in the grand Sophy's court in Persia, when he had been but twice shot through with ordnance, and had two bullets in each thigh: and so quickly, that he was able at night to lie with his wife, the Sophy's niece, and beget a whole church of Christians. And could this be done with raw beef and ink-horns?

Sim. No, sure, this could not have been done without eggs and green sauce, or an oatmeal poultice at least.

Med. The King of Russia had died of the worms, but for a powder I sent him.

2d Schol. Some of that, you mean, that stuck on the bullet which you took out of Sherley's legs.

Med. In the siege of Ostend, I gave the Duchess of Austria a receipt to keep her smock from being animated, when she had not shifted it for a twelve-month.

1st Schol. Believe me, and that was a cure beyond Scoggin's fleas.

---

[1] This passage is quoted in "Old English Jest-Books," vol. ii. ("Scoggin's Jests," p. 84).

Med. I am able, by the virtue of one salve, to heal all the wounds and breaches in Bohemia.

2d Schol. Ay, and close up the bung-hole in the great tub at Heidelberg, I warrant you.

Med. I cured the State of Venice of a dropsy, the Low Countries of a lethargy ; and if it had not been treason, I had cured the fistula, that it should have dropt no more than your nose. By one drachm on a knife's point, I restored Mansfeldt to his full strength and forces, when he had no men left, but was only skin and bones. I made an arm for Brunswick with so great art and skill, as Nature herself could not have mended it ; which, had it not come too late after his death, would have done him as much service as that which was shot off.

2d Schol. I easily believe that, i' faith.

Med. I could make purgation that should so scour the seas, that never a Dunkirk durst show his head.

1st Schol. By my faith, and that would be a good State glyster.

Med. I have done as great wonders as these when I extracted as much chastity from a sanctimony in the English Nunnery as cured the Pope of his lechery.

2d Schol. And yet had as much left as served five cardinals on fasting-days.

Med. And there was no man in the realm of France, either French or Spanish, or Italian doctors, but myself, that durst undertake the King of France his corns ; and afterwards, having cured him, I drank a health to him.

Sim. Would we had the pledging on't. O happy man, that has conferred a note with the King of France !

Med. And do you seem to misdoubt my skill, and speak of my art with ifs and ands ? Do you take me for a mountebank? and hath mine own tongue been so silent in my praise that you have not heard of my skill?

2d Schol. No, pardon us, signior : only the danger our tutor is in makes us so suspicious. We know your skill, sir; we have heard Spain and your own tongue speak loud on't; we know, besides, that you are a traveller, and therefore give you leave to relate your words with authority.[1]

Med. Danger? what danger can there be when I am his surgeon?

1st Schol. His head, sir, is so wonderfully bruised, it is almost past cure.

Med. Why, what if he had never a head? Am not I able to make him one? Or if it were beaten to atoms, I could set it together, as perfectly as in the womb.

Wild-m. Believe me, neighbour, but that would be as great a wonder as the thumb, or Prester John's head.

Med. Why, I'll tell you, sir, what I did—a far greater wonder than any of these—I was a traveller——

2d Schol. There was no such great wonder in that, but what may be believed.

Med. ——and another friend of mine travelled with me; and (to be short) I came into the country of the cannibals, where, missing my friend, I ran to seek him, and came at last into a land, where I saw a company feeding on him. They had eaten half of him. I was very pensive at his misfortune, or rather mine : at last I bethought me of a powder that I had about me. I put it into their wine; they had no sooner drunk of it, but they presently disgorged their stomachs, and fell asleep; I, sir, gathered up

---

[1] Alluding, of course, to the proverb, "A traveller may lie with authority."

the miserable morsels of my friend, placed them together, and restored him to be a perfect man again;
and if he were here still alive, he were able to witness
it himself; and do you think I cannot cure a ten-
groats' damage or a cracked crown?

1st Schol. Good signior, make no such delay; cure
him, and have one wonder more to fill up your legend.

Med. Here, [you] hold the basin, you the napkins,
and you, Master Simplicius, the boxes. What shall
we have to lay his feet upon? By my troth, sir, he
is wonderfully hurt. His pia mater, I perceive, is
clean out of joint; of the twenty bones of the cranium,
there is but three only whole; the rest are miserably
crushed and broken, and two of his sutures are clean
perished. Only the sagittal remains free from violence;
the four tunicles of his eyes are threadbare; the meninx
of his ear is like a cut drum, and the hammer's lost.
There is not a cartilago in his head worth threepence;
the top of his nose is dropt away; there is not a muscle
left in the cavities of his nostrils; his *dentes molares* are
past grinding; his palate is lost, and with it his gur-
gulio. Yet, if he can swallow, I warrant his drinking
safe. Help, open his mouth. So, so; his throat is
sound. He's well, I warrant you; now give him a
cup of sack. So, let me chafe his temples: put this
powder into another glass of sack, and (my life for
his) he is as sound as the best of us all. Let down
his legs. How do you, sir?

Arist. Why, as young as the morning, all life and
soul, not a drachm of body. I am newly come back
from hell, and have seen so many of my acquaintance
there, that I wonder whose art hath restored me to
life again.

1st Schol. The Catholic Bishop of Barbers, the very
Metropolitan of Surgeons, Signior de Medico Campo.

2d Schol. One that hath engrossed all arts to himself, as if he had the monopoly.

1st Schol. The only Hospital of Sores.

2d Schol. And spital-house of infirmities, Signior de Medico Campo.

1st Schol. One that is able to undo the Company of Barber-Surgeons and College of Physicians, by making all diseases fly the country.

2d Schol. Yea, he is able to give his skill to whom he please by act of deed, or bequeath it by legacy; but he is determined as yet to entail it to his heirs male for ever.

1st Schol. Sir, death itself dares not anger him, for fear he should beggar the sextons, by suffering no grave to be made; he can choose whether any shall die or no.

2d Schol. And he does't with such celerity, that a hundred pieces of ordnance in a pitched field could not in a whole day make work enough to employ him an hour. You owe him your life, sir, I'll assure you.

Arist. Sir, I do owe you my life, and all that is mine. Think of anything that lieth in the compass of my philosophy, and 'tis your own.

Med. I have gold enough, sir, and philosophy enough, for my house is paved with philosophers' stones; mine only desire is, that you forgive the rage of this wild man, who is heartily sorry for his offence to you.

Wild-m. O reverend philosopher and alchemy of understanding, thou very sack of sciences, thou noble Spaniard, thou Catholic Monarch of Wines, Archduke of Canary, Emperor of the Sacred Sherry, pardon me, pardon my rudeness; and I will forswear that Dutch heresy of English beer, and the witchcraft of Middleton's water; I'll turn myself into a gown, and be a professed disciple of Aristippus.

Arist. Give him a gown, then, ere we admit him to our lecture hereafter. Now, noble Signior Medico de Campo, if you will walk in, let's be very jovial and

merry. 'Tis my second birthday ; let's in and drink
a health to the company.

[*Exeunt, and sing within.*]

We care not for money, riches, or wealth :
Old sack is our money, old sack is our health.
   Then let's flock hither,
   Like birds of a feather—
To drink, to sting,
To laugh and sing,
   Conferring our notes together,
   Conferring our notes together.
Come let us laugh, let us drink, let us sing,
The winter with us is as good as the spring.
   We care not a feather
   For wind or for weather,
But night and day
We sport and play,
   Conferring our notes together,
   Conferring our notes together.

Sim. Hark, they are drinking your healths within,
and I must have it too. I am only left here to offer
my *supplicat* to you, that my grace may pass ; and
then, if I may commence in your approbation, I will
take a degree in drinking ; and because I am turned
a jovial mad rascal, I have a great desire to be a midsummer bachelor—I was only staying to ask your
leave to go out. [*Exit.*

THE CONCEITED PEDDLER.

FOR the editions of this unique production, see the notice prefixed to "Aristippus," to all the impressions of which it is
annexed.

Dodsley was indebted to Randolph's "Conceited Peddler"
for the idea and outline of his dramatic performance called
"The Toy-Shop."

The Conceited Peddler.

As it was presented in a strange Show.

———o———

GENEROUS GENTLEMEN,—

SUCH is my affection to Phœbus and the ninety-nine Muses, for the benefit of this Royal University I have strodled over three of the terrestrial globes with my geometrical rambling, viz., the Asia of the Dolphin, the Africa of the Rose, and the America of the Mitre, besides the *terra incognita* of many an ale-house. And all for your sakes, whom I know to be the divine brats of Helicon, the lawful-begotten bastards of the thrice-three sisters, the learned filly-foals to Monsieur Pegasus, Arch-hackney to the students of Parnassus. Therefore I charge you, by the seven deadly sciences, which you more study than the three and four liberal sins, that your *ha, ha, he's* may be recompense of my ridiculous endeavours.

I have been long in travail; but, if your laughter give my embryon jests but safe deliverance, I dare maintain it in the throat of Europe, Jeronymo rising from his naked bed was not so good a midwife.[1]

---

[1] An allusion to a well-known declamatory passage in Kyd's " Spanish Tragedy."

But I see you have a great desire to know what profession I am of. First, therefore, hear what I am not. I am not a lawyer, for I hope you see no buckram honesty about me, and I swear, by these sweet lips, my breath stinks not of any stage actions. I am no soldier, although my heels be better than my hands; by the whips of Mars and Bellona, I could never endure the smell of saltpetre since the last gunpowder treason; the voice of a mandrake to me is sweeter music than those maxims of wars, those terrible cannons. I am no townsman, unless there be rutting in Cambridge, for you see my head without horns. I am no alderman, for I speak true English. I am no Justice of Peace, for I swear, by the honesty of a *Mittimus*, the venerable Bench ne'er kissed my worshipful buttocks. I am no alchemist; for, though I am poor, I have not broke out my brains against the philosopher's stone. I am no lord, and yet (methinks) I should, for I have no lands. I am no knight, and yet I have as empty pockets as the proudest of them all. I am no land-lord, but to tenants-at-will. I am no inns-of-court gentleman, for I have not been stewed throughly at the Temple, though I have been half coddled at Cambridge. Now do you expect that I should say I am a scholar? but, I thank my stars, I have more wit than so. Why, I am not mad yet : I hope my better Genius will shield me from a threadbare black cloak, it looks like a piece of Beelzebub's livery. A scholar? What, I do not mean my brains should drop through my nose. No, if I was what I wish I could but hope to be : but I am a noble, generous, understanding, royal, magnificent, religious, heroical, and thrice-illustrious peddler.

But what is a peddler? Why, what's that to you? yet, for the satisfaction of him whom I most respect, my right honourable self, I will define him.

A peddler is an *individuum vagum,* or the *primum mobile* of tradesmen, a walking-burse or movable exchange, a Socratical citizen of the vast universe, or a peripatetical journeyman, that, like another Atlas, carries his heavenly shop on's shoulders.

I am a peddler, and I sell my ware   [*He sings.*
This brave Saint Barthol or in Sturbridge Fair.
I'll sell all for laughter, that's all my gains,
Such chapmen should be laugh'd at for their pains.
Come, buy my wits, which I have hither brought.
For wit is ne'er good till it be bought.
Let me not bear all back, buy some the while;
If laughter be too dear, take't for a smile.
My trade is jesting now, or quibble-speaking;
Strange trade, you'll say, for it's set up with breaking.
My shop and I am all at your command
For lawful English laughter paid at hand.
Now will I trust no more; it were in vain
To break, and make a Craddock of my brain.
Half have not paid me yet: first, there is one
Owes me a quart for his declamation;
Another morning's draught is not yet paid
For four epistles at the election made;
Nor dare I cross him, who does owe as yet
Three ells of jests to line Priorum's wit.
But here's a courtier has so long a bill,
'Twill fright him to behold it; yet I will
Relate the sums.   *Item, he owes me first*
For an Imprimis : *but what grieves me worst,*
A dainty epigram on his spaniel's tail
Cost me an hour, besides five pots of ale.
Item, an anagram on his mistress' name.
Item, the speech wherewith he courts his dame :
And an old blubber'd scowling elegy
Upon his master's dog's sad exequy.

Nor can I yet the time exactly gather,
When I was paid for an epitaph on's father :
Besides he never yet gave me content
For the new-coming of's last compliment.
Should I speak all (be't spoken to his praise),
The total sum is, what he thinks or says.
I will not let you run so much o' th' score,
Poor Duck-Lane brain, trust me, I'll trust no more.
Shall's jest for nought ? have you all conscience lost ?
Or do you think our sack did nothing cost ?
Well, then, it must be done as I have said,
I needs must be with present laughter paid :
I am a free man ; for by this sweet rhyme,
The fellows know I have secured the time.
Yet if you please to grace my poor adventures,
I'm bound to you in more than ten indentures.

But a pox on Skelton's fury ! I'll open my shop
in honester prose ; and first, gentlemen, I'll show
you half a dozen of incomparable points. I would
give you the definition of points, but that I think you
have them at your fingers'-ends ; yet for your better
understanding—a point is no body, a common term,
an extreme friend of a good man's longitude, whose
centre and circumference join in one diametrical
opposition to your equilateral doublet or equicrural
breeches. But to speak to the point, though not to
the purpose :—1. The first point is a point of honesty,
but is almost worn out, and has never been in request
since trunk-hose and codpiece breeches went out of
fashion. It's made of simplicity-ribbon, and tagged
with plain dealing. If there be any knaves among
you (as I hope you are not all fools), faith, buy this
point of honesty, and the best use you can put it to
is to tie the band of affection. But I fear this point
will find no chapman. Some of you had rather sell,
than with Demosthenes buy honesty at too dear a

rate. O, I would wish that the breeches of bursers, stewards, taxers, receivers, and auditors were trussed with these honesty-points; but some will not be tied to it. But whist, Tom; it is dangerous untrussing the time.

2. The next is a point of knavery; but I have enough of them already; yet because I am loth to carry mine any longer about me, who gives me most shall take it, and the devil give him good on't. This point is cut out of villanous sheep's-skin parchment in a scrivener's shop, tagged with the gold of a ring which the pillory robbed him of when it borrowed his ears. If he do but fasten this to the new doublet of a young squire, it will make him grow so corpulent in the middle, that there will be nothing but waste. This point of knavery has been a man in his days, and the best of the parish: fourteen of them go to a baker's dozen.

The definition of him may be this: A point of knavery is an occult quality tied on a riding-knot, the better to play fast and loose; he was born in buckram, he has run through all offices in the parish, and now stands to be president of Bridewell; where I leave him, hoping to see him trussed at Tyburn.

3. Among all my points, the point of ignorance is the very alderman of the dozen. This is the richest point in my pack, and is never out of fashion at inns-of-court. If you buy this point, you are arrant fools; for I'll give you this gift, that you shall have it in spite of your teeth.

4. The next is a point of good manners, that has been long lost amongst a crowd of clowns, because it was only in fashion on this side Trent. This point is almost found in our college, and I thank the heavens for't, it begins to be tagged with Latin; it hath been much defiled, but I hope to see it clean washed away

with the soap of good government. This point, to give you a little inkling of it, begins from the due observance of a fresh man to sophisters ; and there it ends with a *cede majoribus.*

5. Next point is a point of false doctrine, snatched from the codpiece of a long-winded puritan; the breath of Arminius will rot in him. Tag him with a piece of Apocrypha, and he breaks in sunder. Truss him to the surplice, and his breeches will presently fall down with the thought of the Whore of Babylon. He hates unity and church discipline so far, that you cannot tie a true love's-knot on him ; cut off his tags, and he will make excellent strings for a Geneva Bible. I would have these points anathematised from all the religious breeches in the company. 'Tis made of a dangerous stubborn leather, tagged at one end with self-conceit, at the other with wilful opinion. This point is fit for no service, but Lucifer's Cacotruces. But why talk I so long of this point? it is pity it is not licensed.

6. If you like my points, why do you not buy? If you would have a more full point, I can furnish you with a period : I have a parenthesis (but that may be left out). I know not how you affect those points, but I love them so well, that I grieve at the ignorance of my infancy, when my most audacious toes durst play at spurn-point.

> *Who will not pity points, when each man sees*
> *To begging they are fall'n upon their knees?*
> *Though I beg pity, think not I do* [1] *fear*
> *Censuring critic whelps ;* no point, monsieur !
> *If you hate points, and these like merry speeches,*
> *You may want points for to truss up your breeches.*

---

[1] Old copies, *think I do not.*

And from the close stool, maybe, never move,
That hating points doth clasps and keepers love.
But if my points have here at all offended,
I'll tell you a way how all shall be amended.
Speak to the point, and that shall answer.   Friend,
All is not worth a point ; and there's an end.

Then the PEDDLER brought forth a looking-glass.

The next is a looking-glass ; but I'll put it up again; for I dare not be so bold as to show some of you your own faces.   Yet I will, because it hath strange operations, viz., if a cracked chamber-maid dress herself by this looking-glass, she shall dream the next night of kissing her lord, or making her mistress a she-cuckold, and shall marry a chaplain, the next living that falls. If a stale court-lady look on this reflection, she may see her old face through her new complexion.   An usurer cannot see his conscience in it, nor a scrivener his ears.   If a townsman peep into it, his Acteon's furniture is no longer invisible.   Corrupt takers of bribes may read the price of their consciences in it. Some fellows cannot see the face of a scholar in it. If one of our jewel-nosed, carbuncled, rubricked Bonifaces [1] can venture the danger of seeing their own faces in't, the poor basilisks will kill themselves by reflection.   If a blind man see his face in this, he shall recover his eyesight.   But I see no pleasure in the contemplation of it ; for when I look into it, I find myself inclined to such a dangerous disease, that I fear I cannot live here above four years longer. Howsoever, I hope, after my decease we shall drink the parting blow :—

If any this looking-glass disgrace,
It is because he dares not see his face :

---

[1] Old copy, *rubrick bonifac't.*

Then what I am, I will not see, (faith) say;
'Twas the whore's argument, when she threw't away.

Then the PEDDLER brought forth a box of cerebrum.

But now, considering what a philosophical *vacuum* there is in most of our Cambridge noddles, I have here to sell a sovereign box of cerebrum, which by Lullius his alchemy was extracted from the quint-essence of Aristotle's *pericranium*, sod in the *sinciput* of Demosthenes; the fire being blown with the long-winded blast of a Ciceronian sentence, and the whole confection boiled from a pottle to a pint in the pip-kin of Seneca. We owe the first invention of it to Sir John Mandeville, the perfection of it to Tom of Odcombe, who fetched it from the grey-headed Alps in the Hobson's waggon of experience. I swear (as Persians use) by this my coxcomb, this magazine of immortal roguery—but for this box of brains, you had not laughed to-night. Buy this box of brains, and the tenure of your wit shall be socage, whereas now it is but fee-simple. These brains have very admirable virtues and very strange operations : four drops of it in the ear of a lawyer will make him write true Latin ; three grains will fill the capital of an University gander ; the terrestrial head of a High Constable will be content with half a drachm ; three scruples and a half will fill the brain-pan of a Banbury brother.

Come, buy my brains, you ignorant gulls,
And furnish here your empty skulls.
Pay your laughter as it's fit,
To the learned peddler of wit.
Quickly come and quickly buy;
Or I'll shut my shop, and, fools, you'll die.
If your coxcombs you would quoddle,
Here buy brains to fill your noddle.

Who buys brains, learns quickly here
To make a problem in a year :
Shall understand the predicable
And the predicamental rabble :
Who buys them not shall die a fool,
An exoteric in the school :
Who has not these shall ever pass
For a great acromatical ass.
Buy then this box of brains : who buys not it,
Shall never surfeit upon too much wit.

Then the PEDDLER brought forth a whetstone.

But (leaving my brains) I come to a more profitable commodity; for, considering how dull half the wits of the University be, I thought it not the worst traffic to sell whetstones. This whetstone will set such an edge upon your inventions, that it will make your trusty iron brains purer metal than your brazen faces. Whet but the knife of your capacities on this whetstone, and you may presume to dine at the Muses' ordinary, or sup at the Oracle of Apollo. If this be not true, I swear by the doxies' petticoats, that I'll never hereafter presume of a better vocation than to live and die the miserable factor of coney-skins.

Then the PEDDLER brought out gloves.

I have also gloves of several qualities : the first is a pair of gloves made for a lawyer, made of an entire loadstone, that has the virtue to draw gold unto it. They were perfumed with the conscience of an usurer, and will keep scent till wrangling have left Westminster Hall ; they are seamed with indenture by the needlework of mortgage, and fringed with *noverint universi.* I would show you more, but it is against the statute, because a *Latitat* hath been served lately upon them; and few of you need any gloves; for you wear Cordovant hands.

[He brings out] nightcaps.

My next commodities are several nightcaps; but they dare not come abroad by candle-light. The first is lined with fox-fur, which I hope to sell to some of the sophisters. It hath an admirable faculty for curing the crapula, above the virtue of ivy or bitter almonds; nay, the pottage-pot's not comparable unto it. I have another fit for an alderman, which Acteon by his last will and testament bequeathed to the city as a principal charter. It was of Diana's own making: Albumazar's *otacousticon* was but a chamber-pot in comparison. I could fit all heads with nightcaps, except your grave, over-wise, metaphysical heads. Marry, they are so transcendant, that they will not be comprehended within the predicament of a nightcap.

[He brings out] ruffs.

I have also several ruffs. First, a ruff of pure Holland for a Dutch drunkard, a ruff of cobweb-lawn for the University statutes. I have a ruff for the College, too; but by this badge of our college (my reverend lambskins) our backbiters say, our college-ruffs are quite out of stock. I have no more ruffs but one, and that is a ruff of strong hemp; you may have them, who will, at the Royal Exchange of Tyburn. As for plain bands, if you find any in a scrivener's shop, there is good hopes honesty will come in fashion again. But you will not bestow your money on such trifles? why, I have greater wares. Will you buy any parsonages, vicarages, deaneries, or prebendaries? The price of one is his lordship's cracked chamber-maid; the other is the reserving of his worship's tithes : or you may buy the knight's horse three hundred pounds too dear, who, to make you amends in the bargain, will draw you on fairly to a vicarage. There be many tricks ; but the downright way is three years' purchase. Come, bring in your coin. Livings are *majori in pretio* than in the days of Doomsday Book. You must give presents for your presentations. There may be several means for your institutions ; but this is the only way to induction that ever I knew. But I see you are not minded to meddle with any, my honest, levitical farmers.

The PEDDLER took out a wench made of alabaster.

But now expect the treasures of the world, the treasures of the earth digged from the mines of my more than Indian paunch. Wipe your eyes, that no envious clouds of musty humours may bar your sight of the happiness of so rare an object—

Come from thy palace, beauteous Queen of Greece :
Sweet Helen of the world. Rise like the morn,
Clad in the smock of night, that all the stars
May lose their eyes, and then, grow blind,
Run weeping to the man i' th' moon,
To borrow his dog to lead the spheres a begging.
Rare empress of our souls, whose charcoal flames
Burn the poor coltsfoot of amazed hearts,
View the dumb audience thy beauty spies,
And then, amaz'd with grief, laugh out thine eyes.

Here's now rare beauty. O, how all your fingers itch who should be the first chapman ! This will be a dainty friend in a corner. And were't not better to embrace this pretty shambles for beauty, this errant poultry of perfection, than to tumble our soapy laundresses ? Is this like your draggle-tailed bedmakers ? when a man shall lie with sea-coal ashes,

and commit adultery with the dust of his chamber?
Methinks this peerless paragon of complexion should
be better countenanced; she should set a sharper
edge on your appetites than all the threepenny cut-
lers in Cambridge.   I am a man as you are, and this
naughty flesh and blood will never leave tempting;
yet I protest, by the sweet soul of this incomparable
she, I never had any acquaintance with the pretty
libraries of flesh, but only this.   This is the subject of
my muse; this I adorned with costly epigrams and
such curious encomiums as may deserve immortality
in the chamber-pots of Helicon.   And thus my *furor
poeticus* doth accost her—

> *Fair madam, thou, whose everything*
> *Deserves the close-stool of a king:*
> *Whose head is fair as any bone,*
> *White and smooth as pumice-stone.*
> *Whose natural baldness scorns to wear*
> *The needless excrements of hair;*
> *Whose forehead streaks our heart's commands.*
> *Like Dover Cliffs or Goodwin Sands.*
> *While from those dainty glow-worm eyes*
> *Cupid shoots plum-pudding pies,*
> *While from the arches of thy nose*
> *A cream-pot of white nectar flows.*
> *Fair dainty lips, so smooth, so sleek,*
> *And truly alabaster cheek,*
> *Pure saffron teeth—happy the meat*
> *That such pretty millstones eat!*
> *O, let me hear some silent song,*
> *Tun'd by the Jew's-trump of thy tongue.*
> *O, how that chin becomes thee well,*
> *Where never hairy beard shall dwell;*
> *Thy coral neck doth statelier bow,*
> *Than Io's, when she turn'd a cow:*
> *O, let me—or I shall ne'er rest—*

Suck the black bottles of thy breast;
Or lay my head, and rest me still
On that dainty hogmagog hill.
O curious and unfathom'd waist!
As slender as the stateliest mast;
Thy fingers, too, breed my delight,
Each wart a natural margarite.
O, pity then my dismal moan,
Able to melt thy heart of stone.
Thou know'st how I lament and howl,
Weep, snort, condole, look sad, and scowl;
Each night so great my passions be,
I cannot wake for thought of thee.
Thy gown can tell how much I lov'd,
Thy petticoat to pity mov'd.
Then let thy peddler mercy find
To kiss thee once, though it be behind.
Sweet kiss, sweet lips, delicious sense:
How sweet a Zephyrus blows from thence!
Blest petticoat, more blest her smock,
That daily busseth her buttock;
For now the proverb true I find,
That the best part is still behind.
Sweet, dainty soul, deign but to give
The poor peddler this hanging sleeve:
And in thine honour (by this kiss)
I'll daily wear my pack in this,
And quickly so bear thee more fame,
Than Quixote, the knight-errant's dame:
So farewell, sweet; deign but to touch,
And once again rebless my pouch.

Is it not pity such ware should not be bought?
Well, I perceive the fault is in the emptiness of your
learned pockets. Well, I'll to the Court, and see
what I can sell there, and then carry the relics to
Rome.

The PEDDLER calls for his colestaff.

Some friend must now perforce
Make haste, and bid my boy
To saddle me my wooden horse;
For I mean to conquer Troy.

THE JEALOUS LOVERS.

EDITIONS.

The Jealous Lovers.   A Comedie presented to their gracious Majesties at Cambridge, by the Students of Trinity Colledge. Written by Thomas Randolph, Master of Arts, and Fellow of the House.

> —— *valeat res ludicra, si me*
> *Palma negata macrum, donata reducit opimum.*

Printed by the Printers to the Universitie of Cambridge.   Anno Dom. 1632.   4°.

The Iealous Lovers.   A Comedie presented to their gracious Majesties at Cambridge, by the Students of Trinitie-Colledge. Written by Thomas Randolph, Master of Arts, and Fellow of the House.

> —— *valeat res ludicra, si me*
> *Palma negata macrum, donata reducit opimum.*

Printed by the Printers to the Universitie of Cambridge.   Anno Dom. 1634.   *And are to be sold by Rich. Ireland.*   4°.

This piece is annexed to the editions of the " Poems,"printed in 1640–68. That of 1643 has, in the copy employed on the present occasion, a title as follows : " The Jealous Lovers.   A Comedie Presented to Their gracious Majesties at Cambridge by the Students of Trinitie-Colledge.   Written by Thomas Randolph, Master of Arts, and Fellow of the House.   *Valeat . . . .* London, Printed for Richard Royston . . . . 1646."

" This play," says Halliwell ("Dictionary of Old Plays," 1860, in *v.*), " which is esteemed the best of our author's works, is commended by no less than nine copies of English, and seven of Latin, verses from the most eminent wits of both Universities, and was revived with great success in 1682."

The original 4° edition of the " Jealous Lovers," as we learn from the Notice to the Reader, was published at sixpence—the usual price.

TO THE RIGHT WORSHIPFUL
MR DOCTOR COMBER,[1]

*Dean of Carlisle, Vice-Chancellor of the University of
Cambridge, and Master of Trinity College.*

———o———

RIGHT WORSHIPFUL:

I HAVE observed in private families, that the careful father, disposing of his children to several employments, sendeth some to school, some to his plough, some to his flocks, while perchance the youngest, as uncapable of greater business, has the liberty to play in his hall. So is it in our society (which joyfully acknowledgeth you our careful and indulgent parent) : those of stronger abilities, more reading, and longer experience, are busied some in one, some in another of the graver and more serious studies ; while I, the last of that learned body, am tasked to these lighter exercises. Accept, sir, a thing born at your command, and preserved by your patronage. Not but that I vow the fruits of my more precious hours to your service : for when I consider the magnificence of her buildings, the riches of her

---

[1] Thomas Comber, Dean of Carlisle, was presented to that dignity 28th August 1629. He lost all his preferments at the Revolution of 1641, and died in 1653-4. See Le Neve's "Fasti," edit. Hardy, iii. 247.

endowments, the great examples of those before me, and all these blessed in your auspicious government, I find a fire kindled in my breast, whose flame aimeth higher, and telleth me, so glorious a hive the royal founders meant not to shelter drones.   So wishing our whole body long happy in so provident a governor, I rest, what my oath and peculiar engagements have bound me to be, yours devoted in all dutiful observance,

THOMAS RANDOLPH.

TO THE READER.

——o——

CourteoUS Reader :

I BEG thy pardon, if I put thee to the expense of a
sixpence and the loss of an hour. If I could by
mine own industry have furnished the desires of
my friends, I had not troubled the press. 'Tis no
opinion of the worth that wrought me to it. If I find
thee charitable, I acknowledge myself beholding to
thee : if thou condemn it of weakness, I cannot be
angry to see another of my mind. I do not aim at
the name of a poet. I have always admired the free
raptures of poetry, but it is too unthrifty a science for
my fortunes, and is crept into the number of the
seven to undo the other six. That I make so many
dedications, think not that I value it as a present rich
enough to be divided ; but know whom I am in piety
bound to honour. That I admit so many of my
friends' approbations, is not that I itched for praise
and love-rubbing, but that I was willing thou shouldst
have something worth thy reading. Be to me as kind
as my audience who, when they might have used
their censures, made choice of their mercies : and so
I must acknowledge myself indebted to thy clemency.

I confess no heights here, no strong conceits ; I speak the language of the people—

> *Neque, si quis scribat, uti nos,*
> *Sermoni propiora, putes hunc esse poetam.*

No, bestow the honour of this glorious title on those that have abler wits, diviner inventions, and deeper mouths. Leave me to the privacy of my studies, and accept for thy unknown friend

T. R.

To that complete and noble Knight Sir Kenellam Digby.[1]

SIR, when I look on you, methinks I see
    To the full height how perfect man may be.
Sure all the arts did court you, and you were
So courteous as to give to each their share.
While we lie lock'd in darkness, night and day
Wasting our fruitless oil and time away :
Perchance for skill in grammar, and to know
Whether this word be thus declin'd, or no.
Another cheats himself, perchance to be
A pretty youth, forsooth, in fallacy.
This on arithmetic doth hourly lie,
To learn the first great blessing, multiply,
That travels in geometry, and tires,
And he above the world a map admires.
This dotes on music's most harmonious chime,
And studying how to keep it, loses time.
One turns o'er histories, and he can show
All that has been, but knows not what is now.
Many in physic labour ; most of these
Lose health to know the name of a disease.
Some (too high wise) are gazing at a star,
And if they call it by his name, they are
In heaven already ; and another one
That cries Melpomene, and drinks Helicon,
At poetry throws wit and wealth away,
And makes it all his work to write a play.
Nay, on Divinity many spend their powers,
That scarce learn anything, but to stand two hours.

---

[1] The celebrated writer. His name is spelled in this unusual
manner in all the old copies. Randolph, among his poems, has
an elegy on Sir Kenelm's wife, the Lady Venetia Digby.

How must we, sir, admire you then, that know
All arts, and all the best of these can show !
For your deep skill in State, I cannot say ;
My knowledge there is only to obey.
But I believe 'tis known to our best peers,
Amaz'd to see a Nestor at your years.
Mars claims you, too : witness the galleon
That felt your thunderbolts at Scanderon,
When Neptune frighted let his trident fall,
And bid his waves call you their general.
How many men might you divide your store
Of virtues to, and yet not leave you poor,
Though enrich them ! Stay here. How dare I then
To such an able judgment show my pen ?
But 'tis, sir, from a muse that humbly prays,
You'll let her ivy wait upon your bays.

Your admiring servant, T. R.

To the truly noble Knight Sir Chr. Hatton.[1]

TO you (whose recreations, sir, might be
    Others' employments ; whose quick soul can see
There may, besides a hawk, good sport be found,
And music heard, although without a hound)
I send my muse : be pleas'd to hear her strain,
When y' are at truce with time. 'Tis a low vein ;
But were her breast enrag'd with holier fire,
That she could force, when she but touch'd her lyre,

---

[1] Cousin and heir of Queen Elizabeth's dancing Chancellor.
He erected a handsome monument to the poet's memory. In
1643 Sir Christopher was created Baron Hatton of Kirby, Co.
Northampton.

The waves to leap above their clifts, dull earth
Dance round the centre and create new birth
In every element, and outcharm each sphere ;
'Twere but a lesson worthy such an ear.   T. R.

To his honoured friend Mr Anth. Stafford.

SIR, had my muse gain'd leisure to confer
   With your sharp judgment, ere I ventur'd her
On such an audience, that my comedy
Had suffer'd by thy obelisk and thee ;
It needed not of just applause despair,
Because those many blots had made it fair.
I now implore your mercy to my pen,
That should have rather begg'd your rigour then.
                    T. R.

Colendissimo viro, et juris municipalis peritissimo, Magistro Richardo Lane.[1]

SIR, if the Term be done, and you can find
   Leisure to hear my suit, pray be so kind
To give this toy such courteous acceptation,
As to be made your client i' th' vacation.
Then if they say I break the comic laws,
I have an advocate can plead my cause.
                    T. R.

---

[1] Among the poems occurs one in which Randolph apologises for an unfulfilled prediction, that "his Aunt Lane" would have a son. Probably this Richard Lane, a lawyer it appears from the present lines, was that lady's husband.

Venerabili viro Magistro Olboston, Præceptori suo semper observando.

SI bene quid scripsi, tibi debeo ; si malè quicquam,
    Hæc erit in vitiis maxima culpa meis.
Naufragium meruit, qui non bene navigat æquor,
    Cui tu Pierium per freta Tiphys eras.   T. R.

To his dear friend, Thomas Riley.[1]

I WILL not say I on our stage have seen
    A second Roscius ; that too poor had been.
But I have seen a Proteus, that can take
What shape he please, and in an instant make
Himself to anything : be that or this
By voluntary metamorphosis.
When thou dost act, men think it not a play,
But all they see is real. O, that day,

---

[1] Thomas Riley, of Trinity College, Cambridge, an occasional writer of the time, and (as it appears from Randolph's lines to him) a clever actor. He performed in the present drama when placed on the stage at the University. The poet seems to acknowledge himself under obligations to Riley for his able impersonation of the part taken by him. In 1638 appeared a Latin play, entitled " Cornelianum Dolium," purporting on the well-phrased title to be by T. R. "*Lepidissimo hujus ævi Coryphæo.*" It seems to have been *edited* by R. Braithwaite, who added some of his peculiar touches. As Randolph was then dead, his name, printed at length on the first page, could scarcely have failed to stimulate the sale of this little book ; and as Riley was less famous probably in London, and his initials were the same, it becomes a question whether Riley was not really the author of the drama. The evidence is pretty strong, as it seems to me, both against Braithwaite and against Randolph.

(When I had cause to blush that this poor thing
Did kiss a queen's hand, and salute a king)
How often had I lost thee! I could find
One of thy stature, but in every kind
Alter'd from him I knew; nay, I in thee
Could all professions and all passions see.
When thou art pleas'd to act an angry part,
Thou fright'st the audience ; and, with nimble art
Turn'd lover, thou dost that so lively too,
Men think that Cupid taught thee how to woo.
To express thee all would ask a better pen ;
Thou art, though little, the whole map of men.
In deeper knowledge and philosophy
Thou truly art what others seem to be,
Whose learning is all face ; as 'twere thy fate
There not to act where most do personate.
All this in one so small ! Nature made thee
To show her cunning in epitome ;
While others, that seem giants in the arts
(Such as have stronger limbs, but weaker parts)
Are like a volume that contains less in't,
And yet looks big, 'cause 'tis a larger print.
I should myself have too ungrateful shown,
Sent I not thee my book :—Take't, 'tis thine own :
For thus far my confession shall be free,
I write this comedy, but 'twas made by thee.

Thy true friend, T. R.

Amico suo charissimo, ingeniosissimo, T. Randolpho, liberum de ejus Comœdiâ judicium.

A UDEBIT proprios negare odores
   Myrrhæ fasciculus, suásque mellis
Mendicare medulla suavitates,

Priùs quàm his Veneres deesse credam,
Quæ præ se placidos ferunt Amores.
Æternum vigeat, vigens amore.
Quòd si quis lapides loquatur, istum
Jamjam aptum Tumulo scias libellum.
En! noster bona verba portat autor :
Illas vult dare, quas recepit, auras,
Ridentes, niveóque perjocosæ
Vincentes Charitas nitore frontis.
Amores simul elegantiásque
Ad partus properare tum putetis,
Cùm risus popularis et theatri
Plausus suppeditârit obstetricem.

DESERT keeps close, when they that write by
　　guess
Scatter their scribbles and invade the press.
Stage-poets ('tis their hard, yet common hap)
Break out like thunder, though without a clap.
Here 'tis not so ; there's nothing now comes forth,
Which hath not for a licence its own worth.
No swagg'ring terms, no taunts ; for 'tis not right
To think that only toothsome which can bite.
See how the lovers come in virgin dye
And rosy blush, ensigns of modesty !
Though once beheld by such with that content,
They need not fear others' disparagement.
But I'll not tell their fortunes, whate'er't be ;
Thou must needs know't, if skill'd in palmestry.
Thus much—where king applauds, I dare be bold
To say, 'Tis petty treason to withhold.

　　　　　　　　　　　　　EDWARD HIDE.

To his dearest friend the Author, after he had revised his Comedy.

THE more I this thy masterpiece peruse,
  The more thou seem'st to wrong thy noble Muse
And thy free Genius.   If this were mine,
A modest envy would bid me confine
It to my study or the critics' court,
And not make that the vulgar people's sport,
Which gave such sweet delight unto the king,
Who censur'd it not as a common thing.
Though thou hast made it public to the view
Of self-love, malice, and that other crew,
It were more fit it should impaled lie
Within the walls of some great library ;
That if by chance, through injury of time,
Plautus and Terence, and that fragrant thyme
Of Attic wit [1] should perish, we might see
All those reviv'd in this one comedy—
The Jealous Lovers.   Pander, Gull and Whore :
The doting Father, Shark, and many more,
Thy scene doth represent unto the life,
Beside the character of a curst wife :
So truly given, in so proper style,
As if thy active soul had dwelt a while
In each man's body, and at length had seen
How in their humours they themselves demean.
I could commend thy jests, thy lines, thy plot,
Had I but tongues enou' ; thy names—what not ?
But if our poets, praising other men,
Wish for an hundred tongues, what want we then,
When we praise poets ?   This I'll only say,
This work doth crown thee laureate to-day.

---

[1] Aristophanes.

In other things how all, we all know well :
Only in this thou dost thyself excel.

EDWARD FRAUNCES.

To his dear friend Mr Thomas Randolph, on his Comedy called The Jealous Lovers.

FRIEND, I must grieve your poems injur'd be
   By that rare vice in poets, modesty.
If you dislike the issues of your pen,
You have invention, but no judgment then.
You able are to write, but 'tis as true,
Those that were there can judge as well as you.
You only think your gold adulterate,
When every scale of judgment finds it weight,
And every touchstone perfect.   This I'll say,
You contradict the name of your own play.
You are no lover of the lines you writ,
Yet you are jealous still of your own wit.

RICH. BENEFIELD, T.C.

To his ingenuous Friend, the Author, concerning his Comedy.

THE Muses, Tom, thy Jealous Lovers be,
   Striving which has the greatest share in thee.
Euterpe calls thee hers ; such is thy skill
In pastoral sonnets and in rural quill.
Melpomene claims thee for her own, and cries,
Thou hast an excellent vein for elegies.
'Tis true ; but then Calliope disdains,
Urging thy fancy in heroic strains,

Thus all the Nine : Apollo by his laws
Sits judge, in person to decide the cause :
Beholds thy comedy, approves thy art,
And so gives sentence on Thalia's part.
To her he dooms thee only of the Nine ;
What though the rest with jealousy repine ?
Then let thy comedy, Thalia's daughter,
Begin to know her mother Muse by laughter,
Out with't, I say, smother not this thy birth,
But publish to the world thy harmless mirth.
No fretting frontispiece, nor biting satire   [nature.
Needs usher't forth : born tooth'd ? fie ! 'tis 'gainst
Thou hast th' applause of all : king, queen, and Court,
And University, all lik'd thy sport.
No blunt preamble in a cynic humour
Need quarrel at dislike, and (spite of rumour)
Force a more candid censure, and extort
An approbation, maugre all the Court.
Such rude and snarling prefaces suit not thee ;
They are superfluous : for thy comedy,
Back't with its own worth and the author's name,
Will find sufficient welcome, credit, fame.

JAMES DUPORT.[1]

Randolpho suo.

A N *quæram monumenta firmiora*
    Nostri nominis ut supersit ætas,
Cùm scriptus legar in tuo libello,

---

[1] Author of versions of the Psalms and Song of Solomon in Latin, and of occasional verses, most of which were collected in a volume, entitled "Musæ Subsecivæ," 8°, 1696, in which, at p. 469, is an elegy on Randolph, headed : "*In Obitum Thomæ Randolphi, M.A., Collegii Trinitatis Cantab. Socii, Poetæ ingeniosissimi, et qui sæculi sui Ovidius dici meruit.*"

Et tecum similis futurus ævi,
Qui jam vita cluis scholæ et theatri ?
Nolo : Marmor erit mihi poeta.
Mausolæa mihi mei Menandri
O, quàm æterna salìs liber perennis !
Non quæram monumenta firmiora,
Nostri nominis ut supersit ætas.

THOMAS RILEY.

A GMINE non tanto paupertas multa beatam,
*   Divitis et pransam vexat ubique domum,*
Quot tua quotidie pulsarunt limina chartæ ;
*   Fervidus à tergo et quisque rogator adest.*
Prodeat audacter, repetitáque vulnera præli
Fabula, quæ meruit sustinuisse, ferat.
Non horret tantùm tua Musa, aut mutat, ut esset
Turpior ornatu rustica Nympha suo.

CAR. FOTHERBIE, *J. Coll.*

Amico suo ingeniosissimo Tho. Randolph.

F INGITO zelotypos, quos pulchrè fingis, amores ;
*   Sed nil de Musa suspicionis habe.*
Fac dominam ut plures norint, et adultera fiet ;
*   Musa, licèt fuerit publica, casta manet.*

FR. MERES.[1]

---

[1] Was this the same person who wrote "Palladis Tamia," 1598, and a little work called "God's Arithmetic," 8º, 1597? Meres was M.A. of both Universities.

Fratri suo Thom. Randolph.

NON satìs est quòd te dederit natura priorem,
Ni simul et natu major et arte fores?
Illa, sciens noster quàm non sit magnus agellus,
Ingenio tenues jure rependit opes.

Ro. RANDOLPH. *æd. Chr. Oxon.*

Autori.

HEI mihi! quos fluctus, quod tentas æquor, amice?
Queis te jactandum das malesanus aquis?
Irritata juvat quid possit lectio scire?
Æmula vel de te dicere lingua velit?
I felix, oculos dudum prædatus, et aures,
Censurámque ipsam sub juga mitte gravem.
Qui meruit CAROLO plausum spectante, popello
Non est cur metuat displicuisse rudi.
Dirige victorem captivo Cæsare currum,
Augeat et titulos victa MARIA tuos:
Triste supercilium lævo nictantis ocello
Mitte sibi: Momis est placuisse nefas.

THOM. VINCENT.[1]

---

[1] Thomas Vincent, of Trinity College, Cambridge, was the author of a Latin drama, entitled "Paria," acted before Charles I. in 1627, and printed in 1648. See *Retrospective Review*, xii. 34–5.

DRAMATIS PERSONÆ.

—— o ——

TYNDARUS, son of Demetrius, and supposed brother to Pamphilus, enamoured of Evadne.

PAMPHILUS, supposed son to Demetrius, but son indeed to Chremylus.

EVADNE, supposed daughter to Chremylus.

TECHMESSA, daughter to Chremylus.

DEMETRIUS, an Athenian, in the disguise of an astrologer.

CHREMYLUS, an old man.

DIPSAS, his wife.

SIMO, an old doating father.

ASOTUS, his prodigal son.

BALLIO, a pander, and tutor to Asotus.

PHRYNE, a courtesan, and mistress to Asotus.

PHRONESIUM, a merry chamber-maid.

HYPERBOLUS,
THRASYMACHUS, } two soldiers.

BOMOLOCHUS,
CHARYLUS, } two poets.

A Sexton.

STAPHYLA, his wife.

PAGNIUM, a page.

A Priest.

Officers.

Servants.

The Scene, THEBES.

The Jealous Lovers.

—o—

ACT I., SCENE I.

SIMO, ASOTUS, BALLIO.

Sim. HOW thrives my boy Asotus? Is he capable
Of your grave precepts?

Bal. Sir, I never met
A quicker brain, a wit so neat and spruce.

Sim. Well, get thee home, old Simo : go and kneel :
Fall on thy aged knees, and thank the gods
Th' hast got a boy of wax, fit to receive
Any impressions.

Aso. As I am a gentleman,
And first of all our family, you wrong me, dad,
To take me for a dunce.

Sim. No, good Asotus,
It is thy father's care (a provident care),
That wakes him from his sleeps to think of thee ;
And when I brooding sit upon my bags,
And every day turn o'er my heaps of gold,
Each piece I finger makes me start, and cry,
This—this—and this—and this—is for Asotus.

Aso. Take this, and this, and this, and this again :
Can you not be content to give me money,
But you must hit me in the teeth with't, 'slid?

Bal. Nay, good Asotus, such a loving father

That does not bless you with a sweaty palm
Clapt on your head, or some unfruitful prayer;
But lays his blessings out in gold and silver,
Fine white and yellow blessings!

 Aso.   Prythee, Ballio,
I could endure his white and yellow blessings,
If he would leave his prating.

 Sim.   Do you hear him?
How sharp and tart his answers are?   Old Simo,
Th' hast got a witty-witty wag, yet dear one.
When I behold the vastness of my treasure,
How large my coffers, yet how cramm'd with wealth,
That every talent sweats as in a crowd,
And grieves not at the prison, but the narrow-
 ness——

 Aso. If I make not room for 'em, ne'er trust me.
             [Aside.

 Sim. When I see this, I cannot choose but fear
Thou canst not find out ways enou' to spend it:
They will outvy thy pleasures.

 Bal.   Few such fathers!
I cannot choose but stroke my [1] beard, and wonder,
That having so much wealth, you have the wit
To understand for whom you got it.

 Aso.   True:
And I have so much wit to understand
It must be spent, and shall, boys.

 Sim.   Pray heaven it may!

 Aso. I'll live to spend it all; and then—perhaps
 I'll die!
And will not leave the purchase of a sheet,
Or buy a rotten coffin.

 Bal.   Yes, dear pupil,
Buy me an urn; while yet we laugh and live,
It shall contain our drink, and when we die,

---

[1] Old copies, *your*.

It may preserve our dust.   'Tis fit our ashes
Should take a nap there where they took their liquor.
 Sim. Sage counsel this—observe it, boy—observe it.
 Aso. I live in Thebes, yet I dare swear all Athens
Affords not such a tutor : thou may'st read
To all the young heirs in town or city.
 Sim. Ah, Ballio ! I have lived a dunghill wretch,
Grown poor by getting riches, mine own torture—
A rust unto myself, as to my gold :
To pile up idle treasure starv'd my body
Thus to a wrinkled skin and rotten bones,
And spider-like have spun a web of gold
Out of my bowels; only knew the care,
But not the use of gold.   Now, gentle Ballio,
I would not have my son so loath'd a thing.
No, let him live and spend, and buy his pleasures
At any rate.   Read to him, gentle Ballio,
Where are the daintiest meats, the briskest wines,
The costliest garments.   Let him dice, and wench
But with the fairest, be she wife or daughter
To our best burgess : and if Thebes be scarce,
Buy me all Corinth for him.   When I sleep
Within my quiet grave, I shall have dreams—
Fine pleasant dreams, to think with how much pleasure
Asotus spends what I with care have got.
 Aso. Sure, I were a most ungracious child now,
If I should spoil the dreams of a dead father.
Sleep, when thou wilt, within thy quiet urn,
And thou shalt dream thou seest me drink sack plenty,
Encircled round with doxies plump and dainty.
 Sim. How thrives my boy ?   How forward in his
  studies ?
 Bal. Troth, with much industry I have brought
  him now
That he is grown past drinking ?
 Sim. How, man, past drinking ?
 Bal. I mean he is grown perfect in that science.

Sim. But will he not forget?

Aso. No, I warrant you, I know I shan't forget;
Because i' th' morning I ne'er remember
What I did o'er-night.

    Sim.   How feeds my boy?

Bal. Troth, well: I never met
A stomach of more valour, or a tooth
Of such judicious knowledge.

    Sim.   Can he wench, ha?

Bal. To say the truth, but rawly.

    Aso.   Rawly?   I'm sure
I have already made my dad a grandsire
To five and twenty: and if I do not
Out of mere charity people all the hospitals
With my stray babes, then geld me!   Woe to the parish
That bribes me not to spare it.

    Bal.   Then for the die—
He throws it with such art, so pois'd a hand,
That had you left him nothing, that one mystery
Were a sufficient portion.

    Aso.   Will you see me?
Set me a bag.   These were an usurer's bones.

Bal. In this behold what frailty lives in man:
He that rubb'd out a life to gather trash,
Is after death turn'd prodigal.

    Sim.   Throw, Asotus.

Aso. Then have at all, and 'twere a million.   All!
Fortune was kind: the precious dirt is mine.

Sim. And take it, boy—and this—and this, beside.
And, 'cause desert may challenge a reward,
This for your pains, dear Ballio.

    Bal.   My endeavours,
Although to my best power, alas! come short
Of any merit.   Sir, you make me blush,
And this reward but chides my insufficiency.
Pray, urge it not.

    Sim. A modest, honest—honest man:

I'll double it; in faith, I will.   I am
The joyfull'st father!
    Bal.   See how the good man weeps!
    Aso. So he will weep his gold away—no matter.
    Sim. Come hither, dear; come, let me kiss my son.
    Aso. There's a sweet kiss indeed! this 'tis to want
A tutor.   Had you had my education,
You would have ta'en me by the lily hand,
Then gaz'd a while upon my flaming eyes,
As wondering at the lustre of their orbs;
Then humbly begg'd in language strow'd with flowers,
To taste the cherries of my ruby lip—
God-a-mercy for this, tutor.
    Sim. I am o'rejoic'd, I am o'rejoic'd.
                     [*Exit* SIMO.

SCENE II.

ASOTUS, BALLIO.

    Aso. Well, go thy ways, I may have a thousand
      fathers,
And never have the like.   Well, pockets, well,
Be not so sad; though you are heavy now,
You shall be lighter.
    Bal.   Pupil, I must tell you,
I do repent the loss of those good hours,
And would call back the study I have ta'en
In moral alchemy, to extract a gentleman
Almost out of a dunghill.   Still do I see
So much of peasant in you?
    Aso.   Angry, tutor?
    Bal. Teem'd my invention all this while for this?
No better issue of my labouring brain
After so many and such painful throes?
Another sin like this, and be transform'd
Mere clown again!

Aso. The reason, dear instructor?

Bal. Have I not open'd to you all the mysteries,
The precise rules and axioms of gentility,
And all methodical? Yet you still so dull,
As not to know you print eternal stains
Upon your honour, and corrupt your blood
(That cost me many a minute the refining)
By carrying your own money? See these breeches,
A pair of worthy, rich and reverend breeches,
Lost to the fashion by a lump of dross.
I'll be your bailiff rather.

Aso.   Out, infection!

Bal. Who, that beheld those hose, could e'er
        suspect
They would be guilty of mechanic metal?
What's your vocation? Trade you for yourself?
Or else whose journeyman or prentice are you?

Aso. Pardon me, tutor: for I do repent,
And do protest hereafter I will never
Wear anything that jingles—but my spurs.

Bal. This is gentile.

Aso.   Away, mechanic trash!
I'll kick thee, son of earth. Thus will I kick thee
For torturing my poor father. Dirt, avaunt!
I do abandon thee.

Bal.   Blest be thy generous tongue!
But who comes here? This office must be mine:
I'll make you fair account of every drachm.

Aso. I'll not endure the trouble of account:
Say all is spent, and then we must have more.

SCENE III.

Tyndarus, Asotus, Ballio.

Tyn. What Fury shot a viper through my soul
To poison all my thoughts? Civil dissension

Wars in my blood : here Love with thousand bows
And twenty thousand arrows lays his siege
To my poor heart which, mann'd with nought but
    fear,
Denies the great god entrance. O Evadne!
Canst thou, that risest fairer than the morn,
Set blacker than the evening? Weak jealousy!
Did e'er thy prying and suspicious sight
Find her lip guilty of a wanton smile,
Or one lascivious glance dart from her eye?
The blushes of her cheeks are innocent,
Her carriage sober, her discourse all chaste.
No toyish gesture, no desire to see
The public shows, or haunt the theatre!
She is no popular mistress ; all her kisses
Do speak her virgin! such a bashful heat
At several tides ebbs, flows : flows, ebbs again,
As 'twere afraid to meet our wilder flame.
But if all this be cunning (as who knows
The sleights of Syrens?) and I, credulous fool,
Train'd by her songs to sink in her embraces,
I were undone for ever. Wretched Tyndarus!

    Aso. Ha, ha, ha, he! This is an arrant coxcomb,
That's jealous of his wife before he has got her,
And thinks himself a cuckold before marriage.

    Bal. Want of a tutor makes unbridled youth
Run wildly into passions. You have got
A skilful pilot (though I say it), pupil,
One that will steer both you and your estate
Into safe harbour. Pray, observe his humour.

    Tyn. Away, foul sin! 'Tis atheism to suspect
A devil lodg'd in such divinity.
Call snow unchaste, and say the ice is wanton,
If she be so! No, my Evadne, no ;
I know thy soul as beauteous as thy face.
That glorious outside which all eyes adore,
Is but the fair shrine of a fairer saint.

O, pardon me thy penitent infidel !
By thy fair eyes (from whom this little world
Borrows that light it has), I henceforth vow
Never to think sin can be grown so bold
As to assault thy soul.
  Aso.   This fellow, tutor,
Waxes and wanes a hundred times a minute !
In my conscience, he was got in the change of the
  moon.

SCENE IV.

CHREMYLUS, DIPSAS, ASOTUS, BALLIO, TYNDARUS.

  Dip. Rot in thy grave, thou dotard : I defy thee.
Curst be our day of marriage ; shall I nurse
And play the mother to another's brat ?
And she to nose my daughter ? Take Evadne,
Your pretty-precious by-blow, fair Evadne,
The minion of the town. Go and provide her
A place i' th' spital.
  Chrem.   Gentle wife, have patience.
  Dip. Let them have patience that can have
  patience,
For I will have no patience. 'Slid, patience,
  patience !
  Chrem. You know her daughter to our dearest
  friend :
And should my son committed to his care
Thus suffer as the poor Evadne does,
The gods were just so to revenge her wrong.
  Dip. I will not have my house afflicted with her :
She·has more suitors than a pretty wench in an Uni-
  versity,
While my daughter has leisure enough to follow her
  needle.

Chrem. Wife, I must tell you you're a peevish
    woman.

Dip. And I must tell you you're an arrant cox-
    comb
To tell me so. My daughter nos'd by a slut!

Aso. There will be a quarrel, tutor; do you take
The old man's part; I am o' th' woman's side.

Chrem. Were every vein in poor Evadne fill'd
With blood deriv'd from those whose ancestors
Transmitted in that blood a hate to us,
A lineal hate to all our family;
Yet (trusted to my care) she is my daughter,
And shall share equal blessings with mine own.

Dip. Then a perpetual noise shall fill thy house;
I will not let thee sleep, nor eat, nor drink,
But I will torture thee with a peal of chiding.
Thou shalt confess the troubled sea more calm;
That thunder with less violence cleaves the air;
The ravens, screech-owls, and the mandrake's voice
Shall be thy constant music. I can talk.
Thy friends that come to see thee shall grow deaf
With my loud clamours. Heaven be prais'd for
    tongue!
No woman in all Thebes is better weapon'd,
And't shall be sharper; or were any member
Needed [1] besides my tongue, I would employ it
In thy just torment. I am vex'd to think
My best revenge age hath prevented now;
Else every man should read it in thy brow.

Chrem. I will not wind you up, dear 'larum. Go:
Run out your line at length, and so be quiet.
                   [*Exit* CHREMYLUS.

---

[1] Old copies, *Not dead.*

SCENE V.

DIPSAS, TYNDARUS, ASOTUS, BALLIO.

Tyn. Here is an argument, Tyndarus, to incite
And tempt thy free neck to the yoke of love.
Are these the joys we reap i' th' nuptial bed?
First in thy bosom warm the snake, and call
The viper to thy arms.   O gentle death!
There is no sleep blest and secure but thine.
Wives are but fair afflictions; sure, this woman
Was woo'd with protestations, oaths, and vows,
As well as my Evadne—thought as fair,
As wise and virtuous as my soul speaks her?
And may not she or play the hypocrite now,
Or after turn apostate?   Guilty thoughts,
Disturb me not.   For were the sex a sin,
Her goodness were sufficient to redeem
And ransom all from slander.
   Dip.   Gentle sir,
I pity the unripeness of your age,
That cast your love upon a dangerous rock—
My daughter; but I blush to own the birth,
And curse the womb so fruitful to my shame.
You may be wise and happy—or repent.
                                         [*Exit* DIPSAS.

SCENE VI.

TYNDARUS, ASOTUS, BALLIO.

Aso. This woman is a devil, for she hates her own
    children.
Bal. In what an ecstasy stands that grieved wight!
Aso. In troth, I shall into compunction melt.

Will not a cup of Lesbian liquor rouse
His frozen spirits to agility?

Bal. Spoke like a son of Æsculapius!

Aso. My father's angels guard thee! We have gold
To cure thy dumps, although we do not mean
It should profane these breeches. Sure, his soul
Is gone upon some errand, and has left
The corpse in pawn till it come back again.

Tyn. Cold jealousy, I shall account thee now
No idle passion, when the womb that bare her
Shall plead her guilt. I must forget her name.
Fly from me, memory:[1] I will drink oblivion
To lose the loath'd Evadne.

Aso.   Generous sir,
A pottle of elixir at the Pegasus
Bravely carous'd is more restorative.
My tutor shall disburse.

Tyn.   Good impertinent.

Aso. Impertinent? Impertinent in thy face!
Danger accrues upon the word impertinent.
Tutor, draw forth thy fatal steel, and slash
Till he devour the word impertinent.

Bal. The word impertinent will not bear a quarrel;
The epithet of good hath mollified it.

Aso. We are appeas'd, be safe. I say, be safe.

Tyn. Be not rash, Tyndarus. This malicious woman
May as well hate her daughter as her husband.
I am too sudden to conclude her false
On such slight witness. Shall I think the sun
Has lost his crown of light, because a cloud
Or envious night hath cast a robe of darkness
'Twixt the world's eye and mine?

Aso.   Canst thou, royal boy,
Burn out the remnant of a day with us?

Tyn. I am resolved upon a safer trial.

---

[1] Old copies, *my memory.*

Sir, you are courtly, and no doubt the ladies
Fall out about you : for those rare perfections
Can do no less than ravish.
　　Aso.　　　　　　　　I confess
I cannot walk the streets, but straight the females
Are in a tumult.　I must leave thee, Thebes,
Lest I occasion civil wars to rage
Within thy walls ; I would be loth to ruin
My native soil.
　　Bal.　　　　Sir, what with my instructions,
He has the wooing character.
Could you now
But pull the maiden-blossoms of a rose
Sweet as the spring it buds in, fair Evadne ;
Or gain her promise, and that grant confirm'd
By some slight jewel, I shall vow myself
Indebted to the service, and live yours.
　　Aso. She cannot stand the fury of my siege.
　　Bal. At first assault he takes the female fort.
　　Aso. And rides love's conqueror though the streets
of Thebes.　I'll tell you, sir : you would not think
how many gentlemen-ushers have and do daily en-
danger their little legs, by walking early and late to
bring me visits from this lady and that countess.
Heaven pardon the sin !　Ne'er a man in this city
has made so many chambermaids lose their voices as
I ha' done.
　　Tyn. As how, I pray ?
　　Aso. By rising in the cold night to let me in to
their madams.　If you hear a waiting-woman coughing,
follow her : she will infallibly direct you to some that
has been a mistress of mine.
　　Bal. I have read love's tactics to him, and he
　　　knows
The military discipline of wooing :
To rank and file his kisses : how to muster
His troops of compliments, and——

Tyn. I do believe you.
Go on ; return victorious. O poor heart,
What sorrows dost thou teem with ! Here she comes.

SCENE VII.

TYNDARUS, ASOTUS, BALLIO, EVADNE.

Tyn. And is it possible so divine a goddess
Should fall from heaven to wallow here in sin
With a baboon as this is ? My Evadne,
Why should a sadness dwell upon this cheek
To blast the tender roses? spare those tears
To pity others ; thy unspotted soul
Has not a stain in't to be wash'd away
With penitent waters. Do not grieve ; thy sorrows
Have forc'd mine eyes too to this womanish weak-
ness.

Aso. A pretty enemy ! I long for an encounter.
Who would not be valiant, to fight under such colours ?

Evad. My lord, 'tis guilt enough in me to challenge
A sea of tears, that you suspect me guilty.
I would your just sword would so courteous be
As to unrip my heart ; there you shall read
In characters sad lovers use to write,
Nothing but innocence and true faith to you.

Tyn. I have lost all distrust. Seal me my pardon
In a chaste turtle's kiss. The doves that draw
The rosy chariot of the Queen of Love,
Shall not be link'd in whiter yokes than we.
Come let us kiss, Evadne. Out, temptation !
There was too much and that too wanton heat
In thy lascivious lip. Go to the stews ;
I may perchance be now and then a customer,
But do abjure thee from my chaster sheets.

[*Exit* TYNDARUS.

SCENE VIII.

EVADNE, BALLIO, ASOTUS.

Evad. Then from the world abjure thyself, Evadne,
And in thy quiet death secure the thoughts
Of troubled Tyndarus.   My womanish courage
Could prompt me on to die, were not that death
Doubled in losing him.   Th' Elysian fields
Can be no paradise, while he's not there :
The walks are dull without him.
    Aso.   Such a qualm
O' th' sudden !
    Bal.   Fie, turned coward?   Resolution
Is the best sword in war.
    Aso.   Then I will on,
And boldly.   Yet——
    Bal.   What? will you lose the day
Ere you begin the battle ?
    Aso.   Truly, tutor,
I have an ague takes me every day,
And now the cold sits on me.
    Bal.   Go home and blush,
Thou son of fear.
    Aso.   Nay, then I'll venture on,
Were she ten thousand strong.   Hail! heavenly Queen
Of Beauty ; most illustrious Cupid's daughter
Was not so fair.
    Bal.   His mother.
    Aso.   'Tis no matter.
The silly damsel understands no poetry.   [*Aside.*]
Deign me thy lip, as blue as azure bright.
    Bal. As red as ruby bright.
    Aso.   What's that to the purpose ?
Is not azure blue as good as ruby red ?
    Evad. It is not charitable mirth to mock

A wretched lady's griefs.   The gods are just,
And may requite you with a scorn as great
As that you throw on me.
    Aso.   Not kiss a gentleman?
And my father worth thousands!   Resolution,
Spur me to brave achievements.
    Evad.   Such a rudeness
Some ladies by the valour of their servants
Could have redeem'd.   Ungentle God of Love,
Write me not down among the happier names;
I only live a martyr in thy flames.   *[Exit.*
    Aso. This is such a masculine feminine gender.
    Bal. She is an Amazon both stout and tall.
    Aso. Yet I got this by struggling.   If I fit you
      not,   *[A diamond ring out of her ear.*
Proud squeamish coyness!   Tutor, such an itch
Of kissing runs all o'er me.   I'll to Phryne,
And fool away an hour or two in dalliance.
    Ball. Go, I must stay to wait on fair Techmessa:
Who is as jealous of young Pamphilus
As Tyndarus of Evadne.
    Aso.   Surely, tutor,
I must provide me a suit of jealousy:
It will be all the fashion.

SCENE IX.

TECHMESSA, BALLIO.

    Tech. Bless me! what uncouth fancies toss my
      brain!
As in yon arbour sleep had clos'd mine eyes,
Methought within a flowery plain were met
A troop of ladies, and myself was one.
Amongst them rose a challenge, whose soft foot
Should gentliest press the grass, and quickest run,

The prize for which they strove—the heart of Pam-
　　philus.
The victory was doubtful : all perform'd
Their course with equal speed, and Pamphilus
Was chosen judge to end the controversy.
Methought he shar'd his heart, and dealt a piece
To every lady of the troop but me—
It was unkindly done.
　　Bal.　　　　　　　I have descried——
　　Tech. What?
　　Bal.　　　　　A frost in his affections
To you, but heat above the rage of Dog-days
To any other petticoat in Thebes.
I do not think but were the pox a woman
He would not stick to court it.
　　Tech.　　　　　　　　O my soul!
Thou hast descried too much.　How sweet it is
To live in ignorance!
　　Bal.　　　　　　I did sound him home,
And with such words profan'd your reputation,
Would whet a coward's sword.　One that ne'er saw you
Rebuk'd my slanderous tongue—I feel the crab-tree
　　still—
While he sat still unmov'd.
　　Tech.　　　　　　It cannot be.
　　Bal. I'll undertake he shall resign his weapon,
And forswear steel in anything but knives,
Rather than venture one small scratch to salve
Your wounded honour, or (to prove you chaste)
Encounter with a pin.
　　Tech. I am no common mistress, nor have need
To entertain a multitude of champions
To draw in my defence.　Yet, had he lov'd me,
He could not hear me injur'd with such patience.
Ballio, one trial more : bring me his sword
Rather resign'd than drawn in my defence,
And I shall rest confirm'd.

Bal. Here's a fine business.
What shall I do? Go to a cutler's shop,
And buy a sword like that. O, it will not do.
    Tech. Will you do this?
    Bal. It is resolv'd. I will
One way or other. Wit, at a dead lift help me.

SCENE X.

PÆGNIUM, TECHMESSA, BALLIO.

Pæg. Madam, the wretched Pamphilus.
    Tech. What of him?
Pæg. Is through your cruelty and suspicion dead.
Bal. That news revives me.
    Tech. Haste, Techmessa, then:
What dost thou here, when Pamphilus is dead?
Cast off this robe of clay, my soul, and fly
To overtake him; bear him company
To the Elysian groves: the journey thither
Is dark and melancholy: do not suffer him
To go alone.
    Pæg. Madam, I joy to see
With how much sorrow you receive his death.
I will restore you comfort: Pamphilus lives.
    Bal. If Pamphilus lives, then Ballio's dead again.
    Tech. Do you put tricks upon me? we shall have
        you,
On a little counterfeit sorrow and a few drops
Of woman's tears, go and persuade your master
I am deeply in love with him.
    Pæg. If you be not,
You ought in justice.
    Tech. I'll give thee a new feather,
And you tell me what were those three ladies' names
Your master entertain'd last night.

Pæg.   Three ladies ?

Tech. You make it strange now.

Pæg.   Madam, by all oaths

My master bears a love so firmly constant
To you, and only you ; he talks, thinks, dreams
Of nothing but Techmessa.   When he hears
The sound of your blest name, he turns chameleon,
And lives on that sweet air.   Here he has sent me
    [He lays down his sword to pull out his letters.
With letters to you ; which I should deliver
I know not, nor himself.   For first he writes,
And, when the letter likes him not, begins
A second style, and so a third and fourth,
And thus proceeds ; then reads them over all,
And knows not which to send—perchance tears all.
The paper was not fair enough to kiss
So white a hand : that letter was too big,
A line uneven ; all excuse prevail'd.
Language, or phrase, or word, or syllable,
That he thought harsh and rough.   I have heard him
        wish
Above all blessings heaven can bestow
(So strange a fancy has affection taught him)
That he might have a quill from Cupid's wing
Dipp'd in the milk of Venus, to record
Your praises and his love.   I have brought you here
Whole packets of affections.

Bal.   Blessed occasion !
        [He steals away the sword.
Here is a conquest purchas'd without blood.
Though strength and valour fail us, yet we see
There may a field be won by policy.   *[Exit.*

Tech. Go, Pægnium, tell your master I could wish
That I was his ; but bid him choose another.
Tell him he has no hope e'er to enjoy me ;
But bid him not despair.   I do not doubt
His constant love to me ; yet I suspect

His zeal more fervent to some other saint.
Say I receive his letters with all joy,
But will not take the pains to read a syllable. [*Exit.*

Pæg. If I do not think women were got with
riddling, whip me! hocus-pocus, here you shall have
me, and there you shall have me! A man cannot
find out their meaning without the sieve and shears.
I conceive them now to be engendered of nothing but
the wind and the weathercock. What! my sword
gone? Ah, well! This same panderly rogue Ballio
has got it. He sows suspicions of my master here,
because he cudgels him into manners, and that old
scold Dipsas hires him to it. How could such a
devil bring forth such an angel as my Lady Techmessa?
unless it were before her fall. I know all their plots,
and yet they cannot see 'em. Heaven keep me
from love, and preserve my eyesight. Go; plot,
engineers, plot on—
   I'll work a countermine, and 'twill be brave,
   An old rogue overreach'd by a young knave!
                                              [*Exit.*

ACT II., SCENE I.

ASOTUS, BALLIO.

Aso. Revenge, more sweet than muscadine and
     eggs,
To-day I will embrace thee! Healths in blood
Are soldiers' mornings-draughts! Proud, proud
     Evadne
Shall know what 'tis to make a wit her foe,
And such a wit as can give overthrow
To male or female, be they—man or woman.
This can my tutor do, and I or—no man.
   Bal. And Pamphilus shall learn by this dear knock
His liberal valour late bestowed upon me,

Invention lies at safer ward than wit :
This sword shall teach not to provoke the cruel.
   Aso. And by this gem shall I confound a jewel.
'Slid, tutor, I have a wit too. Here was a jest *ex
    tempore !*

SCENE II.

ASOTUS, BALLIO, TYNDARUS.

   Tyn. Physicians say there's no disease so dangerous
As when the patient knows not he is sick.
Such, such is mine : I could not be so ill,
Did I but know I were not well.   The fear
Of dangers but suspected is more horrid
Than present misery.   I have seen a man,
During the storm, shake at the thoughts of death :
Who when his eyes beheld a certain ruin,
Died hugging of the wave.   Were Evadne true,
I were too blest ; or could I say she's false,
I could no more be wretched.   I am well :
My pulse beats music, and my lively blood
Dances a healthful measure.   Ha ! what's this
Gnaws at my heart ?   What viperous shirt of Nessus
Cleaves to my skin, and eats away my flesh ?
'Tis some infection.
   Aso.   Tutor, let's be gone.
O' my life, we are dead men else.
   Tyn.   My Asotus !
   Aso. Keep your infection to yourself.
   Tyn.   'Tis love
Is my infection.
   Aso.   Nay, then I care not, Tyndarus :
For that is an epidemical disease,
And is the finest sickness in the world
When it takes two together.

Tyn. Dear, dear self!
How fares the darling of the age? Say, what success?

Aso. Did not I tell you, sir, that I was born
With a caul upon my face? My mother wrapp'd me
In her own smock. The females fall before me
Like trembling doves before the towering hawk,
While o'er the spoils in triumph thus I walk.

Bal. So he takes virgins with his amorous eye,
As spider's web entraps the tender fly.

Aso. True, tutor, true: for I woo 'em with cobweb-
lawn.

Tyn. I know the rest of women may be frail,
Brittle as glasses: but my Evadne stands
A rock of Parian marble, firm and pure.
The crystal may be tainted, and rude feet
Profane the Milky Way: the phœnix self,
Although but one, no virgin—ere I harbour
Dishonourable thoughts of that bright maid!
No, Tyndarus, reflect upon thyself:
Turn thine eyes inward, see thine own unworthiness,
That does thy thoughts to this suspicion move:
She loves thee not, 'cause thou deserv'st no love.

Aso. I do not know where the enchantment lies,
Whether it be the magic of mine eyes,
Or lip, or cheek, or brow: but I suppose
The conjuration chiefly in my nose.
Evadne, sir, is mine, and woo'd me first.
Troth, 'tis a pretty lass; and for a woman
She courts in handsome words; and now and then
A polite phrase, and such a feeling appetite
That, having not a heart of flint or steel,
As mine's an easier temper, I consented
To give her, in the way of alms, a night
Or so—you guess the meaning.

Tyn. Too-too well.
And must her lust break into open flames,
To lend the world a light to view her shames?

Could not she taste her page? or secretly
Admit a tough-back'd groom into her arms?
Or practice with her doctor, and take physic
In a close room?   But thus, good heavens, to take
Her stallions up i' th' streets!   While sin is modest,
It may be healed; but if it once grow impudent,
The fester spreads above all hopes of cure.
I never could observe so strange a boldness
In my Evadne.   I have seen her cheeks
Blush as if modesty herself had there
Lain in a bed of coral.   But how soon
Is virtue lost in women!
   Bal.   Mistake us not,
Dear Tyndarus: Evadne may be chaste
To all the world—but him.   And as for him,
Diana's self or any stricter goddess
Would lose the virgin-zone.   I have instill'd
Magnetic force into him, that attracts
Their iron hearts, and fashions them, like steel
Upon the anvil, to what shape he please.
He knows the minute—the precise one minute—
No woman can hold out in.   Come to me, sir,
I'll teach you in one fortnight by astrology
To make each burgess in all Thebes your cuckold.
   Aso. As silly lambs do fill the wolves' black jaw,
And fearful harts the generous lions' paw,
As whales eat lesser fries; so may you see
The matrons, maids and widows stoop to me.
   Tyn. O, do not hold me longer in suspense:
The prisoner at the bar may with less fear
Hear the sad sentence of his death pronounc'd,
Than stand the doubtful trial.   Pray, confirm me.
   Aso. Know you this jewel?
   Tyn.   O, my sad heart-strings crack!
   Aso. If your Evadne be a phœnix, Tyndarus,
Some ten months hence you may have more o' th'
    breed.

Tyn. This did I give her, and she vow'd to keep it
By all the oaths religion knew.   No deity
In all the court of heaven but highly suffers
In this one perjury.   The diamond
Keeps his chaste lustre still, when she has soil'd
A glory of more worth than all those toys
Proud folly gave such price to.
   Aso.   This? a pretty toy;
But of no value to my other trophies
That the frail tribe has sent me.   Your best jewels
Are to be found, sir, in the weaker vessels;
And that's a mystery: I have sweat out such
Variety of trifles, their several kinds
Would pose a learned lapidary.   My closet
By some, that knew me not for Cupid's favourite,
Has been mistaken for a jeweller's shop.
   Bal. And then for ribbons, points, for knots and
      shoe-strings,
Or (to slip higher) garters, no Exchange
Affords such choice of wares.
   Aso.   Phœbus, whip
Thy lazy team; run headlong to the west,
I long to taste the banquet of the night.
Sir, if you please, when I am surfeited,
To take a pretty breakfast of my leavings——
   Tyn. Where art thou, patience? Hence, contagious
      mists,
That would infect the air of her pure fame!
My sword shall purge you forth, base dross of men,
From her refined metal.
   Aso.   Bless me, tutor!
This is not the precise minute.
   Tyn.   Why should I
Afflict myself for her? No, let her vanish.
Shall I retain my love, when she has lost
The treasure of her virtue?   Stay, perchance
Her innocence may be wrong'd.   Said I, perchance?

That doubt will call a curse upon my head
To plague my unbelief.   But here's a witness
Of too-too certain truth stands up against her.
Methinks the flame that burnt so bright dies in me.
I am no more a captive : I have shak'd
My fetters off, and broke those gyves of steel
That bound me to my thraldom.   My fair prison,
Adieu !   How sweetly breathes this open air !
My feet, grown wanton with their liberty,
Could dance and caper, till I knock'd at heaven
With my advanced head.   Come, dear Asotus,
There are no pleasures but they shall be ours.
We will dispeople all the elements
To please our palates.   Midnight shall behold
Our nightly cups, and wear a blacker mask,
As envious of our jollities.   The whole sex
Of women shall be ours.   Merchants shall proffer
Their tender brides : mothers shall run and fetch
Their daughters (ere they yet be ripe) to satisfy
Our liquorish lusts.   Then Tyndarus happy call,
That (losing one fair maid) has purchas'd all.

   Aso. You have an admirable method, tutor ;
If this fellow has not been i' my heart, I'll be hang'd,
He speaks my mind so pat.   Ha, *buon corragio !*

   Bal. You see what more than miracles art can do.

   Tyn. And when we have run o'er the catalogue
Of former pleasures, thou and I, and Ballio,
Will sit and study new ones : I will raise
A sect of new and rare philosophers,
Shall from my name be call'd Tyndarides.

   Aso. And I will raise another sect like these,
That shall from me be called Asotides.
Tutor, my fellow-pupil here and I
Must quaff a bowl of rare philosophy,
To pledge the health of his Tyndarides.

   Tyn. Come, blest restorer of my liberty !

   Aso. If any friend of yours want liberty

In such a kind as this, you may command me ;
For if the brave Tyndarides be not free,
Th' Asotides shall grant them liberty.

   Tyn. We will be frolic, boy ; and ere we part,
Remember thee, thou mighty man of art.

                [*Exeunt* TYNDARUS *and* ASOTUS.

SCENE III.

BALLIO, TECHMESSA.

   Bal. There is (besides revenge) a kind of sweet-
      ness
In acting mischief.   I could hug my head,
And kiss the brain that hatches such dear rogueries,
Such loving—loving rogueries.   Silly Pamphilus,
With thine own sword I'll kill thee, and then trample
On thy poor foolish carcass.   Techmessa here ?
Then, fortune, wait on my designs, and crown 'm
With a success as high as they deserve.

   Tech. Methinks sometimes I view my Pamphilus,
Clothed (angel-like) in white and spotless robes ;
And straight upon a sudden my chang'd fancy
Presents him black and horrid, all a-stain,
More loathsome than a leper.

   Bal.   And that fancy
Presents him in his likeness.   All the sinks
And common sewers in Thebes are cleanly to him.

   Tech. Peace, thou foul tongue !

   Ball.   Nay, if you be so squeamish,
I have no womanish itch to prate.   Farewell.

   Tech. Nay, do not leave me unresolv'd, good Ballio.

   Bal. Why, I did set you out in more vile colours
Than ever cunning pencil us'd to limn
Witch, hag, or fury with.

   Tech.   Thou couldst not do't, and live.

Bal. I am no ghost, flesh and blood still.
I said you had a pretty head of hair,
And such as might do service to the State,
Made into halters ! that you had a brow
Hung o'er your eyes like fly-flaps : that your eyes
Were like two powdering-tubs, either running o'er,
Or full of standing brine : your cheeks were sunk
So low and hollow, they might serve the boys
For cherry-pits !

Tech.   Could Pamphilus hear all this,
And not his blood turn choler ?

Bal.   This ? and more—
I said your nose was like a hunter's horn,
And stood so bending up, a man might hang
His hat upon't : that I mistook the year,
And always thought it winter when I saw
Two icicles at your nostrils !

Tech.   Have I lost
All woman, that I can with patience hear
Myself thus injur'd ?

Bal.   I could beat myself
For speaking it ; but 'twas to sound him, madam.
I said you had no neck : your chin and shoulders
Were so good friends, they would ha' nothing part
    'em :
I vow'd your breasts for colour and proportion
Were like a writhel'd pair of o'erworn footballs.
Your waist was slender, but the ambitious buttock
Climbs up so high about, who sees you naked
Might swear you had been born with a vardingale.

Tech. I am e'en frighted with thy strange description.

Bal. I left, asham'd and weary.   He goes on—
There be more chops and wrinkles in her lips
Than on the earth in heat of dogdays ; and her teeth
Look like an old park-pale.   She has a tongue
Would make the deaf man bless his imperfection,
That frees him from the plague of so much noise,

And such a breath (heaven shield us !) as outvies
The shambles and bear-garden for a scent !
   Tech. Was ever such a fury ?
   Bal.   For your shoulders,
He thinks they were ordain'd to underprop
Some beam o' th' Temple ; and that's all the use
Religion can make of you !   Then your feet
(For I am loth to give the full description)
He vows they both are cloven !
   Tech.   Had all malice
Dwelt in one tongue, it could not scandal more.
Is this the man adores me as his saint ?
And pays his morning orisons at my window
Duly, as at the temple ?   Is there such hypocrisy
In love's religion, too ?   Are Venus' doves
But white dissemblers ?   Is this that Pamphilus
That shakes and trembles at a frown of mine
More than at thunder ?   I must have more argument
Of his apostacy, or suspect you false.
   Bal. Whose sword is this ?
   Tech.   'Tis his ; and this I tied
About the hilt, and heard him swear to fight
Under those colours, the most faithful soldier
The fields of Mars or tents of Cupid knew.
False men, resign your arms.   Let us go forth
Like bands of Amazons ; for your valours be
Not upright fortitude, but treachery !
   Bal. I urg'd him in a language of that boldness,
As would have fir'd the chillest veins in Thebes,
To stand in your defence, or else resign
The fruitless steel he wore.   He bid me take it,
He had not so much knight-errant in him,
To vow himself champion to such a doxy.
   Tech. Then, love, I shoot thy arrows back again ;
Return 'em to thy quiver, guide thy arm
To wound a breast will say the dart is welcome,
And kiss the golden pile.   I am possess'd

With a just anger.　Pamphilus shall know
My scorn as high as his.
　　Bal.　　　　　　　　　Bravely resolv'd.
Madam, report not me to Pamphilus
Author of this : for valour should not talk,
And fortitude would lose itself in words.
　　Tech. I need no other witness than his sword.

SCENE IV.

BALLIO, ASOTUS, TYNDARUS, TECHMESSA.

Tyn. Techmessa, never did I understand
The sweets of life till now.　I will pronounce
This for my birthday.
　　Tech.　　　　　　And this happy minute
Has clear'd my soul too of the same disease.
　　Aso. Then do as Tyndarus did, and go with me ;
We'll drink a pottle to Liberty, and another
Pottle to the Asotides, and a pottle
To the Tyndarides, and a fourth to the
She-philosophers yclept Techmessides.

SCENE V.

Enter PAMPHILUS.

Tyn. Pamphilus, welcome ; shake thy sorrows off :
Why in this age of freedom dost thou sit
A captiv'd wretch ?　I do not feel the weight
Of clay about me.　Am I not all air,
Or of some quicker element ?　I have purg'd out
All that was earth about me, and walk now
As free a soul as in the separation.
　　Pam. Brother, if any stream of joy can mix
With such a sea of grief as mine, and lose not

His native sweetness, 'tis a joy for you.
But I am all bitterness.
    Bal.   Now, Asotus, the comedy begins.
    Pam. When will my sufferings
Make my atonement with my angry goddess?
Do you (celestial forms) retain an anger
Eternal as your substance?
    Tech.   O fine hair!
An amorous brow, a pretty lovely eye,
A most delicious cheek, a handsome nose!
How nectar-sweet his lips are! and his teeth,
Like two fair ivory pales, enclose a tongue
Made up of harmony.   Then he has a chin
So full of ravishing dimples, it were pity
A beard should overgrow it : and his feet
Past all expression comely.
    Pam.   Do not add
Contempt to cruelty.   Madam, to insult
Upon a prostrate wretch is harder tyranny
Than to have made him so.
    Tech.   And then a shoulder
Straight as the pine or cedar.
    Pam.   Courteous death,
Take wings; thou art too slow.
    Tech.   I could not hear
Those precious parts defam'd, but I durst fight
In the just quarrel.
    Tyn.   'Tis a touchy tiger.
How happy am I that I have 'scap'd the dens
Of these she-wolves!
    Bal.   Now my safety lies
Upon a ticklish point—a woman's secrecy.
Madam, my reputation is dear to me.
    Pam. In what a maze I wander! how my sorrows
Run in a labyrinth!
    Tech.   I'll unriddle it.
    Bal. Hist, hist! the honour of a man-at-arms.

Tech. Then know, thou perjur'd Pamphilus, I have
  learnt
Neglect from thee.

    Pam.   Madam, I am all love ;
And if the violence of my flame had met
With any heart but marble, I had taught it
Some spark of my affection.

    Bal.   Now it heats.

    Tech. No doubt the flame is violent, and must
  work
Upon a breast so capable as mine.

    Aso. I think Cupid be turned juggler. Here's
nothing but hocus-pocus, *Præsto, begone; Come again,
Jack*, and such feats of activity.

    Tech. But I must tell you, you are false and per-
  jur'd,
Or, what is more, a coward. Tell me, sir,

                         [*To* Asotus.

(For I suppose you of a nobler soul)
If you should hear your mistress by rude tongues
Wrong'd in the graces both of mind and beauty,
Could you have suffered it ?

    Aso.   Madam, were you made
From bones of Hercules and brawn of Atlas,
And daughter were unto Gargantua great,
And wrong my mistress, you should hear my rage
Provoke my blade, and cry, *Blade, canst thou sleep
In peaceful scabbard ? Out, thou beast of terror !
And, lion-like, roar this disdainful wight
To Pluto's shades and ghosts of Erebus !*

    Tech. Yet you, my valiant champion, could resign
This (if you know it) rather than endure
The terror of your own steel to redeem
My bleeding honours.

    Pam.   How am I betray'd,
And fall'n into the toils of treachery !
Give me a man bold as that earthborn race

That bade Jove battle, and besieg'd the gods;
And if I make him not creep like a worm
Upon his belly, and with reverence
Lick up the dust you scatter from your shoe,
May I for ever lose the light I live in,
The sight of you!

    Tech.   I'll try your spirits; Phronesium!
    [*Intrat* PHRONESIUM, *et exeat rursus, et statim intrat*
        cum gladio.

    Tyn. That blood of goats should soften adamant!
And poor weak woman with an idol [1] face
Should make the soldier to forget his valour,
And man his sex!

SCENE VI.

Enter PHRONESIUM.

    Tech.   Here's a champion for you.
    Phron. Come, sir, this sword be yours; and if you
    dare
Maintain in the lists against me, as I fear
Your blood is whey by this time, by your valour
You may redeem your honour and your sword.

    Aso. This is another Hercules come from the
    distaff!

    Phron. If not, I do proclaim thee here no knight,
But mean to post thee up for a vile varlet
And the disgrace of chivalry.

    Pam.   O, my shame!
    Aso. A dainty lady-errant.
    Bal.   A fine piece
Of female fortitude.

---

[1] Old copies, *idle*. *Idol face* appears to be intended in the same sense as we would say a *doll face;* and, in fact, *doll* is merely a corruption of *idol*.

Phron.　　　　　　　If this stir thee not,
Thy mistress is the blemish of her sex,
A dirty, filthy huswife.
　　Pam.　　　　　　Would it were not
Dishonour now to kill thee!
　　Phron.　　　　　　If your valour
Lie in your back-parts, I will make experience
Whether a kick will raise it.　Pray, go fetch him
Some *aqua vitæ :* for the thought of steel
Has put him in a swoon.　Nothing revive you?
Then will I keep thy sword and hang it up
Amongst my buskpoints, pins, and curling-irons,
Bodkins and vardingales, a perpetual trophy.
　　　　　　　　　　　　[Exit PHRONESIUM.
How brave a knight you are !
　　Pam.　　　　　　Where shall I run
And find a desert, that the foot of man
Ne'er wander'd in, to hide from the world's eyes
My shame ; 'sdeath, every page and sweaty footman
And soapy chambermaid will point and laugh at me.
　　Tyn. I joy to think that I shall meet Evadne
Turn'd on the sudden Moor.　How black and vile
She will appear !

SCENE VII.

Enter EVADNE.

　　Tyn.　　　O heavens ! who will not dare
Henceforth to scorn your powers, and call sacrilege
Merit and piety ? I do not see
A hair deform'd, no tooth or nail sustain
The brand of her deserved shame.　You punish'd
The queen of beauty with a mole ; but certainly
Her perjury hath added to her form,[1]

---

[1] In the sense of the Lat. *forma*, beauty.

And that the abus'd gods bribe her with beauty,
As the wrack'd tenant strives to buy the favour
Of his imperious landlord.

Evad.　　　　　　　Gentle Tyndarus,
Load not weak shoulders with too great a burden.

Tyn. O lust ! on what bright altars blaze thy flames,
While chastity lets her cold fires glow out
In deform'd temples and on ruin'd altars !
Tempt me not, strumpet : you that have your hirelings,
And can with jewels, rings, and other toys
Purchase your journeymen-lechers.

Evad.　　　　　　　My chaste ear
Has been a stranger to such words as these.
I have not sin enough to understand 'em,
And wonder where my Tyndarus learn'd that language.

Tyn. I am turn'd eagle now, and have an eye
Dares boldly gaze on that adulterate sun.
I must be short—who durst this ring direct [1]
Into your guilty sheets?

Evad.　　　　　I do not know,
How I should lose that pledge of my lord's love ;
But 'tis not in the power of any thief
To steal away the heart I have vowed yours :
And would to all the gods I had kept it there !

Aso. Come, blush not, bashful belly-piece.　I will
　　meet thee :
I ever keep my word with a fair lady.
I will requite that jewel with a richer.
The glorious heavens, array'd in all their stars,
Shall not outshine thee.　Be not, girl, asham'd.
These are acquainted with it.　I would vex 'em
To-night with the remembrance of those sports

---

[1] We have here, it appears, an allusion to the well-known story first related in English in " A C. Mery Talys " (1525). See " Old English Jest-Book," i. 19, or Webster's Works, by Hazlitt, i. 178–9.　Old copies, *must.*

We shall enjoy.   Then pleasures double rise,
When both we feed, and they shall tantalise.
   Evad. It is not manly in you, sir, to ruin
A virgin's fame with hazard of your own.
   Aso. Tut, lass, no matter, we'll be manly anon.
   Tyn. A fine dissembler!   Ha! what tumult's here?

SCENE VIII.

Enter PÆGNIUM *and* OFFICERS.

   Pæg. That's he; I charge you, apprehend the
   villain.
   1*st Officer.* Villain, we reprehend thee.
   Bal.   Slaves, for what?
   2*d Officer.* For an arrant cutpurse : you stole away
this little gentleman's sword; and being done by
chance-medley, 'tis flat felony by statute.
   Pam. I thank thee, innocence.   Though earth dis-
   claim
Thy title, heaven denies thee not protection.
   Pæg. Confess, or I will have thee instantly
Hang'd for a sign on thine own post.
   Bal.   Well, villany,
Thou wilt not thrive, sir, for 'twas you I wrong'd.
I do confess the sword by which I rais'd
So strange a scandal on you, was by me
Stolen from your page, as he delivered letters
From you to your Techmessa; and the plot
Was fashion'd by her mother, though ill-fortune
Made me the unlucky instrument.
   Aso.   Curs'd tutor!
Thou hast read nothing to me worth the learning,
But th' highway to th' gallows.   There shall we
Hang up like vermin.   Little did I think
To make the women weep and sob to see

Th' untimely end of two such proper men.
This mouth was never made to stand awry,
And sure my neck was long enough before.
Lady, upon my humbled knees I beg
Pardon for faults committed. I acknowledge
That, striving with felonious intent
To steal a kiss or two from your sweet lips,
From your sweet ear I stole a ring away.

    Pæg. For which your sweet neck must endure the
      halter.

    Tyn. I am again thy servant, mighty love!
O my Evadne, how shall I appear
So bold as but to plead in mine own cause?
It is so foul, that none can seal my pardon,
But you that should condemn me.

    Evad.   Sir, you know
The power I have is yours : be your own judge,
And seal your pardon here.

    Tyn.   'Tis double life
Granted by such a seal.

    Tech.   What punishment
Shall we inflict on these?

    Aso.   Gentle lady,
E'en what you please, but hanging ; that's a death
My enemies will hit me in the teeth with.
Besides, it makes a man look like a cat,
When she cries mew.

    Bal.   I'll bark and bite awhile,
Before the dog's death choke me.

    Aso.   Pray, dismiss
This pack of hounds ; and since we both are guilty,
Let us bestow on one another's shoulders
The good and wholesome counsel of a cudgel.

    Pæg. Pray, let me intercede.

    Aso. Thanks, pretty little gentleman.

    Tyn. Officers, you are discharged.

    Aso. Are the mad dogs gone? [*Exeunt* OFFICERS.

Come, tutor, I must read awhile to you
Under correction.   Not so hard, good tutor.

Tyn. Enough.

Aso.   Nay, one bout, I beseech you, more
To make up satisfaction.

Bal.   Well, for this
I'll have one engine more ; my bad intents
Mend not, but gather strength by punishments.

Tyn. Your satisfaction now is full and ample.

Aso. Nay, we must have the health i' th' crab-tree
   cup too.
One to the Tyndarides, another to the Asotides,
And one, my dear instructor, to the Techmessides.

Pam. Nay, now your penance doth exceed your
   crime.

Aso. Say you so ? nay, then here's a health to the
   Pamphilides too ;
And, for his noble sake, to the Evadnides,
And all philosophic sects, whate'er they be.

Evad. Your justice to yourselves is too severe.

Aso. Then I ha' done : farewell, and hearty thanks.
But, tutor, stay ; this little gentleman
Has been forgot.   Pray, sir, what may I call you ?

Pæg. My name is Pægnium.

Aso.   I were most unthankful
To pass o'er you.   To the Pægniades, tutor,
You have brought us to a fair pass, tutor.

Bal.   Tush !
'Twas but to exercise your passive valour.

Aso. Your passive valour ? give me your active
   valour :
I do not like your black-and-blue valour,
When bones shall ache with magnanimity.

                [*Exeunt* ASOTUS, BALLIO, *and* PÆGNIUM.

SCENE IX.

Tyndarus, Pamphilus, Evadne, Techmessa.

Tyn. Brother, I find my soul a troubled sea,
Whose billows are not fully quieted,
Although the storm be over. Therefore, Pamphilus,
By the same womb that bred us, and the breasts
Of our dead mother Lalage, I conjure thee,
With all the charms that love can teach thee,
Assault Evadne's faith. If thou report her
Constant, I end my jealousy ; if frail,
The torrent of my love shall bend his course
To find some other channel.
  Pam.   By that love
That made us twins, though born at several births,
That grew along with us in height and strength,
I will be true. Farewell.
  Tyn. Be sudden, Pamphilus. [*Exit* Tyndarus.
Evad. Methinks this should confirm you.
  Tech.   That he was not
Guilty of this, acquits him not of all.
To prove a man free from an act of theft,
Assoils him not of murder. No, no, sister ;
Tempt him with kisses, and what other dalliance
Craft and indulgent nature hath taught woman
To raise hot youth to appetite ; if he yield not,
I will put off distrust. I do not know
Whom I durst trust but you.
  Evad.   Though mine own love
Find me enough of business, yet in hope
That you will second me in my occasions,
I undertake the task.
  Tech.   Take heed, Evadne,
Lest, while you counterfeit a flame, you kindle
A real fire. I dare not be too confident.
Hence will I closely pry into their actions,

And overhear their language ; for if my sister
See with my eyes, she cannot choose but love him
In the same height with me.   [*Aside.*

SCENE X.

PAMPHILUS, EVADNE, TECHMESSA *in insidiis.*[1]

Pam. It grieves me that a lady of your worth :
Young, soft, and active as the spring—the star
And glory of our nation, should be prodigal
Of your affections, and misplace your love
On a regardless boy.
     Evad.   Sir, the same pity
I must return on you.   Were I a man,
Whom all the ladies might grow rivals for ;
(As less you cannot be) I would not lose
My service to a mistress of so coy
And proud an humour.   True, she is my sister ;
But the same womb produces several natures.
I should have entertain'd so great a blessing
With greater thankfulness.
     Pam.   That my stars should be
So cross unto my happiness !
     Evad.   And my fate
So cruel to me !
     Pam.   Sweet, it is in us
To turn the wheel of Fortune ; she's a goddess
That has no deity, where discretion reigns.
     Evad. But shall I wrong my sister?
     Pam.   Do not I
Give just exchange, and lose a brother for her?
Our sufferings have been equal, and their prides ;
They must be equal necks than can draw even
In the same yoke.

---

[1] *i.e.,* In concealment.

Evad.　　　　I have observ'd the chariot
Of the great Cyprian queen links not together
The dove with sparrows; but the turtle joins
With turtles, and the sparrow has his mate.
　　Pam. See if one softness kiss not in our lips.
　　Evad. One lip not meets the other with more sym-
　　　　pathy
Than yours met mine.
　　Pam.　　　　Let's make the second trial.

SCENE XI.

Enter TECHMESSA *from her concealment.*

Tech. I can endure no longer.　Gentle sister!
　　Evad. I cannot blame your jealousy: for I find——
　　Tech. Too much of sweetness in his amorous lips.
There is no tie in nature; faith in blood
Is but a thing that should be.　Brothers, sisters,
Fathers and mothers, are but specious names
Of love and duty: you and I have been
But guests in the same womb, that at first meeting
Change kind and friendly language, and next morning
Fall out, before they part, or at least ride
Contrary roads.
　　Evad.　　　　Will you then misconstrue
The service I perform'd at your request?
　　Tech. Henceforth I'll set the kite to keep my
　　　　chickens,
And make the wolf my shepherd.

SCENE XII.

Enter TYNDARUS.

Tyn. Pamphilus, how is't?
　　Pam.　　　　I know not how to answer thee.
She met me with more courtship than I tender'd.

Tech. Sir, we are both abus'd, and the same womb
That gave us life was fruitful to our ruin.
Your traitor wears the mask call'd brother : mine
As cunning a disguise—the name of sister :
These eyes are witness, that descried them kissing
Closer than cockles, and in lustful twines
Outbid the ivy or the circling arms
Of winding vines.   Their hot embraces met
So near, and folded in so close a knot,
As if they would incorporate, and grow one.
   Tyn. Then farewell all respect of blood! and, friend-
      ship,
I do pronounce thee stranger.   If there can be
Valour in treachery, put thy trust in steel,
As I do, not in brothers.   Draw, or die.
   Pam.   Brother!
   Tyn. I hate the name : it is a word
Whets my just anger to a sharper edge.
   Pam.   Hear me.
   Tyn. I will no pleading but the sword.
Wert thou protected by Apollo's temple,
Or hadst the altar for security,
Religion should not bind me from thy death.
Couldst thou retreat into my mother's womb,
There my revenge should find thee.   I am sudden,
And talk is tedious.
   Pam.   Bear me witness, heaven ;
This action is unwilling.

SCENE XIII.

Enter to them CHREMYLUS *and* DIPSAS.

Chrem. Put up for shame those rude unhallowed
      blades,
And let not rash opinion of a valour
Persuade you to be patricides.   Pray, remember

You thirst but your own blood.   He that o'ercomes,
Loses the one-half of himself.
   Tyn.   Dear Chremylus,
The reverence to your age hath tied my hands :
But were my thread of life measur'd by his,
I'd cut it off, though we both fell together;
That my incensed soul might follow his,
And to eternity prosecute my revenge.
   Pam. Brother, at your entreaty I adventured
To court Evadne; and, because I found her
(Against my mind) too easy to my suit,
Your rage falls heavy on me.
   Tech.   On my knees
I beg, dear father, cloister me in darkness,
Or send me to the desert to converse
With nothing but a wilderness ; or expose me
To the cold mercy of the wind and wave,
So you will free me from the company
Of a false sister.
   Evad.   Sir, with much persuasion
She wrought on me to personate a love
To Pamphilus, to find if I could stagger
The faith he vow'd to her.   This have I done,
And this so much hath mov'd her.
   Chrem.   Here you see
The fruits of rashness.   Do you find your error ?
But the foul spring, from whence these bitter streams
Had their first head (I fear) is from you, Dipsas.
   Dip. I will no more deny it : I have sown
Those seeds of doubt, wishing to see dissension
Ripe for the sickle.   For what cause, I now
Forbear to speak.   But henceforth I will strive
To clear those jealousies, and conclude their loves
In a blest nuptial.
   Tyn.   O, how frail is man !
One sunny day the exhalation rears
Into a cloud : at night it falls in tears.
          [*Exeunt all save* DIPSAS *and* TYNDARUS.

ACT III., SCENE I.

Dipsas, Tyndarus.

Tyn. If it be not immodesty to demand
So bold a question, I would be resolv'd
Of one doubt yet.
    Dip.   Speak boldly : by all holiness,
My answer shall be true.
    Tyn.   When you were young,
And lively appetite revelled in your blood,
Did you not find rebellion in your veins?
Did not the same embraces tedious grow,
And cause a longing in your thoughts to taste
Varieties of men ?
    Dip.   I blush : I cannot answer
With a denial.   Not a proper gentleman
But forc'd my goatish eye to follow him :
And, when I had survey'd his parts, I would
With any loss of honour, wealth, and friendship,
Have brought him to my bed : and truly, sir,
'Twas cheap at any rate.
    Tyn.   Steel'd impudence !
What fruit can I expect the bough should bear,
That grows from such a stock ?
    Dip.   I had of late
A moneth's mind, sir, to you.   Y' have the right make
To please a lady.
    Tyn.   Sure, this old piece of lust,
When she is dead, will make her grave a brothel,
And tempt worms to adulterate her carcass.
    Dip. And that's the reason I have cross'd my
        daughter
To further mine own love.   Pity me, sir ;
For though the fuel's spent, there is a spark
Rak'd up i' th' embers.   But I now desist.

Please you to go to Ballio's house, my daughter
Shall meet you there. I hope that out of duty
She will not grudge her mother a good turn,
When she is married, now and then. *[Exit.*
    Tyn.   Is there no house
To meet at but this Ballio's? Is Evadne
Acquainted there? Is that the rendezvous
Of her hot meetings. Yet I still suspect
This woman's malice to her child not lost.
I will bestow some time, and go to see
The strange event of this dark mystery. *[Exit.*

SCENE II.

DIPSAS, BALLIO.

    Dip. Ballio!
    Bal.   Madam!
    Dip.   See your house be stor'd
With the deboisest [1] roarers in the city:
Let every room be fill'd with noise and quarrelling,
For Tyndarus is to meet Evadne there.
You guess the rest; if not, this purse of gold
Better inform you. *[Exit.*
    Bal.   Most celestial lady!
Though I have practised villany from my cradle,
And from my dug suck'd mischief more than milk,
This fury still outdoes me. I am vex'd—
Vex'd to the heart, to see a silly woman
Carry more devils in her than myself.
And yet I love thee—thou she-rogue, I love thee.
Had I but such a wife, what a fine brood
Of toads could I beget!

---

[1] Most debauched.

SCENE III.

Enter SIMO.

Bal.   Here comes my mole,
The son of earth, that digs his mother's entrails
To turn up treasure for his boy and me ;
That with industrious eyes searches to hell
To buy us heaven on earth. [*Aside.*] Welcome,
      welcome,
Thou age of gold : how do the bags at home ?
Are all the chests in health ? thrives the purse still ?
And says it to the talents, Multiply ?
   Sim. Thanks to my providence, like a swarm.
      Wealth falls
Not in small drops upon me, as at first,
But (like a torrent) overthrows the bank,
As it would threat a deluge.   Were it not pity
My boy should not invent sluices enou'
To drain the copious stream ?
   Bal.   A thousand pities
That you should lose the fruits of so much care.
   Sim. True, Ballio, true.
   Bal.   Trust me, what art can do
Shall not be wanting.
   Sim.   I'll not be ungrateful.
It lies in you to turn these silver hairs
To a fresh black again, and by one favour
Cut forty years away from the great [1] sum.
   Bal.   I had rather
Cut off all, and be our own carvers.   [*Aside.*
Sir, if I had Medea's charms to boil
An aged ram in some enchanted cauldron
Till he start up a lamb, I would recall

---

[1] Edits., *gray.*

Your youth, and make you (like the aged snake)
Cast off this wrinkled skin, and skip up fresh
As at fifteen.
    Simo.   All this you may, and more.
If you will place me where I may unseen
Make my eye witness of my son's delight :
I shall enjoy the pleasures by beholding 'em.
    Bal. True, sir, you know he's but your second self,
The same you might have been at one-and-twenty :
The bliss is both's alike.
    Simo.   Most philosophical !
    Bal. Place yourself there.
    Simo.   I ha' no words but these
To thank you with.   *[Gives money.*
    Bal.   This is true rhetoric.

SCENE IV.

ASOTUS, BOMOLOCHUS, CHARYLUS, THRASYMACHUS,
   HYPERBOLUS. BALLIO *and* SIMO *in angulis.*[1]

    Aso. Come forth, my rascals.   Let the thriving lord
Confine his family unto half a man,
Yclep'd a page.   Our honour be attended
With men of arts and arms.   Captains and poets
Shall with the Bilboa blade and grey goose-quill
Grace our retinue ; and, when we grow surly,
Valour and wit fall prostrate at our frown.
Crouch, imps of Mars and frogs of Helicon !
    Simo. How they adore him ! and the perilous wag
Becomes his state.   To see what wealth can do
To those that have the blessing how to spend it !
                           [Aside.

---

    [1] *i.e.,* In a corner, or behind a screen.

Bal. Your blessing was the wealth : the art of spending
He had from me.

Simo.   Once more I give thee thanks. [*Aside.*

Thras. Who dares offend thee, lord of fortitude,
And not pay homage to thy potent toe,
Shall be a morsel for the dogs.

Aso.   Stoutly deliver'd,
My brave Thrasymachus !   Thou for this shalt feed.
I will not suffer valour to grow lean,
And march like famine.   I have seen an army
Of such a meagre troop, such thin-chapp'd starvelings,
Their barking stomachs hardly could refrain
From swallowing up the foe, ere they had slain him.

Hyp. If thou command our service, we will dye
Dull earth with crimson, till the tears of orphans,
Widows and mothers wash it white again :
We'll strow thy walks with legs and arms, and thighs,
And pay thee tribute thousand heads a day,
Fresh bleeding from the trunk ; and panting hearts
(Not dead) shall leap in thy victorious paw.

Aso. Then say thou too to Hunger : Friend, adieu !
Ballio, condemn a bag ; let trash away,
See 'em both arm'd in scarlet *cap-a-pie.*
Strike topsail, men-of-war.

Bal.   We must divide :
We that serve great men have no other shifts
To thrive ourselves, but gelding our lords' gifts.

Simo. Now I am rich indeed ; this is true treasure.
                                    [*Aside.*

Aso. Ha ! has Melpomene ta'en cold of late,
That you are silent, my Parnassian beagles ?
Is Clio dumb, or has Apollo's Jew's-trump
By sad disaster lost her melodious tongue ?

Char. Your praise all tongues desire to speak ;
    but some—
Nay all, I fear—for want of art grow dumb.

The harp of Orpheus blushes for to sing,
And sweet Amphion's voice hath crack'd a string.
   Aso. A witty solecism ! reward the error.
Harp and sing, voice and string !
   Bom. Give me a breath of thunder ; let me speak
Sonorous accents, till their clamours break
Rocks with the noise obstreperous.   I will warble
Such bouncing notes shall cleave obdurate marble
Upon Mount Caucasus' heavens-knocking head ;
Boreas shall blow my trumpet, till I spread
Thy fame, grand patron of the thrice-three sisters :
Till envy's ears shall hear it, and have blisters.
   Aso. O rare close ! a high sublime conceit !
For this I'll sheathe thee in a new serge scabbard,
Blade of the fount Pegasean !
   Simo.   What an honour
Will our blood come to !—I have satisfied
For all the orphans, widows, and what others
My sacred hunger hath devour'd.   [*Aside.*
   Aso.   Ballio,
Bless him with twenty drachms : yet forbear.
Money may spoil his poetry.   Give's some wine,
Here is a whetstone both for wit and valour :
A health to all my beadsmen of the sword !
   Thras. Hyp. This will engage the men-of-arms to fight.
   Aso. This to the Muses and their threadbare tribe.
   Char. Bom. Thou dost engage the learn'd troop [1] to
   write.
   Aso. Go, sons of Mars, with young Apollo's brood,
And usher in my Venus : wine hath warm'd
My blood, and wak'd it to an itch of sporting
     [*Exeunt* BOMOLOCHUS, HYPERBOLUS, CHARYLUS,
        THRASYMACHUS, *for to fetch in* PHRYNE.
       ASOTUS *the while is putting on his armour.*
   Bal. Some twenty ages hence 'twill be a question

---

[1] Old copies, *troups.*

Which of the two the world will reverence more :
You for a thriving father, or Asotus
So liberal a son.

 Simo.   Good, Ballio, good !
But which will they prefer ?

 Bal.   They cannot, sir,
But most admire your fist, which grip'd so much
That made his hand so open.

 Simo.   Gracious stars !
How blest shall I be twenty ages hence—
Some twenty ages hence !

 Bal.   You shall be call'd
A doating coxcomb twenty ages hence. [*Aside.*

SCENE V.

CHARYLUS, BOMOLOCHUS, *before, personating two
 Mercuries,* PHRYNE, *in an antique robe and
 coronet, guarded in by* HYPERBOLUS *and* THRA-
 SYMACHUS.

 Aso. How bright and glorious are the beams my
  star
Darts from her eye ! Lead up my queen of beauty—
But in a softer march—sound a retreat.
Lead on again : I'll meet her in that state
The God of War puts on when he salutes
The Cyprian queen : these, that were once the postures
Of horrid battles, are become the muster
Of love and beauty. Say, sweet brace of Mercuries,
Is she th' Olympic or the Paphian goddess ?

 Bal. Where are you, sir, where are you ? [*Aside.*
 Simo.   In Elysium, in Elysium.
 Char. This is no goddess of the Olympic hall.
 Bom. Nor may you her of Neptune's issue call.
 Char. For she nor Syren is, nor Amphitrite.

Bom. Nor wood-nymph that in forest takes delight.
Char. Nor is she Muse.
Bom.   Nor Grace.
Char.   Nor is she one of these
That haunt the springs—the beauteous Naiades.
Bom. Nor Flora, lady of the field, is she.
Char. Nor bright Pomona, th' orchard's deity.
Bom. No, she is none of these.
Char.   O, then prepare
To hear her blessed name.
Both.   'Tis Phryne fair.
Aso. Phryne the fair? O peace! if this be she,
Go forth and sing the world a lullaby.
For thy dear sake, in whom is all delight,
I will no more the trembling nations fright
With bellowing drums and groans of slaughter'd men.
My father brings the golden age again.
Phryne. Pardon me, dreadful deity of war;
'Twas love of you that forc'd me from my sphere,
And made me leave my orb without her influence,
To meet you in the fury of the fight,
Sweating with rage, and reeking in the blood
Of wretches sacrificed to the Stygian flood.
Aso. Come forth, thou horrid instrument of death.
Bal. Do you hear him, sir?   [*Aside.*
Simo.   Ay, to my comfort, Ballio.
Aso. I will dispeople earth, and drown the world
In crimson floods and purple deluges.
The old, the young, the weak, the lusty wight :
Soldiers and scholars, fair and foul together,
Men, women, children, infants—all shall die,
I will have none survive that shall have left
Above one eye, three-quarters of a face,
And half a nose.   I will carve legs and arms,
As at a feast.   Henceforth to all posterity
Mankind shall walk on crutches.
Phryne.   Cruel Mars !

Let the conjunction of my milder star
Temper the too malignant force of thine.
The drum, the fife, and trumpet shall be turn'd
To lutes and citherns.   We will drink in helmets,
And cause the soldier turn his blade to knives,
To conquer capons and the stubble goose :
No weapons in the age to come be known,
But shield of bacon and the sword of brawn.
Deign me a kiss, great warrior.   [*Kisses him.*

   Aso.   Hogsheads of nectar
Are treasur'd in the warehouse of her lips.
That kiss hath ransom'd thousands from the grave.
   Phryne. Let me redeem more thousands with a
      second.   [*Kisses him again.*
   Aso. Rage melts away.   I pardon half the world.
   Phryne. O, let me kiss away all rigour from thee.
                                          [*Kisses him.*
   Aso. Live, mortals, live.   Death has no more
      to do.
And yet (methinks) a little rigour's left.
   Phryne. Thus shall it vanish.   [*Kisses him.*
   Aso.   Vanish, rigour, vanish !
Harness the lions : make my chariot ready.
Venus and I will ride.
   Phryne.   How ? drawn by lions ?
   Aso. Ay, thou shalt kiss 'em till their rigour vanish
(As mine has) into air.   I will have thee play
With ounces, tigers, and the panther's whelp,
As with a squirrel.   Bears shall wait on thee,
And spotted leopards shall thy monkeys be.
Sit down, my queen, and let us quaff a bowl.
Seest thou, my Phryne, what a fair retinue
I have provided thee ?   These for thy defence
'Gainst any lady rivals thee in beauty :
And these on all occasions shall vent forth
Swelling encomiums.   Say, Bomolochus ;
How sings my mistress ?

Bom. The grasshopper chants not his autumn choir
So sweet, nor cricket by the chimney-fire.
Aso. They'll make thee anything. Thou art already
Cricket and grasshopper. Charylus, how does she
    dance?
Char. Have you beheld the little sable beast
Clad in an ebon mantle, hight a flea,
Whose supple joints so nimbly skip and caper
From hem to sleeve, from sleeve to hem again,
Dancing a measure o'er a lady's smock,
With motion quick and courtly equipage?
So trips fair Phryne o'er the flowery stage.
Aso. Now thou art a flea. How snorts she as she
    sleeps?
Bom. Zephyrus breathes not with a sweeter gale
Through a grove of sycamore. The soft spring
Chides not the pebbles that disturb his course
With sweeter murmur. Let Amphion's lute
(That built our Theban walls) be henceforth mute.
Orpheus shall break his harp, and silent be
The reed of Pan, the pipe of Mercury!
Yea, though the spheres be dumb, I care not for't:
No music such as her melodious snort!
Aso. Melodious snort? With what decorum spits
    she?
Char. Like the sweet gums that from electar[1] trees
Distil, or honey of the labouring bees:
Like morning dew, that in a pleasant shower
Drops pearls into the bosom of a flower.
Cupid with acorn-cups close by her sits
To snatch away the nectar that she spits.
Aso. Ballio, present me with the crowns of laurel.
Thus I drop wine the best of Helicon

---

[1] I do not know what is meant by *electar trees*. Perhaps Randolph may have written *elecam tree*, referring to the *elecampane* or *Helenium*, which certainly yields a species of gum.

On your learn'd heads, and crown you thus with bays.
Rise poets-laureate both !   Favour, Apollo !
   Both. The Muses and Asotus be propitious !
   Aso. I will not have you henceforth sneak to
     taverns,
And peep like fiddlers into gentlemen's rooms,
To shark for wine and radishes ; nor lie sentinel
At ordinaries, nor take up at plays
Some novice for a supper.   You shall deal
No more in ballads, to bewail an execution
In lamentable rhythms ; nor beg in elegies ;
Nor counterfeit a sickness to draw in
A contribution ; nor work journey-work
Under some play-house poet, that deals in
Wit by retail ; nor shall you task your brains
To grace a burgess' new post with a rebus ;
Or furnish a young suitor with an anagram
Upon his mistress' name ; nor study posies
For rings and bracelets.   Injure not the bough
Of Daphne : know that you are laureate now.
   Bal. How like you this discourse ?   [*Aside.*
   Simo.   Excellent well.
It is a handsome lass.   If I were young
(As I am not decrepit), I would give
A talent for a kiss.   [*Aside.*
   Phryne.   Come, beauteous Mars,
I'll kemb thy hair smooth as the raven's feather,
And weave those stubborn locks to amorous bracelets ;
Then call a livelier red into thy face,
And soften with a kiss thy rugged lips.
I must not have this beard so rudely grow,
But with my needle I will set each hair
In decent order, as you rank your squadrons.
   Aso. Here's a full bowl to beauteous Phryne's
     health.
What durst thou do, Thrasymachus, to the man
That should deny it ?

Thras.   Dissect him into atoms.

Hyp. I durst do more for beauteous Phryne's sake.

Thras. What, more than I ? Hyperbolus, thou art mortal.

Hyp. Yield, or I see a breakfast for the crows.

Thras. Death to my lungs, I spit upon thy fame.

Hyp. Then with my steel I whip thy rash contempt.

Aso. Brawling, you mastiffs ? Keep the peace at home,
And join your forces 'gainst the common foe.

Phryne. You shall not be angry ; by this kiss you shall not.

Aso. I will, unless you swear again.

Phryne. You shall not.

Simo. [*Aside.*] Ah, Ballio ! age has made me dry as tinder,
And I have taken fire. I burn, I burn !
The spark rak'd up in ashes is broke forth,
And will consume me, Ballio.

Bal.   What's the matter ? [*Aside.*]

Simo. [*Aside.*] Love, cruel love, I must enjoy that lady,
Whatever price it cost me.

Bal.   Your son's mistress ? [*Aside.*]

Simo. Son or not son. Let this entreat, and this.
                                        [*Aside.*]

Bal. This will persuade. I must remove your son,
His fury else will surely stand 'twixt us
And our designs. Old lecher, I will fit you,
And geld your bags for this. You shall be milk'd,
Emptied and pump'd. Sponge, we will squeeze you, sponge,
And send you to suck more. [*Aside. Comes forward.*] Invincible Mars !

Aso. What says the governor of our younger years ?

Bal. You have worn this plot of Mars too stale
   already.
O, shift yourself into all shapes of love.
Women are taken with variety.
What think you of Oberon, the King of Fairies ? [1]
I know 'twill strike her fancy.
   Aso.   Business calls ;
Drink on, for our return shall sudden be.

SCENE VI.

BALLIO, SIMO, THRASYMACHUS, HYPERBOLUS,
CHARYLUS, BOMOLOCHUS, PHRYNE.

Bal. Phryne, here is a boy of wealth, my girl,
The golden bull that got this golden calf,
Deeply in love with her.
   Phryne.   Let me alone ;
I'll fleece him.
   Bal. Melt him, Phryne, melt him.
We must not leave this mine, till we have found
The largeness of the vein.   Suck like an horse-leech.
                                         [*Aside.*
Come, sir, and boldly enter : I have chalk'd out
An easy path to tread in ; 'twill direct you
To your wish'd journey's end, and lodge you safe
In her soft arms.
   Simo.   Thou art my better angel.
Wilt thou eat gold, drink gold, lie in gold,
I have it for thee.   Old men are twice children ;
And so was I ; but I am grown again
Up to right man.   Thou shalt be my tutor too.
Is there no stools or tables ?

---

[1] Randolph introduces the fairies more at large into his
" Amyntas."

Bal. What to do?

Simo. I would vault over them, to show the strength
And courage of my back.

Bal.   Strike boldly in, sir.

Simo. Save you, gentlemen.   If you want gold,
     here's for you.

Give me some wine.   Mistress, a health to you :
Pledge me, and spice the cup with these and these.
Thou shalt have better gowns.

Thras.   A brave old boy !

Hyp. There's mettle in him.

Char.   I will sing thy praise
In lines heroic.

Bom.   I will tune my lyre,
And chant an ode that shall eternise thee.

Phryne. Of what a sweet aspect ! how lovely-look'd
Is this fine gentleman.   I hope you know
It is in Thebes the custom to salute
Fair ladies with a kiss.

Simo.   She is enamour'd.
Sure I am younger than I thought myself.
Fair lady, health and wealth attend thee. [*Kisses her.*

Phryne. Good sir, another kiss.   You have a breath
Compos'd of odours.

Simo.   Buy thee toys with this. [*Gives her money.*
I'll send thee more.

Phryne.   How ravishing is his face !

Simo. That I should have so ravishing a face,
And never know it !   Miser that I was !
I will go home and buy a looking-glass,
To be acquainted with my parts hereafter.

Phryne. Come, lie thee down by me ; here we
     will sit.

How comely are these silver hairs !   This hand
Is e'en as right to my one mind, as if
I had the making of it.   Let me throw
My arms about thee.

Bal.   How the burr cleaves to him !
  Simo. This remnant of my age will make amends
For all the time that I have spent in care.
    Phryne. Give me thy hand.   How smooth a palm
        he has !
How with a touch it melts !
    Bal.   The rogue abuses him
With his greasy fists.
    Phryne.   Let us score kisses up
On one another's lips.   Thou shalt not speak,
But I will suck thy words, ere they have felt
The open air.
    Simo.   That I should live so long,
And ignorant of such a wealth as this !

SCENE VII.

SIMO, THRASYMACHUS, HYPERBOLUS, CHARYLUS,
      BOMOLQCHUS, PHRYNE, ASOTUS.

Aso. Now am I Oberon, prince of fairyland,
And Phryne shall be Mab, my empress fair :
My soldiers two I'll instantly transform
To Will-with-a-wisp and Robin Goodfellow,
And make my brace of poets transmigrate
Into Pigwiggin and Sir Peppercorn.
It were a pretty whimsy now to counterfeit
That I were jealous of my Phryne's love.
The humour would' be excellent, and become me
Better than either Tyndarus or Techmessa.
Thus will I walk as one in deadly dumps.
    Simo. When shall we marry ?   [*Aside.*]
    Phryne.   I can hardly stay
Till morning.   [*Aside.*]
    Aso.   O, what fury shot
A viper through my soul !   Here love with twenty bows

And twenty thousand arrows lays his siege
To my poor heart.   O Phryne, Phryne !
I have no cause why to suspect thy love.
But if all this be cunning, as who knows ?
Away, foul sin !   O eyes, what mischief do you see !
 Bal. O, I could burst with laughter.   Here will be
A pretty scene of mirth.
 Simo.   Thou dost not love me.
My boy Asotus, my young sprightly boy
Has stolen thy heart away.
 Phryne.   He ? a poor mushroom !
Your boy ?   I should have guess'd him for your
   father.
He has a skin as wrinkled as a tortoise,
I have mista'en him often for a hedgehog
Crept out on's skin.   Pray, keep the fool at home.
 Aso. Patience, go live with cuckolds.   I defy
   thee !
Villain, rogue, traitor, do not touch my dear,
So to unsanctify her tender skin,
Nor cast a goatish eye upon a hair,
To make that little thread of gold profan'd,
Or gaze but on her shoe-string that springs up
A real rose from virtue of her foot,
To blast the odours.   Grim-fac'd death shall hurry
   thee
To Styx, Cocytus, and fell Phlegethon.
 Simo. Asotus, good Asotus, I am thy father.
 Aso. I no Asotus am, nor thou my sire,
But angry and incensed Oberon.
 Simo. All that I have is thine, though I could vie
For every silver hair upon my head
A piece in gold.
 Aso.   I should send you to the barbers. [*Aside.*
 Simo. All, all is thine : let me but share
A little in thy pleasures : only relish
The sweetness of 'em.

Aso.   No, I will not have
Two spenders in a house.   Go you and revel,
I will go home and live a drudge's life,
As you ha' done, to scrape up pelf together :
And then forswear all tutors, soldiers, poets,
Women and wine.   I will forget to eat,
And starve myself to the bigness of a polecat.
I will disclaim his faith that can believe
There is a tavern or a religious place
For holy nuns that vow incontinence,
And have their beads to sin by.   Get you home.
You kiss a gentlewoman to endanger
Your chattering teeth.   Go, you have done your
    share
In getting me : to furnish the next age
Must be my province.   Go, look you to yours.
Lie with your musty bags, and get more gold.
'Slid, anger me, and I'll turn drudge for certain.
    Simo. Asotus, good Asotus, pardon me.
    Aso. I wonder you are not ashamed to ask pardon.
    Simo. It was the dotage of my age, Asotus.
    Aso. How did you live until this age of dotage ?
    Simo. I will abjure all pleasures but in thee.
    Aso. This something qualifies.
    Simo.   It shall be my sport to
Maintain thine.   Thou shalt eat for both
And drink for both.
    Aso.   Good ! this will qualify more.
    Simo. And here I promise thee to make a jointure
Of half the land I have to this fair lady.
    Aso. This qualifies all.   You have your pardon,
    sir :
But hear you, sir, it must be paid for, too.
To-morrow, Mab, I thee mine empress crown.
    Bal. All friends : a merry cup go round.   What !
    captains
And poets here, and leave the sack for flies !

SCENE VIII.

BALLIO, ASOTUS, PHRYNE, SIMO, THRASYMACHUS,
  HYPERBOLUS, CHARYLUS, BOMOLOCHUS, TYN-
  DARUS.

Hyp. Thrasymachus, a whole one.
  Thras.   Done, I'll pledge thee.
Though 'twere a deluge.   By my steel, you have left
Enough to drown an island, Charylus.
  Char. And 'twere the famous fount of Hippocrene,
I'd quaff it off all, though the great Apollo
And all the Muses died for thirst, Bomolochus.
  Bom. Come, boys, as deep as is Parnassus high.
  Tyn. What nursery of sin is this? what temple
Of lust and riot?   Was this place alone
Thought a fit witness for the knitting up
Chaste and religious love?   Deeds dark as hell,
Incest and murder, might be acted here!
The holy god of marriage never lighted
His sacred torch at so profane a den.
It is a cage for screech-owls, bats, and ravens,
For crows and kites, and such like birds of prey.
But the chaste turtle, the indulgent pelican,
And pious stork, fly hence as from infection.
Evadne meet me here!   Is she a parcel
Of the damn'd family?   Are there such white devils
Among their Succubas?   No, thou art wrong'd,
      Evadne;
And there be some that scatter snakes amongst us,
Have stung too deep already.

SCENE IX.

BALLIO, ASOTUS, CHARYLUS, SIMO, HYPERBOLUS,
THRASYMACHUS, TYNDARUS, EVADNE.

Tyn.   Bless me, eyes!
My troubled fancy fools me: I am lost
In a distracted dream.   It is not she.
Awake thee, Tyndarus: what strange sleeps are
      these!
Methinks I am in hell, and yet behold
A glorious angel there.   Or have these devils [1]
Broke into Paradise? for the place is such
She blesses with her presence.   Mere contradictions:
Chimeras of a restless brain!
    Evad.   Diana,
And whatsoever goddess else protects
Untouch'd virginity, shield me with your powers.
To what a wilderness have my wandering steps
Betray'd me!   Sure, this cannot be a place
To meet my Tyndarus in.
    Tyn.   'Tis Evadne!
'Tis the fair soul Evadne.   Now, my sword,
That hadst a good edge to defend this woman,
Go send her soul into another mansion,
Black as itself.   It is too foul a tenant [2]
For this fair place.   Stay yet, too forward steel:
Take her encircled in her stallion's arms,
And kill two sins together.   Let 'em be
At hell to bear the punishment of lust,
Ere it be fully acted.
    Evad.   What strange fancies

---

[1] A term which Webster's celebrated drama so-called,
printed in 1612, brought into fashion.

[2] An idea which several writers have employed.   See Hazlitt's Dodsley, x. 173, and Dyce's edition of Ford, i. 143.

My maiden fears present me ! Why, I know not :
But this suspicion seldom bodeth good.

    Thras. A handsome *bona roba,* and my prize.

    Hyp. I do deny't ; she's my monopoly.

    Char. Perchance she may one of the Muses be,
And then claim I a share for poetry.

    Evad. If ever silly lamb thus stray'd before
Into a flock of wolves ; or harmless dove
Not only made the prey, but the contention
Of ravenous eagles—such poor soul am I.

    Thras. Give me a buss, my girl.

    Evad.   If there be here
A gentleman in whom there lives a spark
Of virtue not yet out, I do beseech him,
By all the ashes of his ancestors,
And by the constant love he bears his mistress,
To rescue innocence and virginity
From these base monsters. I for him will pay
A thousand prayers a morning, all as pure
And free from earthly thought as e'er found passage
Through the strict gate of heaven.

    Tyn.   That's a task for me.
Away, foul ravishers ! I will teach my sword
Justice to punish you. Such a troop of harpies
To force a lady's honour ! I will quench
With your own blood the rage of that hot lust
That spurr'd you on to base and bold attempts.

    Aso. Fly, Phryne, fly ! for dangers do surround !

    Simo. This is a pleasure that I care not for.

            [*Exeunt all but* TYNDARUS *and* EVADNE.

SCENE X.

TYNDARUS, EVADNE.

Tyn. Lady, be safe.

Evad.   Sir, may this favour, done

An injur'd maid, call blessings on your head
In plenteous show'rs !
    Tyn.   This courtesy deserves
Some fair requital.
    Evad.   May plum'd victory
Wait on your sword : and if you have a mistress,
May she be fair as lilies, and as chaste
As the sweet morning dew that loads the heads
Of drooping flow'rs. May you have fair children
To propagate your virtues to posterity,
And bless succeeding times !
    Tyn.   Heaven, be not deaf !
    Evad. May you and plenty never live asunder.
Peace make your bed, and——
    Tyn.   Pray'r is cheap reward.
And nothing now bought at a rate so easy
As that same highway ware, *Heaven bless your worship !*
In plain words, lady (I can use no language
But what is blunt), I must do what they would ha'
    done.
    Evad. Call back your words, and lose not that
    reward
Heaven is engag'd to pay you.
    Tyn.   Come ; no circumstance.
Your answer—quick !
    Evad.   I beg it on my knees :
Have a respect to your own soul, that sinks
In this dishonour, sir, as deep as mine.
    Tyn. You are discourteous, lady.
    Evad.   Let these tears
Plead for me : did you rescue me from thieves,
To rob me of the jewel you preserv'd ?
    Tyn. Why do I trifle time away in begging
That may command ?   Proud damsel, I will force
    thee.
    Evad. I thank thee, blest occasion : now I dare
            [*She snatcheth a stilletto out of his pocket.*

Defy thee, devil: here is that shall keep
My chastity secure, and arm a maid
To scorn your strength.

 Tyn.   Be not too masculine, lady.

 Evad. Stand off, or I will search my heart with this,
And force my blood a passage, that in anger
Shall fly into thy face, and tell thee boldly
Thou art a villain !

 Tyn.   Incomparable lady !
By all those pow'rs that the blest men adore,
And the worst fear, I have no black design
Upon your honour; only as a soldier
I did desire to prove whether my sword
Had a deserving cause: I would be loth
To quarrel for light ware. Now I have found you
Full weight, I'll wear his life upon my point
That injures so much goodness.

 Evad.   You speak honour.

 Tyn. Blest be this minute; sanctify it, Time,
'Bove all thy calendar. Now I find her gold;
This touchstone gives her perfect. The discovery
Of new[1]-found kingdoms, where the plough turns up
Rich ore in every furrow, is to this
A poor success. Now all my doubts are clear'd,
And I dare boldly say: Be happy, Tyndarus !

SCENE XI.

Enter PAMPHILUS.

 Pam. Great Queen of Love, sure, when the labour-
  ing sea
Did bring forth thee, before she was deliver'd,
Her violent throes had rais'd a thousand storms.
Yet now (I hope) after so many wracks

---

[1] Old copies, *ne'er*.

That I have suffer'd in thy troubled waves,
Thou now wilt land me safe.

Tyn.   Pamphilus here?
He comes to meet Evadne.   This is their house
Of toleration.   She had spied me out
Through my disguise; and with what studied art,
What cunning language, how well-acted gesture,
How much of that unbounded store of tears,
She wrought on my credulity!   The fox,
Hyæna, crocodile, and all beasts of craft,
Have been distill'd to make one woman up.   [*Exit.*

Evad. And has he left me in this dragon's den,
A spoil to rapine? what defence, poor maid,
Hast thou against these wild and savage beasts?
My stars were cruel: if you be courteous, eyes,
Weep me a flood of tears, and drown me in't,
And be physicians to my sorrows now,
That have too long been heralds of my grief.
My thread of life has hitherto drawn out
More woes than minutes.

Pam.   Health to the fair Evadne!
Evad. Is any left so courteous to wish health
To the distress'd Evadne?   Pamphilus?
Pam. Is my Techmessa here?
Evad.   Now all the gods
Preserve her hence; there is in hell more safety
Among the Furies.   Mischief built this house
For all her family.   Gentle Pamphilus,
See me delivered from this jail, this dungeon,
This horrid vault of lust.

SCENE XII.

PAMPHILUS, TYNDARUS, TECHMESSA, EVADNE.

Pam.   Take comfort, lady.
Your honour stands safe on his guard, while I
Can use a sword.

Evad.   You have confirmed me, sir.

Tyn. How close they wind, like glutinous snakes
    engend'ring !

Tech. Well, sister, I shall study to requite
This courteous treachery.

Evad.   Pamphilus, in me
All stars conspire to make affliction perfect.

Pam. Wait on heaven's pleasure, madam : such a one
The heavens ne'er made for misery ; they but give you
These crosses as sharp sauce to whet your appetite
For some choice banquet. Or they mean to lead you
Thorough a vault dark and obscure as hell,
To make your paradise a sweeter prospect.

                    [*Aside.*]   Thus I feed
Others with hopes, while mine own wounds do bleed.

                [*Exeunt* EVADNE *and* PAMPHILUS.

SCENE XIII.

TYNDARUS, TECHMESSA.

Tech. Why should we toil thus in an endless search
Of what we ne'er [1] behold ?   Let us grow wise.
I loathe false Pamphilus ; yet I could have lov'd him !
And, if he were but faithful, could do still.

Tyn. Sure, were Evadne false, yet Pamphilus
Would not be made the instrument to wrong me.
Or suppose Pamphilus were a treacherous brother,
Methinks Evadne should be kinder to me.
Techmessa, join with me in one search more.

SCENE XIV.

Enter BALLIO *and* ASOTUS.

Tyn. O Ballio, 'tis in you and dear Asotus
To make two wretches happy.

---

[1] Old copies, *now.*

Aso.   Then be happy.

Tyn. I'll make you two joint-heirs of my estate,
And you shall give it out we two are dead
By our own hands, and bear us both this night
To church in coffins : whence we'll make escape,
And bid farewell to Thebes.

Aso.   Would you not both
Be buried in one coffin ? then the grave
Would have her tenants multiply :—hear you, tutor,
Shall not we be suspected for the murder,
And choke with a hempen squincy ?

Tyn.   To secure you,
We'll write before what we intend to act :
Our hands shall witness forth[1] your innocence.

Bal. Well, come the worst, I'll venture ; and per-
    chance
You shall not die in jest again o' th' sudden.

Tyn. What strange meanders Cupid leads us
    through !
When most we forward go, we backward move ;
There is no path so intricate as love.

ACT IV., SCENE I.

BALLIO, ASOTUS ; CHARYLUS *and* BOMOLOCHUS *bear-
    ing the coffin of* TECHMESSA ; HYPERBOLUS *and*
    THRASYMACHUS *bearing the coffin of* TYNDARUS ;
    a Servant.

Bal. Carry these letters unto Chremylus' house.
Give this to Pamphilus, to Evadne that ;
And certify 'em of this sad event.
It will draw tears from theirs, as from my eyes,
Because they are not real obsequies.   [*Aside.*

---

[1] Old copies, *with.*

Aso. So great my grief, so dolorous my disaster,
I know not in what language to express it,
Unless I should be dumb! Sob, sob, Asotus!
Sob till thy buttons break, and crack thy bandstrings
With lamentation and distress'd condoling;
With blubber'd eyes behold this spectacle
Of man's mortality. O my dearest Tyndarus!

Thras. Learn of us captains to outface grim Death,
And gaze the lean-chapp'd monster in the face.

Asot. Ay, and I could but come to see his face,
I'd scratch his eyes out. O the ugly rogue!
Could none but Tyndarus and fair Techmessa
Serve the vile varlet to lead apes in hell?

Hyp. I have seen thousands sigh out souls in
  groans,
And yet have laugh'd : it has been sport to see
A mangled carcass broach'd with so many wounds,
That life has been in doubt which to get out at.

Aso. Are crawling vermin of so choice a diet?
Would I were then a worm, freely to feed
On such a delicate and ambrosian dish,
Fit to be serv'd a banquet to my bed!
But, O Techmessa! Death has swallowed thee :
Too sweet a sop for such a fiend as he!

Char. Chase hence these show'rs; for, since they
  both are dead,
Tears will not bribe the Fates for a new thread.

Bom. Inexorable sisters! Be not sorry :
For Clotho's distaff will be peremptory.

Aso. Go, then, and dip your pens in gall and vinegar
To rail on Mors—cruel, impartial Mors :
The savage tyrant, all-devouring Mors :
The envious, wicked, and malicious Mors :
Mors, that respects not valour : Mors, that cares not
For wit or learning : Mors, that spares not honour :
Mors, whom wealth bribes not : Mors, whom beauty
  tempts not :

Sex.   As worms do, by the dead.

Aso. A witty rascal.   Let's have some discourse
     with him.

Thras. Are any soldiers' bones in garrison here ? [1]

Sex. Faith, sir, but few : they, like poor travellers,
Take up their inn by chance : but some there be.

Thras. Do not those warlike bones in dead of night
Rise up in arms, and with tumultuous broils
Waken the dormice that dull peace hath lull'd
Into a lethargy ?   Dost not hear 'em knock
Against their coffins, till they crack and break
The marble into shivers that entombs 'em ;
Making the temple shake as with an earthquake,
And all the statues of the gods grow pale,
Affrighted with the horror ?

Sex.   No such matter.

Hyp. Do they not call for arms, and fright thee,
     mortal,
Out of thy wits ?   Do they not break the legs,
And crush the skulls that dare approach too near
Their honour'd graves ?   When I shall come to dwell
In your dark family, if a noisome carcass
Offend my nostrils with too rank a scent,
Know I shall rage and quarrel, till I fright
The poor inhabitants of the charnel-house :
That here shall run a toe, a shinbone there :
Here creep a hand, there trolls an arm away.
One way a crooked rib shall halting hie,
Another you shall trundling find a skull.
Like the distracted citizens of a town
Beleaguer'd, and in danger to be taken.

---

1 This is a capital passage, and may remind us of the grave-
digger's scene in Hamlet, as well as of a less-known poem,
printed for the first time in Mr Huth's "Inedited Poetical
Miscellanies," 1870, entitled " A Conference with a Dead Man's
Head."

Aso. For heaven's sake, sexton, lay my quiet bones
By some precise religious officer—
One that will keep the peace. These roaring captains,
With blustering words and language full of dread,
Will make me quit my tomb, and run away
Wrapp'd in my winding-sheet ; as if grim Minos,
Stern Æacus, and horrid Rhadamanth
Enjoin'd the corpse a penance.

Sex.   Never fear it.
This was a captain's skull, one that carried a storm
in his countenance and a tempest in his tongue ; the
great bugbear of the city, that threw drawers down
the stairs as familiarly as quart-pots ; and had a pen-
sion from the barber-chirurgeons for breaking of pates :
a fellow that had ruined the noses of more bawds and
panders than the disease belonging to the trade ; and
yet I remember, when he went to burial, another corse
took the wall of him, and the bandog ne'er grumbled.

Aso. Then, skull (although thou be a captain's skull),
I say thou art a coward, and no gentleman ;
Thy mother was a whore, and thou liest in thy throat.

Hyp. Do not, live hare, pull the dead lion's beard.[1]

Aso. No, good Hyperbolus ; I but make a jest
To show my reading in morality.

Char. Do not the ashes of deceased poets,
Inspir'd with sacred fury, carol forth
Enthusiastic raptures ? Dost not hear 'em
Sing mysteries, and talk of things conceal'd
The rest of mortal judgments ? Dost not see
Apollo and the Muses every night
Dance rings about their tombs ?

Bom.   Do not roses,
Lilies, and violets grow upon their graves ?
Shoots not the laurel, that impal'd their brows,
Into a tree, to shadow their blest marble ?

---

[1] A proverb. See Hazlitt's " Proverbs," 1869, p. 153.

Do not they rise out of their shrouds to read
Their epitaphs? and if they like 'em not,
Expunge 'em, and write new ones? Do they not
Roar in caliginous terms, and vapour forth
From reeking entrails fogs Egyptian,
To puzzle even an oculate intellect?
Prate they not cataracts of insensible noise,
That with obstreperous cadence cracks the organs
Acromatic, till the deaf auditor
Admires the words he hears not?

Sex. This was a poetical noddle. O, the sweet
lines, choice language, eloquent figures, besides the
jests, half-jests, quarter-jests, and quibbles that have
come out o' these chaps that yawn so! He has not
now so much as a new-coined compliment to procure
him a supper. The best friend he has may walk by
him now, and yet have ne'er a jeer put upon him.
His mistress had a little dog deceased the other day,
and all the wit in this noddle could not pump out an
elegy to bewail it. He has been my tenant these
seven years, and in all that while I never heard him
rail against the times, or complain of the neglect of
learning. Melpomene and the rest of the Muses have
a good time on't that he is dead; for while he lived,
he ne'er left calling upon 'em. He was buried (as
most of the tribe) at the charge of the parish, and is
happier dead than alive; for he has now as much
money as the best in the company, and yet has left
off the poetical way of begging, called borrowing.

Aso. I scorn thy lyric and heroic strain,
Thy tart iambic and satiric vein.
Where be the quirks and tricks? show me again
The strange conundrums of thy frisking brain,
Thou poet's skull, and say what's rhyme to chimney?

Sex. Alas! sir, you ha' posed him : he cannot speak
to give you an answer, though his mouth be always
open. A man may safely converse with him now,

and never fear stifling in a crowd of verses. And now a play of his may be freely censured without a libel on the audience. The boys may be bold to cry it down.[1]

Bal. I cannot yet contrive it handsomely.
Methinks the darkness of the night should prompt me
To a plot of that complexion. Ruminate,
Ruminate, Ballio.

Phryne. Pray, sir, how does Death
Deal with the ladies? Is he so unmannerly
As not to make distinction of degrees?
I hope the rougher bones of men have had
More education than to trouble theirs,
That are of gentler stuff.

Sex. Death is a blunt villain, madam; he makes no distinction betwixt Joan and my lady. This was the prime madam in Thebes, the general mistress, the only adored beauty. Little would you think there were a couple of ears in these two auger-holes: or that this pit had been arched over with a handsome nose, that had been at the charges to maintain half a dozen of several silver arches to uphold the bridge. It had been a mighty favour once to have kissed these lips that grin so. This mouth out of all the madam's boxes cannot now be furnished with a set of teeth. She was the coyest, [most] overcurious dame in all the city: her chambermaid's misplacing of a hair was as much as her place came to. O, if that lady now could but behold this physnomy of hers in a looking-glass, what a monster would she imagine herself! Will all her perukes, tires, and dresses; with her chargeable teeth, with her ceruse and pomatum, and the benefit of her painter and doctor, make this idol up again?

Paint, ladies, while you live, and plaister fair;
But when the house is fallen, 'tis past repair.

---

[1] An evident allusion to the fate of Hausted's " Rival Friends."

Phryne. Nò matter, my Asotus : let Death do
His pleasure then ; we'll do our pleasures now.
Each minute that is lost is past recall.
This is the time allotted for our sports,
'Twere sin to pass it.   While our lips are soft,
And our embraces warm, we'll twine and kiss.
When we shall be such things as these, let worms
Crawl through our eyes, and eat our noses off ;
It is no matter—while we lived, we lived.
   Aso. And when we die, we die.   We will be both
     embalm'd.
In precious unguents to delight our sense,
And in our grave we'll buss and hug, and dally,
As we do here : for death can nothing be
To him that after death shall lie with thee.
Sexton, receive these coffins to the temple,
But not inter them ; for they both are guilty
Of their own blood—till we make expiation
T' assoil the fact.   Tutor, reward the sexton ;
I'll come sometimes and talk morality with him.
   Bal. This, sir, my pupil gives you : but hereafter
I'll more than treble it, if you be no enemy
To your own profit.
   Sex.   Profit's my religion.
   Aso. Now you that bore my dead friends to the
     grave,
Usher my living mistress home again.
Thus joy with grief alternate courses shares :
Fortune, I see thy wheel in all affairs.
                [*Exeunt omnes præter* SEXTON.

SCENE IV.

   Sex. Staphyla ! why, Staphyla ! I hope she has [not]
     ta'en her last sleep.   Why, when, Staphyla ?

Enter the Sexton's wife STAPHYLA.

Sta. What a life have I? I, that can never be quiet? I can no sooner lie down to take my rest, but presently, *Staphyla, Staphyla!* What's the news?

Sex. A prize, my rogue, a prize!

Sta. Where? or from whom?

Sex. Why, thou knowest I rob nowhere but on the highway to heaven—such as are upon their last journey thither. Thou and I have been land-pirates these six-and-thirty years, and have pillaged our share of Charon's passengers. Here are a couple of sound sleepers, and perchance their clothes will fit us. Then will I walk like a lord, and thou shalt be my madam, Staphyla.

Sta. Truly, husband, I have had such fearful dreams to-night, that I am persuaded (though I think I shall never turn truly honest again) to rob the dead no more. For (methought) as you and I were robbing the dead, the dead took heart and robbed us.

Sex. Tush! dreams are idle things. There is no felony warrantable but ours; for it is grounded on rules of charity. Is it fitting the dead should be clothed, and the living go naked? Besides, what is it to them whether they lie in sheets or no? Did you ever hear of any that caught cold in his coffin? Moreover, there is safety and security in these attempts. What inhabitant of the grave, that had his house broke open, accused the thief of burglary? Look here! this is a lawyer's skull. There was a tongue in't once, a damnable eloquent tongue, that would almost have persuaded any man to the gallows. This was a turbulent, busy fellow, till death gave him his *quietus est.* And yet I ventured to rob him of his gown and the rest of his habiliments, to the very buckram bag, not leaving him so much as a poor halfpenny to pay for his waftage: and yet the good man ne'er repined at it. Had he been alive, and were to have pleaded against me, how would he have thundered it ! " Behold, most grave judges, a fact of that horror and height in sin, so abominable, so detestable in the eyes of heaven and earth, that never any but this day's cause presented to the admiration of your ears. I cannot speak it without trembling, 'tis so new, unused—so unheard-of a villany. But that I know your lordship's confident of the honesty of your poor orator, I should not hope by all my reasons, grounds, testimonies, arguments, and persuasions to gain your belief. This man—said I a man ?—this monster, rather—but monster is too easy a name—this devil, this incarnate devil, having lost all honesty, and abjured the profession of virtue, robbed (a sin in the action)—but who ?   The dead ! What need I aggravate the fault ? the naming the action is sufficient to condemn him—I say, he robbed the dead.   The dead !   Had he robbed the living, it had been more pardonable ; but to rob the dead of their clothes, the poor impotent dead, that can neither card nor spin, nor make new ones—O, 'tis most audacious and intolerable ! "   Now you have well spoke, why do you not, after all this rhetoric, put your hand behind you to receive some more instructions backward ?   Now a man may clap you o' th' coxcomb with his spade, and never stand in fear of an action of battery.

Sta. For this one time, husband, I am induced ; but in sooth I will not make a common practice of it : knock you up that coffin, and I'll knock up this. Rich and glorious !

Sex. Bright as the sun ! Come, we must strip you, gallants ; the worms are not for having the dishes served up to their table covered.   O, O, O!

Sta. Heaven shield me ! O, O, O !
[TYNDARUS *and* TECHMESSA *rise from the coffins,
and the* SEXTON *and his wife, affrighted, fall
into a swoon.*

SCENE V.

TYNDARUS *and* TECHMESSA.

Tyn. How poor a thing is man, whom death itself
Cannot protect from injuries ! O ye gods !
Is't not enough our wretched lives are toss'd
On dangerous seas, but we must stand in fear
Of pirates in the haven too ? Heaven made us
So many butts of clay, at which the gods
In cruel sport shoot miseries. Yet, I hope,
Their spleen's grown milder, and this blest occasion
Offers itself an earnest of their mercy.
Their sins have furnish'd us with fit disguises
To quiet our perplexed souls. Techmessa,
Let me array you in this woman's robes.
I'll wear the sexton's garments in exchange.
Our sheets and coffins shall be theirs.
 Tech.   Dear Tyndarus !
In all my life I never found such peace
As in this coffin : it presented me
The sweets that death affords. Man has no liberty
But in this prison. Being once lodg'd here,
He's fortified in an impregnable fort,
Through which no doubts, suspicions, jealousies :
No sorrows, cares, or wild distractions
Can force an entrance to disturb our sleeps.
 Tyn. Yet to those prisons will we now commit
These two offenders.
 Tech.   But what benefit
Shall we enjoy by this disguise ?
 Tyn.   A great one.

If my Evadne or thy Pamphilus
E'er lov'd us living, they will haste to make
Atonement for our souls, stain'd with the guilt
Of our own blood; if not, they will rejoice
Our deaths have opened them so clear a passage
To their close loves: and, with those thoughts pos-
    sess'd,
They will forget the torments hell provides
For those that leave the warfare of this life
Without a pass from the great general.
    Tech. I hope they may prove constant.
    Tyn.   So pray I.
I will desire yon statue be so courteous
To part with's beard awhile.   So; we are now
Beyond discovery.
    Sext.   O, O, O!
    Sta.   O, O, O!
    Tyn. Let's use a charm for these.

> *Quiet sleep, or I will make*
> *Erinnis whip thee with a snake,*
> *And cruel Rhadamanthus take*
> *Thy body to the boiling lake,*
> *Where fire and brimstone never slake;*
> *Thy heart shall burn, thy head shall ache,*
> *And every joint about thee quake.*
> *And therefore dare not yet to wake.*

Tech. *Quiet sleep, or thou shalt see*
> *The horrid hags of Tartary,*
> *Whose tresses ugly serpents be,*
> *And Cerberus shall bark at thee,*
> *And all the Furies that are three—*
> *The worst is call'd Tisiphone—*
> *Shall lash thee to eternity.*
> *And therefore sleep thou peacefully.*

[*The* SEXTON *and his wife are placed in the coffins.*

Tyn. But who comes hither? Ballio; what's his
business?

SCENE VI.

Enter BALLIO.

Bal. Sexton, I'll open first thine ears with these,
To make 'em fit to let persuasions in.
Tyn. These, sir, well cure my deafness.
Bal.   Art thou mine?
Tyn. Sir, you have bought me.
Bal.   I'll pay double for thee.
Shall I prevail in my request?
Tyn.   Ask these ——
Bal. Thou art apprehensive : to the purpose, then.
Have you not in the temple some deep vault
Ordain'd for burial?
Tyn.   Yes.
Bal.   Then I proceed :
We have to-night perform'd the last of service
That piety can pay to our dead friends.
Tyn. 'Twas charitably done.
Bal.   We brought 'em hither
To their last home. Now, sir, they both being guilty
Of their own deaths, I fear the laws of Thebes
Deny 'em burial. It would grieve me, sir
(For friendship cannot be so soon forgot :
Especially so firm a one as ours),
To have 'em cast a prey to wolves and eagles.
Sir, these religious thoughts have brought me hither
Now at the dead of night, to entreat you
To cast their coffins into some deep vault,
And to inter 'em. O my Tyndarus !
All memory shall fail me, ere my thoughts
Can leave th' impression of that love I bear thee.
Thou left'st me half of all the land thou hadst ;

And should I not provide thee so much earth
As I can measure by thy length, heaven curse me !

Tyn. Sir, if your courtesy had not bound me yours,
This act of goodness had.

Bal.   So true a friend
No age records. Farewell. This work succeeds.
Posterity, that shall this story get,
May learn from hence an art to counterfeit.

                          [*Exit* BALLIO.

SCENE VII.

TYNDARUS, TECHMESSA.

Tyn. Here was a strange deliverance ! Who can be
So confident of fortune as to say,
I now am safe ?

Tech.   This villain has reveal'd
All our designs to Pamphilus and Evadne ;
And they with bribes and hopes of an inheritance,
If you were dead indeed, have won this rascal
To this black treason. What foul crimes can lust
Prompt her base vassals to ! Here let us end
Our busy search, and travel o'er the world,
To see if any cold and northern climate
Have entertain'd lost virtue, long since fled
Our warmer country.

Tyn.   Ha ! 'Tis so ! 'tis so !
I see it with clear eyes. O cursed plot !
And are you brooding, crocodiles ? I may chance
To break the serpent's egg, ere you have hatch'd
The viper to perfection. Come, Techmessa,
My anger will no longer be confin'd
To patient silence. Tedious expectation
Is but a foolish fire by night, that leads
The traveller out of 's way. Break forth, my wrath ;
Break like a deluge of consuming fire,

And scorch 'em both to ashes in a flame
Hot as their lust.   No.   'Tis too base a blood
For me to spill.   Let 'em e'en live t' engender
A brood of monsters.   May perpetual jealousy
Wait on their beds, and poison their embraces
With just suspicions ; may their children be
Deform'd, and fright the mother at the birth !
May they live long and wretched, all men's hate,
And yet have misery enough for pity !
May they be long a-dying of diseases
Painful and loathsome.   Passion, do not hurry me
To this unmanly womanish revenge.
Wilt thou curse, Tyndarus, when thou wear'st a sword?
But ha ! hark ! observe !

SCENE VIII.

Enter PAMPHILUS *and* EVADNE.[1]

 Pam.   Wait till we call.   [*To Attendants.*
Heaven, if thou hast not emptied all thy treasury
Of wrath upon me, here I challenge thee
To lay on more.   What torments hast thou left,
In which thou hast not exercis'd my patience ?
Yet cast up all the accounts of all my sorrows,
And the whole sum is trebled in the loss
Of dear Techmessa.
 Tech.   If this grief were real !   [*Aside.*
 Tyn. Be not too credulous.   [*Aside.*
 Pam.   I have stood the rest
Of your afflictions : with this one I fell—
Fell like a rock that had repell'd the rage
Of thousand violent billows, and withstood

---

[1] Tyndarus and Techmessa are still disguised in the garments
of the Sexton and his wife.

Their fierce assaults, until the working tide
Had undermin'd him : then he falls, and draws
Part of the mountain with him.
    Evad.   Pamphilus,
When did you see my sweetheart? prythee, tell me,
Is he not gone a-maying?   He will bring me
Some pinks and daisies home to-morrow morning.
Pray heaven he meet no thieves !
    Pam.   Alas, Evadne!
Thy Tyndarus is dead.
    Evad.   What shall I do?
I cannot live without him.
    Tyn.   I am mov'd :
Yet I will make this trial full and perfect.   [*Aside.*
What at this dismal hour, when nothing walks
But souls tormented, calls you from your sheets
To visit our dark cells, inhabited
By death and melancholy?
    Evad.   I am come
To seek my true love here.   Did you not see him?
He's come to dwell with you ; pray, use him well.
He was a proper gentleman.
    Tech.   Sir, what cause
Enforc'd you hither ?
    Pam.   I am come to pay
The tribute of my eyes to a dead love.
    Tyn. Fair lady, may I ask one question of you?
Did you admit no love into your bosom
But only his?
    Evad.   Alas ! you make me weep.
Could any woman love a man but him?
No, Tyndarus, I will not long outlive thee :
We will be married in Elysium,
And arm-in-arm walk through the blessed groves,
And change a thousand kisses—you shan't see us.
    Tyn. I know not whether it be joy or grief
Forces tears from me.

Tech.　　　　Were you constant, sir,
To her whose death you now so much lament?
For by those prodigies and apparitions
That have to-night shak'd the foundations
Of the whole temple, your inconstancy
Hath caus'd your mistress's untimely end.
　　Pam. The sun shall change his course, and find
　　　new paths
To drive his chariot in : the loadstone leave
His faith unto the north : the vine withdraw
Those strict embraces that enfold the elm
In her kind arms—but if I change my love
From my Techmessa, may I be recorded
To all posterity love's great apostate
In Cupid's annals.
　　Evad.　　　　If you see my Tyndarus,
Pray, tell him I will make all haste to meet him.
I will but weep awhile first.
　　Tyn.　　　　　　Pretty sorrow!　　[*Aside.*
　　Tech. Sir, you may veil your falsehood in smooth
　　　language,
And gild it o'er with fair hypocrisy :
But here has been such groans : ghosts that have
　　cried
In hollow voices, *Pamphilus, O false Pamphilus!*
Revenge on Pamphilus! Such complaints as these
The gods ne'er make in vain.
　　Pam. Then there is witchcraft in't; and are the
　　　gods
Made parties too against me?　Pardon, then,
If I grow stubborn.　While they press'd my shoulders
No more than I could bear, they willingly
Submitted to the burden.　Now they wish
To cast it off.　What treachery has brib'd you,
Celestial forms, to be my false accusers?
I challenge you (for you can view my thoughts,
And read the secret characters of my heart)

Give in your verdict ; did you ever find
Another image graven in my soul
Besides Techmessa ?   No !   'Tis hell has forg'd
These sly impostures ! all these plots are coin'd
Out of the devil's mintage.
  Tech.   Certainly,
There's no false fire in this.   [*Aside.*]
  Tyn.   There cannot be. [*Aside.*]
  Evad. Pray, sir, direct me where I may embalm
My Tyndarus with my tears.
  Tyn.   There, gentle lady.
  Evad. Is this a casket fit to entertain
A jewel of such value ?
  Pam.   Where must I
Pay my devotions ?
  Tech.   There your dead saint lies.
  Evad. Hail, Tyndarus, may earth but lightly press
   thee :
And may'st thou find those joys th' art gone to
   taste
As true as my affection.   Now I know
Thou canst not choose but love me, and with longing
Expect my quick arrival : for the soul,
Freed from the cloud of flesh, clearly discerns
Forms in their perfect nature.   If there be
A guilt upon thy blood, thus I'll redeem it.
        [*Offers to kill herself.*
And lay it all on mine.
  Tyn.   What mean you, lady ?
  Evad. Stay not my pious hand.
  Tyn.   Your impious, rather.
If you were dead, who then were left to make
Lustration for his crime ? shall foolish zeal
Persuade you to a hasty death, and so
Leave Tyndarus to eternity of flames ?
  Evad. Pardon me, Tyndarus ; I will only see
That office done, and then I'll follow thee.

Pam. Thou gentle soul of my deceased love,
If thou still hover'st hereabouts, accept
The vows of Pamphilus.   If I ever think
Of woman with affection but Techmessa,
Or keep the least spark of a love alive
But in her ashes, let me never see
Those blessed fields where gentle lovers walk
In endless joys.   Why do I idly weep?
I'll write my grief in blood.   [*Offers to kill himself.*]
    Tech.   What do you mean?
    Pam. Techmessa, I am yet withheld; but sud-
    denly
I'll make escape to find thee.
    Tech.   O blest minute !   [*Aside.*

SCENE IX.

Enter DIPSAS.

Dip. Where shall I fly to hide me from my guilt?
It follows me, like those that run away
From their own shadows : that which I would shun,
I bear about me.   Whom shall I appease,
The living or the dead? for I have injur'd
Both you and them.   O Tyndarus, here I kneel,
And do confess myself thy cruel murd'ress,
And thine, Techmessa.   Gentle daughter, pardon
    me ;
But how shall I make satisfaction,
That have but one poor life, and have lost two?
O Pamphilus ! my malice ruin'd thee,
But most Evadne : for at her I aim'd,
Because she is no issue of my womb,
But trusted by her father to my care.
Her have I followed with a step-dame's hate,
As envious that her beauty should eclipse

My daughter's honour.   But the gods in justice
Have ta'en her hence to punish me.   My sins
March up in troops against me.   But this potion
Shall purge out life and them.
   Tyn.   Be not too rash:
I will revive Techmessa.   *[Discovers her.]*
   Dip.   O sweet daughter!
   Pam. Thou hast reviv'd two lives at once.
   Evad.   But I
Still live a widowed virgin.
   Tyn.   No, Evadne;
               [Discovering himself.]
Receive me, new-created of a clay
Purg'd from all dregs; my thoughts do all run clear.
Take hence these coffins; I will have them borne
Trophies before me, when we come to tie
The nuptial knot: for death has brought us life.
Suspicion made us confident, and weak jealousy
Hath added strength to our resolved love.
Cupid hath run his maze: this was his day.
But the next part Hymen intends to play.   *[Exeunt.*

ACT V., SCENE I.

Demetrius *solus.*

Hail, sacred Thebes, I kiss thy blessed soil,
And on my knees salute thy seven gates.
Some twenty winters now have glaz'd thy floods
Since I beheld thy turrets batter'd then
With wars that sought the ruin of those walls
Which music built.[1]   When Minos' cruel tribute
Robb'd mothers of their dearest babes, to glut
His ravenous minotaur, I for safety fled

---

[1] Alluding to the legend of Amphion.

With my young sons, but call'd my country's hate
Upon my head, whom misery made malicious.
Each father had a curse in store for me,
Because I shar'd not in the common loss,
Yet would have willingly chang'd fortunes with me.
I dare not meet the vulgars' violent rage
Eager against me.   I will therefore study
Some means to live conceal'd.

SCENE II.

Enter ASOTUS.

Aso.   I have heard my mother,
Who had more proverbs in her mouth than teeth,
(Peace with her soul, where'er it be !) affirm :
Marry too soon, and you'll repent too late.
A sentence worth my meditation ;
For marriage is a serious thing.   Perchance
Fair Phryne is no maid ; for women may
Be beauteous, yet no virgins.   Fair and chaste
Are not of necessary consequence ;
Or being both fair and chaste, she may be barren ;
And then, when I am old, I shall not have
A boy to doat on as my father does.
    Dem. Kind fortune fan you with a courteous wing.
    Aso. A pretty compliment ! What art thou, fellow ?
    Dem. A register[1] of heaven, a privy councillor
To all the planets : one that has been tenant
To the Twelve Houses,[2] tutor to the Fates,
That taught 'em the art of spinning : a live almanac,
One that by speculation in the stars
Can foretell anything.

---

[1] *i.e.*, Registrar.
[2] Alluding to the twelve houses into which the old astro-
nomers and astrologers divided the starry system.

Aso.   How ! foretell anything ?
How many years are past since Thebes was built ?
  Dem. That is not to foretell : you state the ques-
    tion
Of times already past.
  Aso.   And cannot you
As well foretell things past as things to come ?
Say, register of heaven and privy councillor
To all the planets, with the rest of your titles,
(For I shall ne'er be able to repeat 'em all)
Shall I, as I intend, to-day be married ?
  Dem. Th' Almutes, or the lord of the ascendant,
I find with Luna corporally join'd
To the Almutes of the seventh house,
Which is the matrimonial family :
And therefore I conclude the nuptials hold.
And yet the aspect is not in trine or sextile,
But in the quartile radiation
Or tetragon, which shows an inclination
Averse, and yet admitting of reception.
It will, although encountered with impediment,
At last succeed.
  Aso.   Ha ! what bold impediment
Is so audacious as to encounter me ?
Be he Almutes of what house he please ;
Let his aspect be sextile, trine, or quartile ;
I do not fear him with his radiations,
His tetragons, and inclinations :
If he provoke my spleen, I'll have him know
I soldiers feed shall mince him, and my poets
Shall with a satire, steep'd in gall and vinegar,
Rhyme 'em to death, as they do rats in Ireland.
  Dem. Good words !
There's no resistance to the laws of fate.
This sublunary world must yield obedience
To the celestial virtues.
  Aso.   One thing more

I would desire to know : whether my spouse
(That shall be) be immaculate ?   I'd be loth
To marry an advowson that has had
Other incumbents.

    Dem.   I'll resolve you instantly.
The Dragon's tail stands where the head should be—
A shrewd suspicion she has been strongly tempted.

    Aso. The Dragon's tail puts me in a horrible fear :
I feel a kind of sting in my head already.

    Dem. And Mars being landlord of th' eleventh
        house,
Plac'd in the Ram and Scorpion, plainly signifies
The maid has been in love ; but the aspect
Being without reception, lays no guilt
Of act upon her.

    Aso.   I shall be jealous presently :
For the Ram is but an ill sign in the head :
And you know what Scorpio aims at in the almanac.

    Dem. But when I see th' ascendant and his lord,
With the good Moon in angles and fix'd signs,
I do conclude her virgin pure and spotless.

    Aso. I thank th' ascendant and his noble lord,
He shall be welcome to my house at any time,
And so shall Mistress Moon, with all her angles
And her fix'd signs.   But how come you to know
All this for certain ?

    Dem.   Sir, the learned Cabalists
And all the Chaldees do conclude it lawful :
As Asla, Baruch, and Abohali,
Caucaph, Toz, Arcaphan, and Albuas,
Gasar, with Hali, Hippocras, and Lencuo,
With Ben, Benesaphan, and Albubetes.

    Aso. Are Asla, Baruch, and Abohali,
With all the rest of th' jury, men of credit ?

    Dem. Their words shall go as far i' th' zodiac, sir,
As another's bond.

    Aso.   I am beholding to 'em.

Another scruple yet.   I would have children too,
Children to doat on, sir, when I grow old ;
Such as will spend when I am dead and gone,
And make me have such fine dreams in my grave.
 Dem. Sir, y' are a happy man.   I do not see
In all your horoscope one sign masculine ;
For such portend sterility.
 Aso.   How's that, man ?
Is't possible for any man to ha' children
Without a sign masculine ?
 Dem.   Sir, you mistake me :
You are not yet initiate.   The Almutes
Of the ascendant is not elevated
Above the Almutes of the filial house :
Venus is free, and Jove not yet combust :
And then, the signifier being lodg'd
In watery signs, the Scorpion, Crab and Fish
Foreshow a numerous issue of both sexes.
And Mercury in's exaltations,
Plac'd in their angles and their points successive,
Beholds the lords of the triplicity
Unhind'red in their influence.   You were born
Under a getting constellation—
A fructifying star.   Sir, I pronounce you
A joyful father !
 Aso.   Happy be the hour
I met with thee ! I'll ha' thee live with me.
Thou shalt be my domestical astronomer
I have a brace of poets, as fit as may be,
To furnish thee with verses for each month.
Sir, since the gracious stars do promise me
So numerous a troop of sons and daughters,
'Tis fit I should have my means in my own hands
To provide for 'em all : therefore I fain would know
Whether my father be long-liv'd or no.
 Dem. The planet Mars is oriental now
To Saturn ; but in reference to the Sun

He bears a westerly position.
Which Ylem linking Saturn with the Sun
In opposition, both sinisterly
Fall'n from their corners, plainly signifies
He cannot long survive.
    Aso.   Why, who can help it?
There's no resistance to the laws of fate:
This sublunary world must yield obedience
To the celestial virtues. Were't not providence
To bespeak mourning-clothes against the funeral?
    Dem. 'Tis good to be in readiness.
    Aso.   If thou be
So cunning a prophet, tell me, do I mean
To entertain thee for my wizard?
    Dem.   Sir,
I do not see the least Azymenes
Or planetary hindrance. Alcocoden
Tells me you will.

Enter THRASYMACHUS, HYPERBOLUS.

    Aso.   Tell Alcocoden then
He is i' th' right. Thrasymachus, Hyperbolus!
We have increas'd our family: see him enroll'd.
He is a man of merit, and can prophesy.
    Thras. We'll drench him in the welcome of the
            cellar,
And try if he can prophesy who falls first.   [*Exeunt.*
    Aso. How will the world admire me, when they see
My house an academy, all the arts
Wait at my table, every man of quality
Take sanctuary here! I will be patron
To twenty liberal sciences.

SCENE III.

Enter BALLIO.

Bal.   A fair sun
Shine on the happy bridegroom.
   Aso.   *Quondam* tutor
(For I am past all tuition but my wife's),
Thanks for your wishes ; have you studied yet
How with one charge (for ceremonious charge
I care not for) I may express my grief
At the sad funerals of my friends deceas'd,
And yet proclaim with how much joy I wed
The beauteous Phryne?
   Bal.   I have beat my brain
To find out a right garb.   Wear these two cloaks :
This sable garment, sorrow's livery,
Speaks funeral : this richer robe of joy
Says 'tis a nuptial solemnity.
   Aso. A choice device : I'll practise.
   Bal.   Rarely well.

SCENE IV.

Enter SIMO.

Simo. Good morrow, boy : how flows thy blood,
   Asotus,
Upon thy wedding-day? is it springtide?
Find'st thou an active courage in thy bones?
Wilt thou at night create me grandsire, ha?
O, I remember with what sprightly courage
I bedded thy old mother, and that night
Bid fair for thee, boy : how I curs'd the ceremonies,
And thought the youngsters scrambled for my points
Too slowly !   'Twas a happy night, Asotus.

Aso. How sad a day is this! methinks the sun
Affrighted with our sorrows should run back
Into his eastern palace, and for ever
Sleep in the lap of Thetis. Can he show
A glorious beam, when Tyndarus is dead
And fair Techmessa? I will weep a flood
Deep as Deucalion's; and again the chaos
Shall muffle up the lamentable world
In sable cloaks of grief and black confusion!

Sim. What ails my boy? unseasonable grief
Shall not disturb thy nuptials. Good Asotus,
Be not so passionate.

Bal. What incomparable mirth
Would such a dotard and his humorous son
Make in a comedy, if a learned pen
Had the expression! *[Aside.]*

Aso. Now the t'other cloak,
In what a verdant weed the spring arrays,
Fresh Tellus in! how Flora decks the fields
With all her tapestry, and the choristers
Of every grove chant carols! Mirth is come
To visit mortals. Everything is blithe,
Jocund, and jovial. All the gods arrive
To grace our nuptials. Let us sing and dance,
That heaven may see our revels, and send down
The planets in a masque, the more to grace
This day's solemnity.

Sim. Ay, this, Asotus.
There's music, boy, in this.

Aso. Now this cloak again.
Ye gods, you overload mortality,
And press our shoulders with too great a weight
Of dismal miseries. All content is fled
With Tyndarus and Techmessa. Ravens croak
About my house; ill-boding screech-owls sing
Epithalamiums to my spouse and me.
Can I dream pleasures, or expect to taste

The comforts of the married bed, when Tyndarus
And fair Techmessa from the world are gone?
No, pardon me, you gentle ghosts; I vow
To cloister up my grief in some dark cell:
And there, till grief shall close my blubber'd eyes,
Weep forth repentance.
  Sim.   Sure, he is distracted!
Asotus, do not grieve so: all thy sorrows
Are doubled in thy father. Pity me,
If not thyself; O, pity these grey hairs!
Pity my age, Asotus.
  Aso.   What a silly fellow
My father is, that knows not which cloak speaks!
Father, you do forget this is our nuptial!
Cast off those trophies of your wealthy beggary,
And clad yourself in rich and splendent weeds,
Such as become my father. Do not blemish
Our dignity with rags. Appear to-day
As glorious as the sun. Set forth yourself
In your bright lustre.
  Sim.   So I will, my boy;
Was there ever father so fortunate in a child?
            [*Exit* SIMO.
  Aso. Do not I vary with decorum, Ballio?
  Bal. I do not think but Proteus, sir, begot you
On a chameleon.
  Aso.   Nay, I know my mother
Was a chameleon; for my father allowed her
Nothing but air to feed on. [*Puts on the other cloak.*

SCENE V.

Enter PHRYNE.

 Phryne. Rises Aurora with a happy light
On my Asotus?

Aso.　　　　　　　Beauteous Phryne, welcome.
Although the dragon's tail may scandal thee,
And Mars corrupt the scorpion and the ram ;
Yet the good moon in angles and fix'd signs
Gives thee a good report.
　　Phryne.　　　　　　What means my dear ?
　　Aso. Thy dear, my beauteous Phryne, means the
　　　same
With Hali, Baruch, and Abohali,
Caucaph, Toz, Arcaphan, and Albuas,
Gafar, with Afla, Hippocras, and Lencuo,
With Ben, Benesaphan, and Albubetes.
　　Phryne. I fear you ha' studied the black art of late.
　　Aso. Ah, girl !　Th' almutes of the filial house
Is not depress'd, Venus is free, and Jove
Not yet combust : the signs are watery signs,
And Mercury beholds the trine aspect
Unhinder'd in his influence.
　　Phryne.　　　　　　What of all this ?
　　Aso. We shall have babies plenty : I am grown
Learned of late.　Go, Phryne, be in readiness ;
I long to tie the knot : at night we'll make
A young Asotus.
　　Phryne.　　　Health attend you, sir.
　　　　　　　　　　　　　[*Exit* PHRYNE.

SCENE VI.

DIPSAS, TYNDARUS, EVADNE, PAMPHILUS, TECHMESSA,
　　ASOTUS, BALLIO, PHRONESIUM, PRIESTS *and sacri-*
　　fice, and Hymen's statue discovered.

　　Aso.　　　　　　Tyndarus living ?
Here, take this cloak away ! we have no use on't.
　　Bal. The more sorrow is mine !
　　Tyn.　　　　　　How does my friend Asotus ?

Aso. You are welcome from the dead, sir.
I hope our friends in Elysium are in good health?
    Tyn. Ballio, I thank you heartily,
You had an honest and religious care
To see us both well buried.
    Bal.   I shall be hanged.   [*Exit.*

The song and sacrifice.

Priest. Hymen, thou God of union, with smooth
    brow
Accept our pious orgies.   Thou that tiest
Hearts in a knot, and link'st in sacred chains
The mutual souls of lovers, may it please
Thy deity to admit into the number
Of thy chaste votaries this blessed pair.
          [*He presents* TYNDARUS *and* EVADNE.
Mercy, you gods, the statue turns away!
    Tyn. Why should this be?   The reason is apparent.
Evadne has been false, and the chaste deity
Abhors the sacrifice of a spotted soul.
Go, thou dissembler, mask thyself in modesty,
Wear virtue for a veil, and paint false blushes
On thy adulterate cheek.   Though thou may'st cosen
The eyes of man, and cheat the purblind world,
Heaven has a piercing sight.   Hymen, I thank thee
Thou stoppedst my foot stepping into the gulf.
How near was I damnation!
    Evad.   Gentle Hymen,
What sin have I unwillingly committed
To call heaven's anger on me?
    Priest.   If there be
A secret guilt in these, that hath offended
Thy mighty godhead, wilt thou please to prove
          [*He presents* PAMPHILUS *and* TECHMESSA.
This other knot?   The statue turns again!
What prodigies are these!

Pam.   Celestial powers,
You tyrannise o'er man : and yet 'tis sin
To ask you why you wrong us.
 Tech.   Cunning Pamphilus,
Though, like a snake, you couch yourself in flowers,
The gods can find your lurking, and betray
The spotted skin.
 Priest.   Above this twenty years
Have I attended on thy sacred temple,
Yet never saw thee so incens'd, dread Hymen.
  Tyn. To search the reason, will you please to proffer
These to his godhead?
 Priest.   Will thy godhead deign
These two the blessings of the genial sheet?
     [*He presents* PAMPHILUS *and* EVADNE.
He beckons 'em.
 Tyn.   There the faith is plighted.
False Pamphilus, the honour of the temple,
And the respect I bear religion,
Cannot protect thee.   I will stain the altars,
And sprinkle every statue in the shrine
With treacherous blood.
 Priest.   Provoke not Jove's just thunder.
  Tyn. Well, you may take Evadne ; heaven give you joy.
 Pam. Religion is mere juggling.   This is nothing
But the priest's knavery : a kind of holy trick
To gain their superstition credit.   Hymen,
Why dost thou turn away thy head?   I fear
Thy bashful deity is asham'd to look
A woman in the face.   If so, I pardon thee :
If out of spite thou cross me, know, weak godhead,
I'll teach mankind a custom that shall bring
Thy altars to neglect.   Lovers shall couple
(As other creatures) freely, and ne'er stand
Upon the tedious ceremony, marriage :

And then thou, priest, may'st starve.   Who in your
    temple
Will light a cere-candle, or for incense burn
A grain of frankincense ?
    Chrem.   Heaven instruct our souls
To find the secret mystery !
    Aso.   I have entertain'd
One that, by Ylem and Aldeboran,
With the almutes, can tell anything.
I'll fetch him hither : he shall resolve you.
                                        [*Exit* ASOTUS.
    Chrem. Man is a ship that sails with adverse winds,
And has no haven till he land at death.
Then, when he thinks his hands fast grasp the bank,
Comes a rude billow betwixt him and safety,
And beats him back into the deep again.

SCENE VII.

Enter ASOTUS, *with* DEMETRIUS : *manent cæteri.*

    Aso. Here's another figure to cast, sir.   These two
    gentlemen.
    Dem. A sudden joy o'ercomes me.   [*Aside.*]
    Aso.   Are to marry
Old Chremylus' daughters.   This is Tyndarus,
And he should have Evadne : and this Pamphilus,
That has a moneth's mind to Techmessa; but that
    Hymen
Looks with a wry neck at 'm.   If the ascendant,
With all his radiations and aspects,
Know anything, here's one that can unfold it.
I must go fit myself for mine own wedding.   [*Exit.*
    Dem. Fly from the temple, you unhallowed troop
That dare present your sins for sacrifice
Before the gods !

Chrem.   What should this language mean?

Dem. Think you that heaven will ever sign a grant
To your incestuous matches?

Chrem.   How incestuous?

Dem. This is not Tyndarus, but Demetrius' son,
Call'd Clinias, and fair Evadne's brother!
Evadne trusted in exchange to Chremylus,
For young Timarchus, whom Demetrius took
With him to Athens, when he fled from Thebes
To save the infants from the monster's jaws—
The cruel Minotaur.   Marvel not the gods
Forbid the banns, when in each match is incest.

Chrem. I wonder he should know this.

Tyn.   I am amaz'd.

Dem. I will confirm your faith.

Tyn.   My father? [*He pulls off his disguise.*

Pam.   My father?

Dem. No, good Timarchus, ask thy blessing there.
Sir, if I not mistake me, you are Chremylus.
Pray, let me see that ring.   Sir, I must challenge it,
And in requital will return you this.

Chrem. Demetrius! welcome.   Now my joys are full,
When I behold my son and my old friend.

Dem. Which is Evadne?   Blessings on thy head.
Now, Chremylus, let us conclude a marriage
As we at first intended; my Clinias
With your Techmessa, and your son Timarchus
With my Evadne.

Chrem. Heaven has decreed it so.

Dem. Are the young people pleas'd?

Pam. Evad. Tyn. and Tech. The will of heaven
Must be obey'd.

Dem. Now try if Hymen please
To end all troubles in a happy marriage.

                            [*The statue assents.*

Priest. Hymen, we thank thee, and will crown thy
    head

With all the glorious chaplets of the spring:
The firstborn kid and fattest of our bullocks
Shall bleed upon thy altars (if it be
Lawful to sacrifice in blood to thee,
That art the means to life) 'cause thy provident mercy
Prevented this incestuous match.   Deign now
Propitious looks to this more holy knot.
This virgin offers up her untouch'd zone,
And vows chaste love to Clinias.   All joy to you!
The fair Evadne too is come to hang
Her maiden girdle at thy sacred shrine,
And vows herself constant to the embraces
Of young Timarchus.   Happiness wait on both!
    Tyn. I see our jealous thoughts were not in vain.
Nature, abhorring from so foul a sin,
Infus'd those doubts into us.

SCENE VIII.

Enter ASOTUS *in arms, with a drum and trumpet,*
    attended by THRASYMACHUS, HYPERBOLUS, BOMO-
    LOCHUS, CHARYLUS, SIMO, PHRYNE.

    Aso. If there be any knight that dares lay claim
To beauteous Phryne (as I hope there's none),
I dare him to th' encounter; let him meet me
Here in the lists.   If he be wise, he dare not,
But will consider danger in the action.
I'll win her with my sword: mistake me not,
I challenge no man.   He who dares pretend
A title to a hair shall sup with Pluto:
'Twere cooler supping in another place.
No champion yet appear?   I would fain fight.
    Phron. Sir, if you want a champion, I am for you.
    Aso. I ha' no quarrel to thee, Amazon.
    Phron. I must have a husband, too, and I will have

a husband; ay, and I will have you : I can hold out no
longer : I am aweary of eating chalk and coals, and
begin to dislike the feeding on oatmeal. The thought
of so many marriages together has almost lost my
maidenhead.

    Aso. Why, thou shalt have my father : though he
      be old,
He's rich, and will maintain thee bravely. Dad,
What think you on't?
    Sim.   Thou'lt make me, boy, too happy.
She shall have anything.
    Phron.   You will let me make
My own conditions.
    Sim.   What thou wilt, my girl.
    Phron. I will feed high, go rich, have my six horses
And my embroider'd coach ; ride where I list,
Have all the gallants in the town to visit me,
Maintain a pair of little legs to go
On idle messages to all the madams.
You shall deny no gentleman entertainment.
And when we kiss and toy, be it your cue
To nod and fall asleep.
    Sim.   With all my heart.
    Aso. Then take him, girl : he will not trouble thee
      long ;
For Mars being oriental unto Saturn,
And occidental to the sun, proclaims
He is shortlived.
    Phron.   Well, sir, for want of a better
I am content to take you.
    Aso.   Join them, priest.
    Priest. Thus I conjoin you in religious bands.
    Aso. Now usher Phryne to my amorous arms.
    Priest. The generous Asotus and fair Phryne
Present their vows unto thee, gracious Hymen.
    Sex. I forbid the banns.   [*They speak out of*
    Sta. I forbid the banns.   *the coffin.*

Aso. And can there be no weddings without pro-
    digies?
This is th' impediment the Azymenes
Or planetary hindrance threatened me.
By the almutes of the seventh house,
In an aspect of tetragon radiation,
If Luna now be corporally join'd,
I may o'ercome th' averseness of my stars.
    Tyn. Sir, as you clear'd our doubts, I will clear
    yours,
See you these ghosts?   Well, sexton, take heed here-
    after
How you rob the dead ; some of 'em may cozen you.
    Sex. Pardon me, sir ; I seriously vow
Henceforth to rob no creature but the living.
    Tyn. Well, you shall both fast to-night, and take
penance at the lower end of the table in these sheets ;
and that shall be your punishment.
    Aso. Phryne, I take you for my loving spouse.
    Phryne. And I take you for my obedient husband.
    Priest. And I conclude the tie.
    Aso.   Ha! you sweet rogue!

SCENE IX.

Enter BALLIO, *with a halter about his neck.*

    Aso. Why, how now, tutor, a rope about your
    neck?
I have heard that hanging and marrying go by destiny ;
But I never thought they had come together before.
    Bal. I have cast a serious thought upon my guilt,
And find myself an arrant rogue.   The gallows
Was all the inheritance I was ever born to.
E'en use me as you please.
    Aso. Pray, sir, let me beg my tutor's pardon.

Spare me to-day : for when the night comes on,
There's sweeter executions to be done.

    Tyn. You have prevail'd.   No man be sad to-day.
Come, you shall dine with me.

    Aso.   Pardon me, sir :
I will not have it said by the malicious
That I ate at another man's table
The first day I set up housekeeping.
No, you shall all go home and dine with me.

    Tyn. Come, then: our joys are ripen'd to perfection.
Let us give heaven the praise ; and all confess
There is a difference 'twixt the jealousy
Of those that woo and those that wedded be.
This will hatch vipers in the nuptial bed,
But that prevents the aching of the head.

    [*Exeunt cum choro cantantium in laudem Hymenis.*

EPILOGUS.

—o—

Asotus, Astrologer.

Aso. How now? Will our endeavours give satisfaction?

Ast. I find by the horoscope, and the elevation of
the bright Aldeboran, a sextile opposition; and that
th' almutes is inclining to the enemy's house.

Aso. Away with your almutes, horoscopes, eleva-
tions, Aldeborans, sextiles, and oppositions! I have
an art of mine own to cast this figure by.

> The lovers now jealous of nothing be
> But your acceptance of their comedy.
> I question not heaven's influence : for here
> I behold angels of as high a sphere.
> You are the stars I gaze at ; we shall find
> Our labours blest, if your aspects be kind.

THE MUSES' LOOKING-GLASS.

EDITIONS.

The Muse's Looking-Glass. By T. R. Oxford. Printed by Leonard Lichfield, for Francis Bowman. 1638.

It seems certain, from Sir Aston Cokain's verses, printed presently, that the "Muse's Looking-Glass" was originally known and acted under the name of the "Entertainment;" that the performance—at least when Cokain witnessed it—occupied two hours; and that the piece was a sort of translation or adaptation by Randolph from a prose—and prosy—original. As regards the time taken to represent the piece, it may be mentioned that in the Epilogue to Barrey's "Ram-Alley," 1611 (Hazlitt's Dodsley, x. 380), that somewhat lengthy drama is said to have been also a two-hours' performance. For the other editions, see the bibliographical account of the "Poems." No separate impression is known to exist.

The "Muse's Looking-Glass" was republished in 1706, 12°, with a preface by Jeremy Collier; and it was revived at Covent Garden, March 14, 1748, and again, March 9, 1749. In 1758 appeared an altered version of the piece, under the title of the "Mirrour."

Gildon pays a high compliment to the "Muse's Looking-Glass," observing that "the source of all humours that are in nature may be found in it;" and Dodsley remarks that "it has always been esteemed an excellent commonplace book for authors, to instruct them in the art of drawing characters." Bishop Hurd, in speaking of Jonson's "Every Man out of his Humour," adds, "And Randolph, in particular, was so taken with the design, that he seems to have formed his "Muse's Looking-Glass" in express imitation of it.

Geneste's account of this play is as follows :—" The scene lies in the playhouse at Blackfriars. Bird and Mistress Flowerdew, two Puritans, who serve the theatre with feathers and other small wares, enter; they express their abhorrence of playhouses; Roscius joins them; he prevails on them to see the representation of the play; Roscius explains the drift of it to them as it proceeds. At the conclusion, they agree that a play may be productive of moral good—they are exquisite characters. When Roscius says that he means to present the several virtues, Bird replies—

> ‘ I hope there be no cardinal-virtues there !
> I hate a virtue that will be made a cardinal.’

This play has no plot ; the object of it is to show that all virtues, and every commendable passion, proceed from mediocrity, or a just medium between two extremes."—*Some Account of the English Stage,* iv. 250.

The often-quoted writer in the *Retrospective Review,* vi. 74, assigns to the " Muse's Looking-Glass " the highest rank among the poet's dramatic productions. He remarks : " The piece of highest merit is the ‘ Muse's Looking-Glass,’ which hardly can be called a drama, though written for the stage. It contains a great number of contrasted portraits of the extremes of the virtues and vices of morality, which are worked into a slender framework, like that of the " Rehearsal," and such pieces. It is from this that all our extracts will be taken ; but they are such rich and striking pieces of portraiture, that they well deserve the space allotted to them. . . . . The whole of this play is particularly well worth reading."

It has further to be stated that the " Muse's Looking-Glass " forms part of all the editions of Dodsley's " Old Plays " except the last, from which it was intentionally excluded when a collected reprint of the poet was decided upon. The text of this piece is given (with certain corrections) as it appears in Dodsley, with all the notes of the commentators.

DRAMATIS PERSONÆ.

—— o ——

ROSCIUS, a player.
BIRD, a feather-man.
MISTRESS FLOWERDEW, a haberdasher of small-wares.
A DEFORMED FELLOW.
COMEDY.
TRAGEDY.
MIME.
SATIRE.
COLAX.
DYSCOLUS.
DEILUS.
APHOBUS.
ACOLASTUS.
ANAISTHETUS.
ASOTUS.

ANELEUTHERUS.
CAUNUS.
MICROPSYCHUS.
ORGYLUS.
AORGUS.
ALAZON.
EIRON.
PHILOTIMIA.
LUPARUS.
ANAISKINTIA.
KATAPLEITUS.
Justice NIMIS and Justice NIHIL.
PLUS and PARUM, their clerks.
AGROICUS, a clown.
BOMOLOCHUS.
MEDIOCRITY.

To my friend Mr Thomas Randolph, on his Play called the Entertainment printed by the name of the Muses' Looking-Glass.[1]

Some austere Catos be, that do not stick
To term all poetry base that's dramatic :
These contradict themselves ; for bid them tell,
How they like poesy, and they'll answer, well.
But as a stately fabric, raised by
The curious science of Geometry,
If one side of the machine perish, all
Participate with it a ruinous fall :
So they are enemies to Helicon
That vow they love all Muses, saving one.
Such supercilious humours I despise,
And like Thalia's harmless comedies.
Thy Entertainment had so good a fate,
That whosoe'er doth not admire thereat,
Discloseth his own ignorance ; for no
True moralist would be suppos'd thy foe.
In the pure Thespian spring thou hast refin'd
Those harsh, rude rules thy author hath design'd ;
And made those precepts, which he did rehearse
In heavy prose, to run in nimble verse.

---

[1] These lines are printed in Sir Aston Cokain's " Poems,"
8°, 1658, pp. 98-9, but are not in the editions of Randolph. Compare what appears in the Memoir as to the acquaintance between
Randolph and Cokain.

The Stagyrite will be slighted : who doth list
To read or see't becomes a moralist ;
And if his eyes and ears are worth thine ore,
Learn more in two hours than two years before.
Thou hast my suffrage, friend, and I would fain
Be a spectator of thy scenes again.

The Muses' Looking-Glass.

—o—

ACT I., SCENE I.

Enter BIRD, *the feather-man, and* MISTRESS FLOWER-
DEW, *wife to a haberdasher of small-wares; the
one having brought feathers to the playhouse, the
other pins and looking-glasses; two of the sanctified
fraternity of Blackfriars.*[1]

Mis. Flo. See, brother, how the wicked throng and
crowd
To works of vanity !   Not a nook or corner
In all this house of sin, this cave of filthiness,
This den of spiritual thieves, but it is stuff'd,

---

[1] Notwithstanding the vicinity of the playhouse, Blackfriars
appears to have been a place celebrated for the residence of
many Puritans. It was equally remarkable for being inhabited
by the feather-makers. Both these circumstances appear in
Ben Jonson's plays.

Thus in " The Alchemist," act i. sc. 1—

> " A whoreson, upstart, apocryphal captain,
> Whom not a *puritan* in *Black-Friers* will trust
> So much as for a *feather*."

And again, in " Bartholomew Fair," act v. sc. 3 : " [What
say you to your feather-makers in the] Friers, that are of your
faction of faith.   Are not they with their perukes and their puffs,
their fans and their huffs, as much pages of Pride and waiters
upon Vanity ? "

Stuff'd, and stuff'd full, as is a cushion,
With the lewd reprobate.

   Bird. Sister, were there not before inns—
Yes, I will say inns, for my zeal bids me
Say filthy inns—enough to harbour such
As travell'd to destruction the broad way ;
But they build more and more—more shops of Satan ?

   Mis. Flo. Iniquity aboundeth, though pure zeal
Teach, preach, huff, puff, and snuff at it ; yet still,
Still it aboundeth.   Had we seen a church,
A new-built church, erected north and south,
It had been something worth the wondering at.

   Bird. Good works are done.

   Mis. Flo.   I say no works are good ;
Good works are merely popish and apocryphal.

   Bird. But th' bad abound, surround, yea, and con-
     found us.
No marvel now if playhouses increase ;
For they are all grown so obscene of late,
That one begets another.

   Mis. Flo.   Flat fornication !
I wonder anybody takes delight
To hear them prattle.

   Bird.   Nay, and I have heard,
That in a tragedy—I think they call it,
They make no more of killing one another,
Than you sell pins.

   Mis. Flo.   Or you sell feathers, brother ;
But are they not hang'd for't ?

   Bird.   Law grows partial,
And finds it but chance-medley : and their comedies
Will abuse you, or me, or anybody.
We cannot put our moneys to increase
By lawful usury, nor break in quiet,
Nor put off our false wares, nor keep our wives
Finer than others, but our ghosts must walk
Upon their stages.

Mis. Flo.　　　　　　　Is not this flat conjuring,
To make our ghosts to walk ere we be dead?
　Bird. That's nothing, Mistress Flowerdew: they
　　will play
The knave, the fool, the devil and all, for money.
　Mis. Flo. Impiety! O, that men endu'd with
　　reason
Should have no more grace in them!
　Bird.　　　　　　　　Be there not other
Vocations as thriving and more honest?
Bailiffs, promoters, jailors, and apparitors,[1]
Beadles and marshal's-men, the needful instruments
Of the republic; but to make themselves
Such monsters! for they are monsters, th' are monsters;
Base, sinful, shameless, ugly, vile, deform'd,
Pernicious monsters!
　Mis. Flo.　　　　　I have heard our vicar
Call playhouses the colleges of transgression,
Wherein the seven deadly sins are studied.
　Bird. Why, then, the city will, in time, be made
An university of iniquity.
We dwell by Blackfriars College, where I wonder,
How that profane nest of pernicious birds
Dare roost themselves there in the midst of us,
So many good and well-disposed persons.
O impudence!
　Mis. Flo.　　It was a zealous prayer
I heard a brother make concerning playhouses.
　Bird. For charity, what is't?
　Mis. Flo.　　　　　　　That the Globe,[2]

---

[1] "A serjeant, beadle, or sumner; but most commonly used for an inferior officer, that summoned in delinquents to a spiritual court."—*Blount's "Glossographia."*

[2] These were the names of several playhouses then in being: the Globe was situate on the Bank-side, and was the same house for which a licence was granted in 1603 to Shakespeare and others, to enable them to perform there. The Phœnix

Wherein (quoth he) reigns a whole world of vice,
Had been consum'd : the Phœnix burnt to ashes :
The Fortune whipp'd for a blind whore : Blackfriars,
He wonders how it 'scap'd demolishing
I' th' time of reformation : lastly, he wish'd
The Bull might cross the Thames to the Bear Garden,
And there be soundly baited.

> *Bird.*   A good prayer.

> *Mis. Flo.* Indeed it something pricks my conscience
> I come to sell 'em pins and looking-glasses.

> *Bird.* I have their custom too for all their feathers :
> 'Tis fit that we, which are sincere professors,
> Should gain by infidels.

SCENE II.

Enter ROSCIUS, *a Player.*

> *Bird.* Master Roscius, we have brought the things
> you spake for.

> *Ros.* Why, 'tis well.

> *Mis. Flo.*   Pray, sir, what serve they for ?

> *Ros.* We use them in our play.

> *Bird.*   Are you a player ?

> *Ros.* I am, sir : what of that ?

> *Bird.*   And is it lawful ?

---

stood in Drury Lane. The Fortune was near Whitecross Street,
and had belonged to the célebrated Edward Alleyn, who rebuilt
it. Blackfriars probably had the *same* proprietors as the Globe ;
and the Red Bull was at the upper end of St John's Street.
The Bear Garden, or, as it is as often called, *Paris Garden,* was
near the Globe playhouse, as may be seen in the " South View of
London," taken in 1599. It there appears to have been an
octagon building, with a flag flying at the top of it, in the same
manner as at the playhouses. On the sale of the Church lands,
January 14, 1647, it produced £17,831, 15s.

Good sister, let's convert him. [*Aside.*] Will you use
So fond a calling?
   Mis. Flo.   And so impious?
   Bird.   So irreligious?
   Mis. Flo. So unwarrantable?
   Bird.   Only to gain by vice?
   Mis. Flo.   To live by sin?
   Ros. My spleen is up. And live not you by sin?
Take away vanity, and you both may break.
What serves your lawful trade of selling pins,
But to joint gewgaws, and to knit together
Gorgets, strips, neckcloths, laces, ribbands, ruffs,
And many other suchlike toys as these,
To make the baby pride a pretty puppet?
And you, sweet feather-man, whose ware, though
    light,
O'erweighs your conscience, what serves your trade,
But to plume folly, to give pride her wings,
To deck vainglory? spoiling the peacock's tail
T' adorn an idiot's coxcomb! O dull ignorance!
How ill 'tis understood what we do mean
For good and honest! They abuse our scene,
And say we live by vice. Indeed, 'tis true,
As the physicians by diseases do,
Only to cure them. They do live, we see,
Like cooks, by pamp'ring prodigality,
Which are our fond accusers. On the stage
We set an usurer to tell this age,
How ugly looks his soul: a prodigal
Is taught by us, how far from liberal
His folly bears him. Boldy, I dare say,
There has been more by us in some one play
Laugh'd into wit and virtue, than hath been
By twenty tedious lectures drawn from sin
And foppish humours: hence the cause doth rise,
Men are not won by th' ears so well as eyes.
First see what we present.

Mis. Flo.   The sight is able
T' unsanctify our eyes, and make them carnal.
    Ros. Will you condemn without examination?
    Bird. No, sister; let us call up all our zeal,
And try the strength of this temptation.
Satan shall see we dare defy his engines.
    Mis Flo.   I am content.
    Ros. Then take your places here : I will come to you,
And moralise the plot.
    Mis. Flo.   That moralising
I do approve ; it may be for instruction.

SCENE III.

Enter a DEFORMED FELLOW.

    Def. Fel. Roscius, I hear you've a new play to‑
day.
    Ros. We want you to play Mephistopheles.[1]
A pretty natural vizard !
    Def. Fel.   What have you there?
    Ros. A looking-glass or two.
    Def. Fel.   What things are they?
Pray, let me see them.   Heaven, what sights are here !
I have seen a devil.   Looking-glasses call you them !
There is no basilisk but a looking-glass.
    Ros. 'Tis your own face you saw.
    Def. Fel.   My own? thou liest :
I'd not be such a monster for the world.
    Ros. Look on it now with me : what see'st thou
now?

---

[1] The familiar attending Dr Faustus, in the old play of that
name by Christopher Marlowe.
    This reply by Roscius shows the figure of the person that
presented Mephistopheles.—*Gilchrist.*   [Old copy, *not you.*]·

Def. Fel. An angel and a devil.

Ros.   Look on that
Thou call'dst an angel ; mark it well, and tell me
Is it not like my face ?

    Def. Fel.   As 'twere the same.

    Ros. Why, so is that like thine. Dost thou not see,
'Tis not the glass, but thy deformity,
That makes this ugly shape : if they be fair,
That view the glass, such the reflections are.
This serves the body : the soul sees her face
In comedy, and has no other glass.

    Def. Fel. Nay, then, farewell ; for I had rather see
Hell than a looking-glass or comedy.

                      [*Exit* DEFORMED FELLOW.

    Ros. And yet, methinks, if 'twere not for this glass,
Wherein the form of man beholds his grace,
We could not find another way to see
How near our shapes approach divinity.
Ladies, let they who will your glass deride,
And say it is an instrument of pride :
I will commend you for it ; there you see,
If you be fair, how truly fair you be :
Where, finding beauteous faces, I do know
You'll have the greater care to keep them so.
A heavenly vision in your beauty lies,
Which nature hath denied to your own eyes.
Were it not pity you alone should be
Debarr'd of that others are bless'd to see ?
Then take your glasses, and yourselves enjoy
The benefit of yourselves : it is no toy,
Though ignorance at slight esteem hath set her,
That will preserve us good, or make us better.
A country-slut (for such she was, though here
I' th' city may be some, as well as there)
Kept her hands clean (for, those being always seen,
Had told her else, how sluttish she had been),
But had her face as nasty as the stall

Of a fishmonger, or an usurer's hall
Daub'd o'er with dirt : one might have dar'd to say
She was a true piece of Promethean clay,
Not yet inform'd ; and then her unkemb'd hair,
Dress'd up with cobwebs, made her haglike stare.
One day within her pail (for country lasses,
Fair ladies, have no other looking-glasses)
She spied her ugliness, and fain she would
Have blush'd, if thorough so much dirt she could.
Asham'd, within that water that (I say)
Which show'd her filth, she wash'd her filth away.
So comedies, as poets do intend them,
Serve first to show our faults, and then to mend them.
Upon our stage two glasses oft there be ;
The comic mirror and the tragedy :
The comic glass is full of merry strife,
The low reflection of a country life.
Grave tragedy, void of such homely sports,
Is the sad glass of cities and of courts.
I'll show you both.   Thalia, come ; and bring
Thy buskin'd sister, that of blood doth sing.

SCENE IV.

COMEDY, TRAGEDY, MIME, SATIRE.

Com. Why do you stop ?   Go on.
Tra.   I charge him stay.
My robe of state, buskins, and crown of gold,
Claim a priority.
Com.   Your crown of gold
Is but the wreath of wealth ; 'tis mine of laurel
Is virtue's diadem.   This grew green and flourish'd,
When nature, pitying poor mortality,
Hid thine within the bowels of the earth.

Men looking up to heaven found this that's mine :
Digging to find out hell, they lit on thine.
  Tra. I know you've tongue enough.
  Com.   Besides, my birthright
Gives me the first possession.
  Tra.   How, your birthright ?
  Com. Yes, sister, birthright ; and a crown besides,
Put on before the altar of Apollo
By his dear priest Phemonoe : [1] she that first,
Full of her god, rag'd in heroic numbers.
  Tra. How came it, then, the magistrate decreed
A public charge to furnish out my chorus,
When you were fain t' appear in rags and tatters,
And at your own expenses ?
  Com.   My reward
Came after, my deserts went before, yours.
  Tra. Deserts ? yes ! what deserts ? when like a
        gipsy
You took a poor and beggarly pilgrimage
From village unto village ; when I then,
As a fit ceremony of religion,
In my full state contended at the tomb
Of mighty Theseus.
  Com.   I before that time
Did chant out hymns in praise of great Apollo,
The shepherds' deity, whom they reverence
Under the name of Nomius ; [2] in remembrance,
How with them once he kept Admetus' sheep.
And, 'cause you urge my poverty, what were you ?

---

  [1] One of the sylphs who first uttered oracles at Delphos, and
invented heroic measure.   So in the "Sylvæ" of Statius, l. 2,
v. 38—
              " Reseretque arcana pudicos
        Phemonoe *fontes."*
—*Steevens.*
  [2] Apollo was so called (from *νομεὺς*, pastor) while he kept the
flocks of Admetus, in Thessaly.—*Steevens.*

Till Sophocles laid gilt upon your buskins,
You had no ornaments, no robes of state,
No rich and glorious scene.   Your first benefactors,
Who were they, but the reeling priests of Bacchus;
For which a goat gave you reward and name.

  Tra. But, sister, who were yours, I pray, but such
As chanted forth religious bawdy sonnets,
In honour of the fine chaste god Priapus?

  Com. Let age alone; merit must plead our title.

  Tra. And have you then the forehead to contend?
I stalk in princes' courts : great kings and emperors,
From their close cabinets and council-tables,
Yield me the fatal matter of my scene.

  Com. Inferior persons and the lighter vanities
(Of which this age, I fear, has grown too fruitful)
Yield subjects various enough to move
Plentiful laughter.

  Tra.   Laughter ! a fit object
For poetry to aim at !

  Com. Yes, laughter is my object : 'tis a property
In man essential to his reason.

  Tra.   So ;
But I move horror, and that frights the guilty
From his dear sins.   He that sees Œdipus
Incestuous, shall behold him blind withal.
Who views Orestes as a parricide,
Shall see him lash'd with furies too : the ambitious
Shall fear Prometheus' vulture ; daring gluttony
Stand frighted at the sight of Tantalus ;
And every family, great in sins as blood,
Shake at the memory of Pelops' house.
Who will rely on fortune's giddy smile,
That hath seen Priam acted on the stage?

  Com. You move with fear ; I work as much with shame—
A thing more powerful in a generous breast.
Who sees an eating parasite abus'd ;

A covetous bawd laugh'd at ; an ignorant gull
Cheated ; a glorious soldier knock'd and baffl'd : [1]
A crafty servant whipp'd ; a niggard churl
Hoarding up dicing-moneys for his son ;
A spruce, fantastic courtier, a mad roarer,
A jealous tradesman, an o'erweening lady,
A[2] corrupt lawyer—rightly personated ;
But (if he have a blush) will blush, and shame
As well to act those follies as to own them.

 Tra. The subject of my scene is in the persons
Greater, as in the vices : atheists, tyrants,
O'erdaring favourites, traitors, parasites,
The wolves and cats of state, which in a language
High as the men, and loud as are their crimes,
I thunder forth with terror and amazement
Unto the ghastly wondering audience.

 Sat. And, as my lady takes deserved place
Of thy light mistress, so yield thou to me,
Fantastic Mime.

 Mime.   Fond Satire, why to thee ?

 Sat. As the attendant of the nobler dame,
And of myself more worthy

 Mime.   How more worthy ?

 Sat. As one, whose whip of steel can with a lash
Imprint the characters of shame so deep,
Even in the brazen forehead of proud sin,
That not eternity shall wear it out.

---

 [1] [*Glorious* here is used in the sense of *vainglorious*, boastful, like the Latin *gloriosus*.] *Knocked and baffled* here means *beaten and disgraced*. The allusion is, I believe, more immediately to the *miles gloriosus* of Plautus. In Randolph's " Aristippus," the Wild-man enters with two brewers, when the former says, " There they be : now for the valour of brewers, *knock 'em* soundly." They then fall on, and the stage direction informs us, *they beat out Aristippus and the scholars.—Gilchrist.*
 [2] [Old copy, *Or.*]

When I but frown'd in my Lucilius' brow,[1]
Each conscious cheek grew red, and a cold trembling
Freez'd the chill soul ; while every guilty breast
Stood fearful of dissection, as afraid
To be anatomis'd by that skilful hand,
And have each artery, nerve, and vein of sin,
By it laid open to the public scorn.
I have untruss'd the proudest : greatest tyrants
Have quak'd below my powerful whip, half-dead
With expectation of the smarting jerk,
Whose wound no salve can cure. Each blow doth leave
A lasting scar, that with a poison eats
Into the marrow of their fames and lives ;
Th' eternal ulcer to their memories !
What can your apish fine gesticulations,
My manlike-monkey Mime, vie down to this ?[2]
   Mime. When men through sins were grown unlike
      the gods,
Apes grew to be like men ; therefore, I think,
My apish imitation, brother beadle,
Does as good service to reform bad manners,
As your proud whip, with all his firks and jerks.
The Spartans, when they strove t' express the loath-
      someness
Of drunkenness to their children, brought a slave,
Some captive Helot, overcharg'd with wine,
Reeling in thus :—his eyes shot out with staring ;
A fire in his nose ; a burning redness
Blazing in either cheek ; his hair upright ;
His tongue and senses falt'ring, and his stomach
O'erburden'd, ready to discharge her load

---

[1] *i.e.*, Brow like that of the Roman satirist : "*Secuit Lucilius urbem.*"—Persius, Sat. I. l. 114.—*Steevens.* Dryden says,
"Luclius wrote long before Horace, who imitates his manner of
satire, but far excels him in the design."
[2] To *vie* is a term used at the game of gleek.

In each man's face he met. This made 'em see
And hate that sin of swine, and not of men.
Would I express a complimental youth,
That thinks himself a spruce and expert courtier,
Bending his supple hams, kissing his hands,
Honouring shoestrings, screwing his writh'd face
To all the several postures of affection,
Dancing an entertainment to his friend,
Who would not think it a ridiculous motion?[1]
Yet such there be, that very much please themselves
In suchlike antic humours. To our own sins
We will be moles, even to the grossest of 'em;
But in another's life we can spy forth
The least of faults with eyes as sharp as eagles,[2]
Or the Epidaurian serpent. Now in me,
Where self-love casts not her Egyptian mists,
They find this unbecoming foppishness,
And afterwards apply it to themselves.
This (Satire) is the use of Mimic elves.

   Tra. Sister, let's lay this poor contention by,
And friendly live together: if one womb
Could hold us both, why should we think this room
Too narrow to contain us? On this stage
We'll plead a trial; and in one year contend
Which shall do best: that past, she then that shall,
By the most sacred and impartial judgment
Of our Apollo, best deserve the bays,
Shall hold th' entire possession of the place.

   Com. I were unworthy if I should
Appeal from this tribunal: be it so.
I doubt not but his censure runs with me.

---

  [1] *i.e.*, Puppet. See a note to Marmion's "Antiquary," act i.
sc. 1, in Hazlitt's Dodsley, xiii.

    [2] " *Cur in amicorum tam cernis acutum,*
      Quam aut aquila—*aut* serpens Epidaurius?"

—Horace Sat. lib. i. 3.—*Steevens.*

Never may anything that's sad and tragical
Dare to approach his presence : let him be
So happy as to think no man is wretched,
Or that there is a thing call'd misery.

 Tra. Such is my prayer ; that he may only see,
Not be the subject of a tragedy !
Sister, a truce till then.   That vice may bleed,
Let us join whips together.

  Com.   'Tis agreed.

 Mime. Let it be your office to prepare
The masque which we intended.

  Sat.   'Tis my care.   [*Exeunt.*

 Mis. Flo. How did she say? a mass?   Brother,
  fly hence !
Fly hence, idolatry will overtake us.

 Ros. It was a masque she spake of; a rude dance
Presented by the seven deadly sins.

 Bird. Still 'tis a mass, sister !   Away, I tell you ;
It is a mass ; a mass of vile idolatry !

 Ros. 'Tis but a simple dance, brought in to show
The native foulness and deformity
Of our dear sin ; and what an ugly guest
He entertains, admits him to his breast.

Song *and* Dance.[1]

> *Say in a dance how shall we go.*
> *That never could a measure know ?*
> *How shall we sing to please the scene,*
> *That n..ver yet could keep a mean ?* [2]
> *Disorder is the masque we bring,*
> *And discords are the tunes we sing,*
> *No sound in our harsh ears can find a place.*
> *But highest trebles or the lowest base.*

---

[1] By the Seven Deadly Sins.—*Gilchrist.*
[2] *i.e.,* Tenor.—*Steevens.*

Mis. Flo. See, brother, if men's hearts and con-
   sciences
Had not been sear'd and cauteris'd, how could they
Affect these filthy harbingers of hell?
Those Proctors of Beelzebub, Lucifer's hench-boys,[1]
   Ros. I pray ye, stow[2] yourselves within awhile.

[Exeunt.

Roscius *solus.*

And here———unless your favourite mildness
With hope of mercy do encourage us,
Our author bids us end.   He dares not venture,
Neither what's pass'd, nor that which is to come,
Upon his country; 'tis so weak and impotent,
It cannot stand a trial; nor dares hope
The benefit of his clergy : but if rigour
Sit judge, must of necessity be condemn'd
To Vulcan or the sponge.   All he can plead
Is a desire of pardon ; for he brings you
No plot at all, but a mere Olla Podrida,[3]

---

[1] Blount says that a *henchman* or *heinsman* "is a German
word, signifying a domestic, or one of a family.   It is used with
us for one that runs on foot, attending on a person of honour."
He also observes that " from hence comes our word *hine* or
hinde, a servant for husbandry."   *Henchmen* are mentioned in
"Jack Drum's Entertainment," 1616, sig. B 4 : " He whose
phrases are as neatly deckt as my Lord Mayor's *hens-
men."*
   They are also excepted out of the stat. 4 Edward IV. c. v.
concerning excess of apparel :   " Provided also, that *henchmen*,
heralds, pursuivants, sword-bearers to mayors, messengers, and
minstrels, nor none of them, nor players in their interludes,
shall not be comprised within this statute."   A like exception,
24 Henry VIII. c. xiii.   See also the notes of Mr Steevens
and Mr Tyrrwhit to " Midsummer Night's Dream," act ii.
sc. 2.
   See Hakluyt, 1589, p. 270.—*Reed.*
   [2] [Or bestow.   Edits., *stir.*   Mr Collier's correction.]
   [3] " Olla Podrida properly consists of beef, mutton, bacon,
hog's-feet, pullet, partridge, black-puddings, sausages, *garvancos,*

A medley of ill-plac'd and worse-penn'd humours.
His desire was in single scenes to show
How comedy presents each single vice
Ridiculous ; whose number, as their character,
He borrows from the man to whom he owes
All the poor skill he has, great Aristotle.
Now, if you can endure to hear the rest,
You're welcome : if you cannot, do but tell
Your meaning by some sign, and all farewell.
If you will stay, resolve to pardon first ;
Our author will deserve it by offending.
Yet if he miss a pardon (as in justice
You cannot grant it, though your mercy may),
Still he hath this left for a comfort to him ;
That he picks forth a subject of his rhyme,
May lose perchance his credit, not his time.   [*Exit.*

ACT II., SCENE I.

Roscius, Bird, Mistress Flowerdew.

*Ros. Receive your places.   The first that we present
are the extremes of a virtue necessary in our conversation, called Comitas or courtesy, which, as all other virtues, hath her deviations from the mean.   The one*

---

a sort of Spanish pease, turkeys, and cabbage ; all very well
boiled, or rather stewed together, and duly seasoned with salt
and spice " (Stevens's " Spanish Dictionary "). Howell, in his
" Letters," adds other ingredients, p. 229, edit. 1754 ; recom-
mending a cook, he says, " He will tell your ladyship, that
the reverend matron the *Olla Podrida* hath intellectuals and
senses ; mutton, beef, and bacon, are to her as the will, understanding, and memory are to the soul ; cabbage, turnips, arti-
chokes, potatoes, and dates, are her five senses, and pepper, the
common sense : she must have marrow to keep life in her, and
some birds to make her light ; by all means she must go
adorned with chains of sausages."

Colax, that to seem over-courteous, falls into a servile flattery; the other (as fools fall into the contraries which they shun) is Dyscolus who, hating to be a slavish parasite, grows into peevishness and impertinent distaste.

Mis. Flo. I thought you taught two vices for one virtue.

Ros. So does philosophy : but the actors enter.

COLAX, DYSCOLUS.

Col. How far they sin against humanity
That use you thus ! believe me, 'tis a symptom
Of barbarism and rudeness, so to vex
A gentle, modest nature as yours is.
Dys. Why dost thou vex me then?
Col.   I ?   Heaven defend !
My breeding has been better ; I vex you !
You that I know so virtuous, just, and wise,
So pious and religious, so admired,
So lov'd of all?
Dys.   Wilt thou not leave me then,
Eternal torture? could your cruelty find
No back but mine, that you thought broad enough
To bear the load of all these epithets?
Pious? religious? he takes me for a fool.
Virtuous and just? sir, did I ever cheat you,
Cosen, or gull you, that you call me just
And virtuous? I am grown the common scoff
Of all the world—the scoff of all the world !
Col. The world is grown too vile, then.
Dys.   So art thou.
Heaven ! I am turn'd ridiculous.
Col.   You ridiculous?
But 'tis an impious age : there was a time
(And pity 'tis so good a time had wings
To fly away), when reverence was paid

To a grey head; 'twas held a sacrilege [1]
Not expiable to deny respect
To one, sir, of your years and gravity.

    Dys. My years and gravity! why, how old am I?
I am not rotten yet, or grown so rank
As I should smell o' th' grave. O times and manners!
Well, Colax, well; go on: you may abuse me,
Poor dust and ashes, worm's meat. Years and
    gravity!
He takes me for a carcass! what see you
So crazy in me? I have half my teeth:
I see with spectacles, do I not? and can walk too
With the benefit of my staff: mark if I cannot!—
But you, sir, at your pleasure, with years and gravity
Think me decrepit.

    Col.   How? decrepit, sir!
I see young roses bud within your cheeks;
And a quick active blood run free and fresh
Thorough your veins.

    Dys.   I am turn'd boy again!
A very stripling school-boy! have I not
The itch and kibes? am I not scabb'd and mangy
About the wrists and hams?

    Col.   Still, Dyscolus——

    Dys. Dyscolus! and why Dyscolus? when were we
Grown so familiar? Dyscolus! by my name?
Sure, we are Pylades and Orestes, are we not?
Speak, good Pylades.

    Col.   Nay, worthy sir,
Pardon my error: 'twas without intent
Of an offence. I'll find some other name
To call you by——

    Dys.   What do you mean to call me?

---

[1] " *Credebant tum grande nefas, et morte piandum,*
    Si juvenis vetulo non assurrexerat."

—Juv. " Sat." XIII. v. 54.—*Steevens.*

Fool, ass, or knave ? my name is not so bad,
As that I am asham'd on't.

   Col. Still you take all worse than it was meant,
You are too jealous.

   Dys. Jealous ? I ha' not cause for't ; my wife's
     honest.

Dost see my horns ? Doest ? if thou doest,
Write cuckold in my forehead ; do, write cuckold
With aquafortis, do. Jealous ! I am jealous—
Free of the company ! wife, I am jealous.

   Col. I mean suspicious.

   Dys.   How ! suspicious ?
For what ? for treason, felony, or murder ?
Carry me to the justice : bind me over
For a suspicious person : hang me too
For a suspicious person ! O, O, O !
Some courteous plague seize me, and free my soul
From this immortal torment ! everything
I meet with is vexation ; and this, this
Is the vexation of vexations ;
The hell of hells, and devil of all devils !

   Mis. Flo. For pity's sake, fret not the good old
     gentleman.

   Dys. O, have I not yet torments great enough,
But you must add to my affliction ?
Eternal silence seize you !

   Col.   Sir, we strive
To please you, but you still misconstrue us.

   Dys. I must be pleas'd ? a very babe, an infant !
I must be pleas'd ? give me some pap or plums ;
Buy me a rattle or a hobby-horse,
To still me, do ! Be pleas'd ? wouldst have me get
A parasite to be flatter'd ?

   Col.   How ? a parasite ?
A cogging, flattering, slavish parasite ?
Things I abhor and hate. 'Tis not the belly
Shall make my brains a captive. Flatterers !

Souls below reason will not stoop so low
As to give up their liberty ; only flatterers
Move by another's wheel.   They have no passions
Free to themselves : all their affections,
Qualities, humours, appetites, desires,
Nay wishes, vows, and prayers, discourse and thoughts,
Are but another's bondman.   Let me tug
At the Turks' galleys ; be eternally
Damn'd to a quarry : in this state my mind
Is free : a flatterer has no soul nor body.
What shall I say ?—No, I applaud your temper,
That in a generous braveness takes distaste
At such whose servile nature strives to please you.
'Tis royal in you, sir.
 Dys.   Ha ! what's that ?
 Col. A feather stuck upon your cloak.
 Dys.   A feather !
And what have you to do with my feathers ?
Why should you hinder me from telling the world
I do not lie on flock beds ?
 Col.   Pray, be pleas'd ;
I brush'd it off for mere respect I bear you.
 Dys. Respect ! a fine respect, sir, is it not,
To make the world believe I nourish vermin ?
O death, death, death ! if that our graves hatch worms
Without tongues to torment us, let 'm have,
What teeth they will.   I meet not here an object,
But adds to my affliction !   Sure, I am not
A man ; I could not then be so ridiculous :
My ears are overgrown, I am an ass ;
It is my ears they gaze at.   What strange Harpy,
Centaur, or Gorgon am I turn'd into ?
What Circe wrought my metamorphosis ?
If I be beast, she might have made me lion,
Or something not ridiculous ! O Acteon !
If I do branch like thee, it is my fortune !
Why look they on me else ?   There is within

A glass, they say, that has strange qualities in it;
That shall resolve me.   I will in to see,
Whether or no I man or monster be.   [*Exit.*

SCENE II.

To them DEILUS, APHOBUS.

Bird. Who be these? they look like Presumption
and Despair.

Ros. And such they are.   That is *Aphobus, one that
out of an impious confidence fears nothing: the other
Deilus, that from an atheistical distrust shakes at the
motion of a reed. These are the extremes of Fortitude,
that steers an even course between overmuch daring and
overmuch fearing.*

Mis. Flo. Why stays this reprobate Colax?

Ros.   Any vice
Yields work for flattery.

Mis. Flo.   A good doctrine, mark it.

Dei. Is it possible? did you not fear it, say you?
To me the mere relation is an ague.
Good Aphobus, no more such terrible stories;
I would not for a world lie alone to-night,
I shall have such strange dreams!

Aph.   What can there be
That I should fear?   The gods?   If they be good,
'Tis sin to fear them; if not good, no gods;
And then let them fear me.   Or are they devils,
That most affright ye?[1]

Dei.   Devils! where, good Aphobus?
I thought there was some conjuring abroad,
'Tis such a terrible wind!   O, here it is;
Now it is here again! O still, still, still!

---

[1] [Old copy, *must—me.*]

Aph. What is the matter?

Dei.   Still it follows me!
The thing in black : behind, soon as the sun
But shines, it haunts me.   Gentle spirit, leave me!
Cannot you lay him, Aphobus? what an ugly look it
    has!
With eyes as big as saucers, nostrils wider
Than barbers' basins!

Aph.   It is nothing, Deilus,
But your weak fancy, that from every object
Draws arguments of fear.   This terrible black thing——

Dei. Where is it, Aphobus?

Aph.   Is but your shadow, Deilus.

Dei. And should we not fear shadows?

Aph.   No! why should we?

Dei. Who knows but they come leering after
    us
To steal away the substance?   Watch him, Apho-
    bus.

Aph. I nothing fear.

Col.   I do commend your valour,
That fixes your great soul fast as a centre,
Not to be mov'd with dangers : let slight cock-
    boats
Be shaken with a wave, while you stand firm
Like an undaunted rock, whose constant hardness
Rebeats the fury of the raging sea,
Dashing it into froth.   Base fear doth argue
A low, degenerate soul.[1]

Dei.   Now I fear everything.

Col. 'Tis your discretion : everything has danger,
And therefore everything is to be fear'd.
I do applaud this wisdom : 'tis a symptom
Of wary providence.   His too confident rashness

---

[1] *Degeneros animos timor* arguit — Virg. "Æn." iv. 13.
—*Steevens.*

Argues a stupid ignorance in the soul,
A blind and senseless judgment.   Give me Fear
To man the fort, 'tis such a circumspect
And wary sentinel——
   Mis. Flo.   Now shame take thee, for
A lukewarm formalist.
   Col.   ——But daring valour,
Uncapable of danger, sleeps securely,
And leaves an open entrance to his enemies.
   Dei. What, are they landed?
   Aph.   Who?
   Dei.   The enemies
That Colax talks of.
   Aph.   If they be, I care not;
Though they be giants all, and arm'd with thunder.
   Dei. Why, do you not fear thunder?
   Aph.   Thunder? no!
No more than squibs and crackers.
   Dei.   Squibs and crackers?
I hope there be none here.   'Slid, squibs and
     crackers!
The mere epitomes of the gunpowder-treason:
Faux in a lesser volume.
   Aph.   Let fools gaze
At bearded stars, it is all one to me,
As if they had been shav'd.   Thus, thus would I
Outbeard a meteor! for I might as well
Name it a prodigy, when my candle blazes.
   Dei. Is there a comet, say you? nay, I saw it:
It reach'd from Paul's to Charing, and portends
Some certain imminent danger to th' inhabitants
'Twixt those two places.   I'll go get a lodging
Out of its influence.
   Col.   Will that serve?   I fear
It threatens general ruin to the kingdom.
   Dei. I'll to some other country.
   Col.   There's danger to cross the seas.

Dei. Is there no way, good Colax,
To cross the sea by land? O, the situation—
The horrible situation of an island!

Col. You, sir, are far above such frivolous thoughts:
You fear not death.

Aph.   Not I.

Col.   Not sudden death?

Aph. No more than sudden sleeps: sir, I dare die.

Dei. I dare not; death to me is terrible.
I will not die.

Aph.   How can you, sir, prevent it?

Dei. Why,—I will kill myself.

Col.   A valiant course;
And the right way to prevent death indeed!
Your spirit is true Roman!—But yours 's greater,
That fear not death, nor yet the manner of it.
Should heaven fall—

Aph.   Why then we should have larks.[1]

Dei. I shall never eat larks again while I breathe.

Col. Or should the earth yawn like a sepulchre,
And with an open throat swallow you quick?

Aph. 'Twould save me the expenses of a grave.

Dei. I'd rather trouble my executors by th' half.

Aph. Cannons to me are pot-guns.

Dei.   Pot-guns to me
Are cannons: the report will strike me dead.

Aph. A rapier's but a bodkin.

Dei.   And a bodkin
Is a most dangerous weapon: since I read
Of Julius Cæsar's death, I durst not venture
Into a tailor's shop for fear of bodkins.[2]

---

[1] This was proverbial. [See Hazlitt's "Proverbs," 1869, p. 462].

[2] So in "The Serpent of Division," prefixed to the 4º edition of "Gorboduc," 1590: "And the cheef woorker of this murder was Brutus Cassius, associed with two hundreth and sixtye of the

Aph. O, that the valiant giants would again
Rebel against the gods, and besiege heaven,
So I might be their leader!
Col.   Had Enceladus
Been half so valiant, Jove had been his prisoner.
Aph. Why should we think there be such things as
        dangers?
Scylla, Charybdis, Python, are but fables;
Medea's bull and dragon very tales;
Sea-monsters, serpents, all poetical figments;
Nay, Hell itself and Acheron mere inventions.
Or were they true, as they are false, should I be
So timorous as to fear these bugbear Harpies,
Medusas, Centaurs, Gorgons?
Dei.   O good Aphobus,
Leave conjuring, or take me into the circle!
What shall I do, good Colax?
Col.   Sir, walk in:
There is, they say, a looking-glass; a strange one,
Of admirable virtues, that will render you
Free from enchantments.
Dei.   How! a looking-glass?
Dost think I can endure it? Why, there lies
A man within't in ambush to entrap me:

---

senate: all having *bodkins* in their sleeves: and, as it is written
in stories, he had twentye fower deadly woundes as he sat in
the Capitall."
    Again, *ibid.*—

> "With *bodkins* was Cæsar Julius
> Murdred at Rome of Brutus Cassius.
> When many a region he had brought full lowe.
> Lo: who may trust Fortune any throw?"

Lyly has it ("Euphues," 1581, p. 46): "Asiarchus, forsaking
companie, spoiled himselfe with his owne *bodkin*."
    And in "Euphues and his England," 1582, p. 10: "And in
this you turne the point of your owne *bodkin* into your own
bosome."
    See also Mr Steevens's note on "Hamlet," act iii. sc. 1.

I did but lift my hand up, and he presently
Catch'd at it.

 Col.   'Twas the shadow, sir, of yourself—
Trust me, a mere reflection.

 Dei. I will trust thee.   [*Exit.*

 Aph.   What glass is that?

 Col.   A trick to fright the idiot
Out of his wits : a glass so full of dread.
Rendering unto the eye such horrid spectacles,
As would amaze even you. Sir, I do think
Your optic nerves would shrink in the beholding.
This if your eye endure, I will confess you
The prince of eagles.

 Aph. Look to it, eyes ! if you refuse this sight,
My nails shall damn you to eternal night. [*Exit.*

 Col. Seeing no hope of gain, I pack them hence :
'Tis gold gives flattery all her eloquence.

SCENE III.

ACOLASTUS, ANAISTHETUS.

 Ros. *Temperance is the mediocrity of enjoying plea-*
sures when they are present, and a moderate desire
of them, being absent; and these are the extremes of that
virtue. Acolastus, a voluptuous epicure, that out of an
immoderate and untamed desire seeks after all pleasures
promiscuously, without respect of honest or lawful. The
other, Anaisthetus, a mere anchorite, that delights in
nothing, not in those legitimate recreations allowed of by
God and nature.

 Aco. O, now for an eternity of eating !
Fool was he that wish'd but a crane's short neck ;
Give me one, Nature, long as is a cable
Or sounding-line ; and all the way a palate,

To taste my meat the longer.   I would have
My senses feast together : Nature envied us
In giving single pleasures ; let me have
My ears, eyes, palate, nose, and touch at once
Enjoy their happiness.   Lay me in a bed
Made of a summer's cloud ; to my embraces
Give me a Venus hardly yet fifteen,
Fresh, plump, and active ; she that Mars enjoy'd
Is grown too stale : and then, at the same instant
My touch is pleas'd, I would delight my sight
With pictures of Diana and her nymphs,
Naked and bathing, drawn by some Apelles :
By them some of our fairest virgins stand,
That I may see whether 'tis art or nature
Which heightens most my blood and appetite.
Nor cease I here : give me the seven orbs
To charm my ears with their celestial lutes ;
To which the angels, that do move those spheres,
Shall sing some amorous ditty.   Nor yet here
Fix I my bounds : the sun himself shall fire
The phœnix' nest to make me a perfume,
While I do eat the bird, and eternally
Quaff off ethereal [1] nectar.   These (single) are
But torments ; but together, O, together !
Each is a paradise !   Having got such objects
To please the senses, give me senses too
Fit to receive those objects : give me therefore
An eagle's eye, a bloodhound's curious smell,
A stag's quick hearing ; let my feeling be
As subtle as the spider's, and my taste
Sharp as a squirrel's : then I'll read the Alcoran,
And what delights that promises in the future,
I'll practise in the present.
  Bird.   Heathenish glutton !
  Mis. Flo. Base belly-god ! licentious libertine !

---

[1] [Old copy, *of eternal.*]

Ana. And I do think there is no pleasures at all
But in contemning pleasures. Happy Niobe
And blessed Daphne, and all such as are
Turn'd stocks and stones ! would I were laurel too,
Or marble ; ay, or anything insensible !
It is a toil for me to eat or drink,
Only for nature's satisfaction ;
Would I could live without it. To my ear
Music is but a mandrake : [1] to my smell
Nard scents of rue and wormwood ; and I taste
Nectar with as much loathing and distaste,
As gall or aloes, or my doctor's potion.
My eye can meet no object but I hate it.
    Aco. Come, brother Stoic, be not so melancholy.
    Ana. Be not so foolish, brother epicure,
    Aco. Come, we'll go and see a comedy, that will
    raise
Thy heavy spirits up.
    Ana.   A comedy ?
Sure, I delight much in those toys : I can
With as much patience hear the mariners
Chide in a storm. [2]
    Aco.   Then let's go drink awhile.
    Ana. 'Tis too much labour. Happy Tantalus,
That never drinks.
    Aco.   A little venery
Shall recreate thy soul.
    Ana.   Yes, like an itch ;
For 'tis no better. I could wish an heir,
But that I cannot take the pains to get one.

---

[1] The shriek supposed to be given by the *mandrake* when torn
out of the earth was esteemed fatal to those who heard it. [See
" Popular Antiquities of Great Britain," 1870, iii. 321.]
  [2] To *chide*, in this instance, does not signify to *reprehend*, but
to *make a noise*. See note on " Midsummer Night's Dream,"
iii. 96, edit. 1778.

Aco. Why, marry, if your conscience be so tender
As not to do it otherwise ; then 'tis lawful.

Ana. True : matrimony's nothing else indeed
But fornication licens'd, lawful adultery.
O heavens ! how all my senses are wide sluices
To let in discontent and miseries !
How happy are the moles, that have no eyes !
How bless'd the adders, that they have no ears ![1]
They never see nor hear aught that afflicts them.
But happier they, that have no sense at all—
That neither see, nor hear, taste, smell, nor feel,
Anything to torment them.   Souls were given
To torture bodies : man has reason, too,
To add unto the heap of his distractions.
I can see nothing without sense and motion,
But I do wish myself transform'd into it.

Col. Sir, I commend this temperance : your arm'd
    soul
Is able to contemn these petty baits,
These slight temptations which we title pleasures,
That are indeed but names.   Heaven itself knows
No suchlike thing : the stars nor eat nor drink,
Nor lie with one another, and you imitate
Those glorious bodies ; by which noble abstinence
You gain the name of moderate, chaste, and sober ;
While this effeminate gets the infamous terms
Of glutton, drunkard, and adulterer ;
Pleasures that are not man's, as man is man,
But as his nature sympathies with beasts.
You shall be the third Cato ; this grave look
And rigid eyebrow will become a censor.
But I will fit you with an object, sir,
My noble Anaisthetus, that will please you :
It is a looking-glass, wherein at once

---

[1] [The deafness of the adder is a popular fallacy.]

You may see all the dismal groves and caves :
The horrid vaults, dark cells, and barren deserts,
With what in hell itself can dismal be.

    Ana. That is indeed a prospect fit for me. [*Exit.*
    Aco. He cannot see a stock or stone, but pre-
        sently
He wishes to be turn'd to one of those.
I have another humour : I cannot see
A fat, voluptuous sow with full delight
Wallow in dirt, but I do wish myself
Transform'd into that blessed epicure :
Or when I view the hot, salacious sparrow
Renew his pleasures with fresh appetite,
I wish myself that little bird of love.

    Col. It shows you a man of a soft moving clay,
Not made of flint.   Nature has been bountiful
To provide pleasures, and shall we be niggards
At plenteous boards ?   He's a discourteous guest
That will observe a diet at a feast.
When Nature thought the earth alone too little
To find us meat, and therefore stor'd the air
With winged creatures : not contented yet,
She made the water fruitful to delight us :
Nay, I believe the other element too
Doth nurse some curious dainty for man's food,
If we would use the skill to catch the salamander :
Did she do this to have us eat with temperance ?
Or when she gave so many different odours
Of spices, unguents, and all sorts of flowers,
She cried not : stop your noses.   Would she give us
So sweet a choir of wing'd musicians
To have us deaf ?   Or when she plac'd us here,
Here in a paradise, where such pleasing prospects,
So many ravishing colours entice the eye,
Was it to have us wink ?   When she bestow'd
So powerful faces, such commanding beauties,
On many glorious nymphs, was it to say :

Be chaste and continent ? Not to enjoy
All pleasures and at full, were to make Nature
Guilty of that she ne'er was guilty of—
A vanity in her works.

Aco.   A learned lecture !
'Tis fit such grave and solid argument
Have their reward.   Here, half of my estate
T' invent a pleasure never tasted yet,
That I may be the first to make it stale.

Col. Within, sir, is a glass, that by reflection
Doth show the image of all sorts of pleasures
That ever yet were acted ; more variety
Than Aretine's pictures.[1]

Aco.   I will see the jewel ;
For though to do most moves my appetite,
I love to see, as well as act delight.   [*Exit.*

Bird. These are the things indeed the stage doth
      teach :
Dear heart, what a foul sink of sins runs here !

Mis. Flo. In sooth, it is the common shore of lewd-
      ness.

SCENE IV.

ASOTUS, ANELEUTHERUS.

Ros. *These are Aneleutherus, an illiberal, niggardly
usurer, that will sell heaven to purchase earth ; that his
son Asotus, a profuse prodigal, that will sell earth to
buy hell—the extremes of liberality, which prescribes a
mediocrity in the getting and spending of riches.*

---

[1] These celebrated pieces of obscenity are likewise mentioned
by Sir Epicure Mammon in the " Alchemist," who says he will
have pictures—

> " Richer than those Tiberius took
>   From Elephantis, and dull *Aretine*
>   But coldly imitated."

—*Steevens.*

Anel. Come, boy, go with me to the scrivener's, go.

Aso. I was in hope you would have said a bawdy-
house.

Anel. Thence to th' Exchange.

Aso.   No, to the tavern, father.

Anel. Be a good husband, boy, follow my counsel.

Aso. Your counsel? No, dad, take you mine,
And be a good fellow. Shall we go and roar?
'Slid, father, I shall never live to spend
That you have got already. Pox of attorneys,
Merchants, and scriveners! I would hear you talk
Of drawers, punks, and panders.

Anel.   Prodigal child!
Thou dost not know the sweets of getting wealth.

Aso. Nor you the pleasure that I take in spending
   it :
To feed on caveare,[1] and eat anchovies!

Anel. Asotus, my dear son, talk not to me
Of your anchovies or your caveare.
No : feed on widows; have each meal an orphan
Serv'd to your table, or a glibbery heir [2]
With all his lands melted into a mortgage.
The gods themselves feed not on such fine dainties :
Such fatting, thriving diet.

Aso.   Trust me, sir,
I am ashamed, la, now to call you father;
Ne'er trust me, now I'm come to be a gentleman ;
One of your havings,[3] and thus cark and care !

---

[1] See note to "The Ordinary" in Haylitt's "Dodsley," xii.

[2] So in Marston's "First Part of Antonio and Mellida," act
ii.—

> "Milk, milk, ye *glibbery* urchin, is food for infants."

[3] *i.e.*, One possessed of your estate or property. So in "Every
Man in his Humour," act i. sc. 4—

> "Lie in a water-bearer's house ! '
> A gentleman of his *havings !*"

Come, I will send for a whole coach or two
Of Bank-side ladies,[1] and we will be jovial.
Shall the world say you pine and pinch for nothing?
Well, do your pleasure, keep me short of moneys;
When you are dead (as die, I hope, you must)
I'll make a shift to spend one-half, at least,
Ere you are coffin'd, and the other half,
Ere you are fully laid into your grave.
Were not you better help away with some of it?
But you will starve yourself, that, when you're rotten,
One have-at-all of mine may set it flying:
And I will have your bones cut into dice,
And make you guilty of the spending of it;
Or I will get a very handsome bowl
Made of your skull, to drink away in healths.

 Anel. That's not the way to thrive. No, sit and
  brood
On thy estate: as yet it is not hatch'd
Into maturity.

 Aso.   Marry, I'll brood upon it,
And hatch it into chickens, capons, hens,
Larks, thrushes, quails, woodcocks, snites, and phea-
  sants,
The best that can be got for love or money.
There is no life to drinking!

 Anel.   O yes, yes.
Exaction, usury, and oppression,
Twenty i' th' hundred is a very nectar,
And wilt thou, wasteful lad, spend in a supper
What I with sweat and labour, care and industry,
Have been an age a-scraping up together?
No, no, Asotus, trust greyhead experience;

And in "The Devil is an Ass," act iii. sc. 3—

  "We then advise the party, if he be
   A man of means and *havings*, that forthwith
   He settle his estate."

[1] Where the stews formerly stood.

As I have been an ox, a painful ox,
A diligent, toiling, and laborious ox,
To plough up gold for thee ; so I would have thee——
   Aso. Be a fine silly ass to keep it.
   Anel. Be a good watchful dragon to preserve it.
   Col. Sir, I overheard your wise instructions,
And wonder at the gravity of your counsel.
This wild, unbridled boy is not yet grown
Acquainted with the world ; he has not felt
The weight of need : that want is virtue's clog ;
Of what necessity, respect, and value
Wealth is ; how base and how contemptible
Poverty makes us. Liberality
In some circumstances may be allow'd ;
As when it has no end but honesty,
With a respect of person, quantity,
Quality, time, and place ; but this profuse,
Vain, injudicious spending speaks him idiot.
And yet the best of liberality
Is to be liberal to ourselves ; and thus
Your wisdom is most liberal, and knows
How fond a thing it is for discreet men
To purchase with the loss of their estate
The name of one poor virtue, liberality ;
And that, too, only from the mouth of beggars !
One of your judgment would not, I am sure,
Buy all the virtues at so dear a rate.
Nor are you, sir, I dare presume, so fond
As for to weigh your gains by the strict scale
Of equity and justice, names invented
To keep us beggars. I would counsel now
Your son to tread no steps but yours ; for they
Will certainly direct him the broad way
That leads unto the place where plenty dwells,
And she shall give him honour.
   Anel.   Your tongue is powerful ;
Pray, read this lecture to my son. I go

To find my scrivener, who is gone, I hear,
To a strange glass, wherein all things appear.   [*Exit.*
   Aso. To see if it can show him his lost ears.
Now to your lecture.
   Col.   And to such an one
As you will be a willing pupil to.
Think you I meant all that I told your father ?
No, 'twas to blind the eyes of the old hunks.
I love a man like you, that can make much
Of his bless'd genius.   Miracle of charity !
That open hand becomes thee : let thy father
Scrape, like the dunghill-cock, the dirt and mire,
To find a precious gem for thee (the chicken
Of the white hen) to wear.   It is a wonder
How such a generous branch as you could spring
From that old root of damned avarice !
For every widow's house the father swallows,
The son should spew a tavern.   How are we
Richer than others ?   Not in having much,
But in bestowing,
And that shines glorious in you.   The chuff's
      crowns,[1]
Imprison'd in his rusty chest, methinks
I hear groan out, and long till they be thine,
In hope to see the light again.   Thou can'st not
Stand in a flood of nectar up to th' chin,
And yet not dare to sup it ; nor can'st suffer
The golden apples dangle at thy lips,
But thou wilt taste the fruit.   'Tis generous this.
   Aso. Gramercy, thou shalt be doctor o' th' chair.

---

[1] It is observed by Mr Steevens (note to "First Part of
Henry IV.," act ii. sc. 2), that this term of contempt is always
applied to rich and avaricious people.   He supposes it a corruption of *chough*, a thievish bird [now very rare], that col-
lects its prey on the seashore.   [But this etymology, if not in-
admissible, is at least very doubtful.]

Here—'tis too little, but 'tis all my store,
I'll in to pump my dad, and fetch thee more.   [*Exit.*

   Col. How like you now my art? Is't not a subtle
     one.

   Mis. Flo. Now, out upon thee, thou lewd repro-
     bate!
Thou man of sin and shame, that sewest cushions
Unto the elbows of iniquity.

   Col. I do commend this zeal; you cannot be
Too fervent in a cause so full of goodness.
There is a general frost hath seiz'd devotion;
And without suchlike ardent flames as these
There is no hope to thaw it.   The word Puritan,
That I do glorify and esteem reverend,
As the most sanctified, pure, and holy sect
Of all professors, is by the profane
Us'd for a name of infamy, a byword, a slander.
That I soothe vice![1] I do but flatter them;
As we give children plums to learn their prayers,
T' entice them to the truth, and by fair means
Work out their reformation.   [*Exit.*

   Bird.   'Tis well done.
I hope he will become a brother, and make
A separatist!

   Mis. Flo. You shall have the devotions
Of all the elders.   But this foppishness
Is wearisome: I could at our Saint Anth'lins,[2]
Sleeping and all, sit twenty times as long.

   Ros. Go in with me to recreate your spirits,

---

   [1] [There is some corruption here, but where it lies is not very
obvious.   The present passage might be improved, perhaps, if
we should read—

              " A byword, a slander,
       That I soothe vices!   I but flatter them."]

   [2] The Church of St Antholin, or St Antlin, was one of the
principal resorts of the Puritans.—*Collier.*

(As music theirs) with some refreshing song,
Whose patience our rude scene hath held too long.
                                            [*Exeunt.*

ACT III., SCENE I.

ROSCIUS, BIRD, *and* MISTRESS FLOWERDEW.

Bird. I will no more of this abomination.

Ros. The end crowns every action, stay till that ;
Just judges will not be prejudicate.

Mis. Flo. Pray, sir, continue still the moralising.

ROS. *The next we present are the extremes of Magnificence, who teaches a decorum in great expenses, as liberality in the lesser : one is Banausus, out of a mere ostentation vaingloriously expensive; the other Microprepes, one in glorious works extremely base and penurious.*

BANAUSUS, MICROPREPES.

Ban. Being born not for ourselves, but for our
    friends,
Our country and our glory, it is fit
We do express the majesty of our souls
In deeds of bounty and magnificence.

Mic. The world is full of vanity; and fond
    fools
Promise themselves a name from building churches,
Or anything that tends to the republic :
'Tis the *re-private* that I study for.

Ban. First, therefore, for the fame of my re-
    public,
I'll imitate a brave Egyptian king,
And plant such store of onions and of garlic,
As shall maintain so many thousand workmen

To th' building of a pyramid at Saint Albans,
Upon whose top I'll set a hand of brass
With a scroll in't, to show the way to London,
For the benefit of travellers.
  Col.   Excellent !
'Tis charity to direct the wand'ring pilgrim.
  Mic. I am churchwarden, and we are this year
To build our steeple up ; now, to save charges,
I'll get a high-crown'd hat with five low bells,
To make a peal shall serve as well as Bow.
  Col.   'Tis wisely cast,
And like a careful steward of the church,
Of which the steeple is no part—at least
No necessary.
  Bird. Verily, 'tis true.
They are but wicked synagogues, where those instru-
  ments
Of superstition and idolatry ring
Warning to sin, and chime all in—to the devil.
  Ban. And, 'cause there be such swarms of here-
  sies rising,
I'll have an artist frame two wondrous weathercocks
Of gold, to set on Paul's and Grantham steeple.[1]
To show to all the kingdom, what fashion next
The wind of humour hither means to blow.
  Mic. A wicker chair will fit them for a pulpit.
  Col. It is the doctrine, sir, that you respect.
  Mis. Flo. In sooth, I have heard as wholesome
  instructions
From a zealous wicker chair, as e'er I did
From the carv'd idol of wainscot.
  Ban.   Next, I intend to found an hospital
For the decay'd professors of the suburbs ;
With a college of physicians too at Chelsea,

---

[1] [See Hazlitt's " Proverbs," 1869, p. 248, where the present passage from Randolph is cited.]

Only to study the cure of the French pox : [1]
That so the sinners may acknowledge me
Their only benefactor, and repent.

    Col. You have a care, sir, of your country's health.

    Mic. Then I will sell the lead to thatch the chancel.

    Ban. I have a rare device to set Dutch windmills [2]
Upon Newmarket Heath and Salisbury Plain,[3]
To drain the fens.

    Col.   The fens, sir, are not there.

    Ban. But who knows but they may be ?

    Col.   Very right.
You aim at the prevention of a danger.

    Mic. A porter's frock shall serve me for a surplice.

    Mis. Flo. Indeed a frock is not so ceremonious.

    Ban. But the great work, in which I mean to glory,
Is in the raising a cathedral church :
It shall be at Hog's Norton ; [4] with a pair
Of stately organs ; more than pity 'twere
The pigs should lose their skill for want of practice.

    Bird. Organs ! fie on them for Babylonian bag-
    pipes.

    Mic. Then for the painting, I bethink myself

---

[1] Qy. If here be not a fling at Sutcliff's project for a College at Chelsea ?

[2] In the reign of James I., and the beginning of his successor's, many schemes were proposed, and some adopted, though never carried into execution, for draining the fens. Among others, a Dutchman, Sir Cornelius Vermuiden, was employed. But I believe his scheme was different from that alluded to in the text.

[3] [See a long note in Gifford's Ben Jonson, v. 42.]

[4] It appears that to say *You were born at Hog's Norton,* conveyed an insinuation of boorish rustical behaviour. The true name of the town is *Hoch Norton,* and it is situated in the county of Oxford. Nash, in "The Apologie of Pierce Pennilesse," 4°, 1593, sig. K 4, says, "If thou bestowst any curtesie on mee, and I do not requite it, then call mee *cut,* and I was brought up at *Hogge Norton, where pigges play on the organs.*" [See Hazlitt's "Proverbs," 1869, pp. 315–16.]

That I have seen in Mother Redcap's hall,
In painted cloth, the story of the Prodigal.[1]
   Col. And that will be for very good use and
     moral.
Sir, you are wise; what serve Egyptian pyramids,
Ephesian temples, Babylonian towers,
Carian Colosses,[2] Trajan's water-works,
Domitian's amphitheatres, the vain cost
Of ignorance and prodigality?
Rome flourish'd when her Capitol was thatch'd,
And all her gods dwelt but in cottages :
Since Parian marble and Corinthian brass
Enter'd her gaudy temple, soon she fell
To superstition, and from thence to ruin.
You see that in our churches glorious statues,
Rich copes, and other ornaments of state,
Draw wond'ring[3] eyes from their devotion
Unto a wanton gazing ; and that other
Rich edifices and such gorgeous toys
Do more proclaim our country's wealth than safety,
And serve but like so many gilded baits
T' entice a foreign foe to our invasion.
Go in, there is a glass will show you, sir,
What sweet simplicity our grandsires used :
How in the age of gold no church was gilded.
                     [*Exit* MICROPREPES.

---

[1] Mother Redcap's hall probably stood where a house between London and Hampstead is still distinguished by the sign
of this old lady's head.   The story of the Prodigal in painted
cloth was a very common one.   Falstaff says to Mrs Quickly,
"For thy walls, ... a pretty slight drollery, or the *story of
the Prodigal*, or the German hunting *in water work*, is worth a
thousand of those bed-hangings, and these fly-bitten tapestries."
"Old Mother Redcap's," is mentioned as famous for good ale,
in "Bacchus' Bountie," 1593, reprinted in "Harleian Miscellany," ii. 303.—*Gilchrist*.
  [2] [Old copy, *Colossus*.]
  [3] [Old copies read *wandering*.]

Ban. O, I have thought on't: I will straightway
    build
A free school here in London ; a free school
For the education of young gentlemen,
To study how to drink and take tobacco ;
To swear, to roar, to dice, to drab, to quarrel.
'Twill be the great Gymnasium of the realm,
The Frontisterium [1] of Great Britainy.
And for their better study, I will furnish them
With a large library of draper's books.

Col. 'Twill put down Bodley [2] and the Vatican.
Royal Banausus ! how many spheres fly you
Above the earthly dull Microprepes !
I hope to live to see you build a stew
Shall outbrave Venice : to repair old Tyburn,
And make it cedar.　This magnificent course
Doth purchase you an immortality.
In them you build your honour, to remain
The example and the wonder of posterity ;
While other hidebound churls do grudge themselves
The charges of a tomb.

Ban.　　　　　　　But I'll have one,
In which I'll lie embalm'd with myrrh and cassia,
And richer unguents than the Egyptian kings :
And all that this my precious tomb may furnish
The land with mummy.[3]

Col.　　　　　　Yonder is a glass
Will show you plots and models of all monuments
Form'd the old way.　You may invent a new ;
'Twill make for you more glory.

Ban.　　　　　　Colax, true.　[*Exit.*

---

[1] *Frontisterium* signifies a cloister, a college.　The word
occurs in " Albumazar."—*Steevens.*

[2] [Old copy, *Bodley's.*]

[3] See Chambers' " Dictionary," *voce* Mummy.

SCENE II.

Ros. *These are the extremes of Magnanimity. Chau-*
nus, a fellow so highly conceited of his own parts, that
he thinks no honour above him; the other Micropsychus,
a base and 'low-spirited fellow, that, undervaluing his
own qualities, dares not aspire to those dignities that
otherwise his merits are capable of.

CHAUNUS, MICROPSYCHUS.

Chau. I wonder that I hear no news from court.
Col. All hail unto the honourable Chaunus !
Chau. The honourable Chaunus ! 'Tis decreed
I am a privy councillor. Our new honours
Cannot so alter us, as that we can
Forget our friends. Walk with us, our familiar.
Mic. It puzzles me to think what worth I have,
That they should put so great an honour on me.
Col. Sir, I do know and see, and so do all
That have not wilful blindness, what rare skill
Of wisdom, policy, judgment, and the rest
Of the state-virtues sit within this breast,
As if it were their parliament; but as yet
I am not, sir, the happy messenger
That tells you, you are call'd unto the helm;
Or that the rudder of Great Britainy
Is put into your hands, that you may steer
Our floating Delos, till she be arriv'd
At the bless'd port of happiness; and surnam'd
The *Fortunate Isle* from you that are the Fortunate.
Chau. 'Tis strange that I, the best-experienc'd,
The skilfull'st and the rarest of all carpenters,
Should not be yet a privy councillor !
Surely the state wants eyes; or has drunk opium,
And sleeps : but when it wakes, it cannot choose
But meet the glorious beams of my deserts,

Bright as the rising sun, and say to England :
England, behold thy light!

    Mic.   Make me a constable!
Make me, that am the simplest of my neighbours,
So great a magistrate, so powerful an officer !
I blush at my unworthiness.   A constable!
The very prince o' th' parish!   You are one, sir,
Of an ability to discharge it better ;
Let me resign to you.

    Chau.   How! I a constable?
What might I be in your opinion, sir?

    Mic. A carpenter of worship.

    Chau.   Very well :
And yet you would make me a constable.
I'll evidently demonstrate, that of all men
Your carpenters are best statesmen : of all carpenters
I, being the best, am best of statesmen too.
Imagine, sir, the commonwealth a log
Or a rude block of wood : your statesman comes
(For by that word I mean a carpenter)
And with the saw of policy divides it
Into so many boards or several orders—
Of prince, nobility, gentry, and the other
Inferior boards, call'd vulgar ; fit for nothing
But to make stiles or planks to be trod over,
Or trampled on.   This adds unto the log,
Call'd commonwealth, at least some small perfection :
But afterwards he planes them, and so makes
The commonwealth, that was before a board,
A pretty wainscot.   Some he carves with titles
Of lord, or knight, or gentleman ; some stand plain,
And serve us more for use than ornament :
We call them yeomen (boards now out of fashion) :
And, lest the disproportion break the frame,
He with the pegs of amity and concord
As with the glue-pot of good government,
Joints 'em together : makes an absolute edifice
Of the republic.   State-skill'd Machiavel

Was certainly a carpenter : yet you think
A constable a giant-dignity.
   Mic. Pray heaven that, Icarus-like, I do not melt
The waxen plumes of my ambition !
Or that from this bright chariot of the sun
I fall not headlong down with Phaeton,
I have aspir'd so high.   Make me a constable,
That have not yet attain'd to the Greek tongue!
Why 'tis his office for to keep the peace—
His majesty's peace.   I am not fit to keep
His majesty's hogs,[1] much less his peace, the best
Of all his jewels.   How dare I presume
To charge a man in the king's name.   I faint
Under the burthen of so great a place,
Whose weight might press down Atlas.   Magistrates
Are only sumpter-horses.   Nay, they threaten me
To make me warden of the church.
Am I a patriot ? or have I ability
To present knights-recusant, clergy-reelers,
Or gentlemen fornicators ?
   Col.   You have worth,
Richly enamelled with modesty ;
And, though your lofty merit might sit crown'd
On Caucasus or the Pyrenean mountains,
You choose the humbler valley, and had rather
Grow a safe shrub below than dare the winds,
And be a cedar.   Sir, you know there is not
Half so much honour in the pilot's place,
As danger in the storm.   Poor windy titles
Of dignity, and offices that puff up
The bubble pride, till it swell big and burst,
What are they but brave nothings ?   Toys, call'd
   honours,

---

[1] Some of the later of the old copies read—

                " I am not fit to keep,
        His Majesty's *logs*."
—*Collier.*

Make them on whom they are bestow'd no better
Than glorious slaves, the servants of the vulgar.
Men sweat at helm as much as at the oar.
There is a glass within shall show you, sir,
The vanity of these silkworms, that do think
They toil not, 'cause they spin so fine a thread.
    Mic. I'll see it. Honour is a baby's rattle ;
And let blind Fortune, where she will, bestow her :
Lay me on earth, and I shall fall no lower.   [*Exit.*
    Chau. Colax, what news ?
    Col.   The Persian emperor
Is desperately sick.
    Chau.   Heaven take his soul !
When I am the Grand Sophy (as 'tis likely
I may be), Colax, thou art made for ever.
    Col. The Turk, they say, prepares again for Poland.
    Chau. And I am no bashaw yet ! Sultan, repent it !
    Col. The state of Venice, too, is in distraction.
    Chau. And can that state be so supinely negligent,
As not to know whom they may choose their duke ?
    Col. Our merchants do report, th' inhabitants there
Are now in consultation for the settling
The crown upon a more deserving head
Than his that bears it.
    Chau.   Then my fortunes rise
On confident wings, and all my hopes fly certain.
Colax, behold !¹ thou see'st the Prester John.
Woe,² England, of all countries in the world,
Most blind to thine own good ! Other nations
Woo me to take the bridle in my hands
With gifts and presents. Had I liv'd in Rome,
Who durst with Chaunus stand a candidate ?
I might have choice of Ædile, Consul, Tribune,

----

¹ [The 4º of 1638, *be bold*, corrected in the later copies properly to *behold.*]
² [Edits., *Well.*]

Or the perpetual Dictator's place.
I could discharge 'em all : I know my merits
Are large and boundless.   A Cæsar might be hew'd
Out of a carpenter, if a skilful workman
But undertook it.
    Col.   'Tis a worthy confidence.
Let birds of night and shame, with their owls' eyes,
Not dare to gaze upon the sun of honour ;
They are no precedents for eagles.   Bats,
Like dull Micropsychus, things of earth and lead,
May love a private safety ; men, in whom
Prometheus has spent much of his stol'n fire,
Mount upwards like a flame, and court bright honour,
Hedg'd in with thousand dangers.   What's a man
Without desert ?   And what's desert to him,
That does not know he has it ?   Is he rich
That holds within his house some buried chests
Of gold or pearl, and knows not where to look them ?
What was the loadstone, till the use was found,
But a foul dotard on a fouler mistress ?
I praise your Argus' eyes, that not alone
Shoot their beams forwards, but reflect and turn
Back on themselves, and find an object there
More worthy their intentive contemplation.
You are at home no stranger, but are grown
Acquainted with your virtues, and can tell
What use the pearl is of, which dunghill-cocks
Scrape into dirt again.   This searching judgment
Was not intended to work wood, but men.
Honour attends you : I shall live to see
A diadem crown that head.   There is within
A glass that will acquaint you with all places
Of dignity, authority, and renown,
The state and carriage of them : choose the best—
Such as deserve you, and refuse the rest.
    Chau. I go, that want no worth to merit honour :
'Tis honour that wants worth to merit me.

Fortune, thou arbitress of human things,
Thy credit is at stake : if I but rise,
The world's opinion will conceive th' hast eyes. [*Exit.*

SCENE III.

ORGYLUS, AORGUS.

Ros. *These are the extremes of Meekness. Orgylus,
an angry, quarrelsome man, moved with the least shadow
or appearance of injury. The other in defect, Aorgus,
a fellow so patient, or rather insensible of wrong, that
he is not capable of the grossest abuse.*

Org. Persuade me not: he has awak'd a fury
That carries steel about him. Dags[1] and pistols.
To bite his thumb at me [2]

 Aor.   Why, should not any man
Bite his own thumb?

 Org.   At me ! Wear I a sword
To see men bite their thumbs? Rapiers and daggers !
He is the son of a whore.

 Aor.   That hurts not you.
Had he bit yours, it had been some pretence
T' have mov'd this anger: he may bite his own,
And eat it too.

 Org.   Muskets and cannons ! eat it?
If he dares eat it in contempt of me,
He shall eat something else too, that rides here.
I'll try his ostrich stomach.[3]

 Aor.   Sir, be patient.

---

[1] [Daggers.]

[2] Which is a disgrace to them, if they bear it ; as it is explained by Shakespeare. See "Romeo and Juliet," act i. sc. I, and Mr Steevens's note thereto.

[3] Alluding to the power of the stomach of an ostrich to digest iron.

Org. You lie in your throat, and I will not.

Aor. To what purpose is this impertinent madness?
Pray, be milder.

Org. Your mother was a whore, and I will not put it up.

Aor. Why should so slight a toy thus trouble you?

Org. Your father was hang'd, and I will be reveng'd.

Aor. When reason doth in equal balance poise
The nature of two injuries, yours to me
Lies heavy, when that other would not turn
An even scale; and yet it moves not me:
My anger is not up.

Org.   But I will raise it.
You are a fool.

Aor.   I know it: and shall I
Be angry for a truth?

Org.   You are besides
An arrant knave.

Aor.   So are my betters, sir.

Org. I cannot move him: O my spleen, it rises:
For very anger I could eat my knuckles.

Aor. You may—or bite your thumb, all's one to me.

Org. You are a horned beast, a very cuckold.

Aor. 'Tis my wife's fault, not mine: I have no reason
Then to be angry for another's sin.

Org. And I did graft your horns: you might have come,
And found us glued together like two goats,
And stood a witness to your transformation.

Aor. Why, if I had, I am so far from anger,
I would have e'en fall'n down upon my knees,
And desir'd Heav'n to have forgiven you both.

Org. Your children are all bastards : not one of
   them,
Upon my knowledge, of your own begetting.
   Aor. Why, then, I am the more beholden to them
That they will call me father.   It was lust,
Perchance, that did beget them ; but I am sure
'Tis charity to keep the infants.
   Org.   Not yet stirr'd !
'Tis done of mere contempt ; he will not now
Be angry, to express his scorn of me.
'Tis above patience this—insufferable !
Proclaim me coward if I put up this ;
Dotard, you will be angry, will you not ?
   Aor. To see how strange a course fond wrath
   doth go ;
You will be angry, 'cause I am not so.
   Org. I can endure no longer.   If your spleen
Lie in your breech, thus I will kick it up——
                            [*He kicks him.*
   Aor. *Alpha, Beta, Gamma, Delta, Epsilon, Zeta,
Eta, Theta, Iota, Kappa, Lambda, Mu, Nu, Xi,
Omicron, Pi, Ro, Sigma, Tau, Upsilon, Phi, Chi, Psi,
Omega.*
   Org. How ! what contempt is this ?
   Aor.   An antidote.
Against the poison anger.   'Twas prescrib'd
A Roman emperor, that on every injury
Repeated the Greek alphabet :[1] that being done,
His anger too was over.   This good rule
I learn'd from him, and practise.

---

[1] Compare Molière, " L'Ecole des Femmes, act ii. sc. 4—

      " Un certain Grec disoit à l'Empereur Auguste,
      Comme une instruction utile autant que juste,
      Que, lorsqu'une aventure en colere nous met,
      Nous devons, avant tout, dire notre alphabet ;
      Afin que dans ce temps la bile se tempère,
      Et qu'on ne fasse rien que l'on ne doive faire.
      J'ai suivi sa leçon," &c.
—*Gilchrist.*

Org.   Not yet angry!
Still will you vex me? I will practise too. [*Kicks again.*
    Aor. *Aleph, Beth, Gimel.*
    Org.   What new alphabet
Is this?
    Aor.   The Hebrew alphabet that I use:
A second remedy.
    Org.   O my torment still!
Are not your buttocks angry with my toes?
    Aor. For aught I feel, your toes have more occasion
For to be angry with my buttocks.
    Org.   '   Well,
I'll try your physic for the third assault;
And exercise the patience of your nose.
    Aor. *A, B, C, D, E, F, G, H, I, K, L, M, N,
O, P, Q, R, S, T, U, W, X, Y, Z.*
    Org. Are you not angry now?
    Aor. Now, sir? why now?
Now, have you done?
    Org.   O, 'tis a mere plot this,
To jeer my tameness! will no sense of wrong
Waken the lethargy of a coward's soul?
Will not this rouse her from her dead sleep, nor this?
                        [*Kicks him again and again.*
    Aor. Why should I, sir, be angry, if I suffer
An injury?   It is not guilt of mine!
No, let it trouble them that do the wrong
Nothing but peace approaches innocence.
    Org. A bitterness o'erflows me: my eyes flame,
My blood boils in me, all my faculties
Of soul and body move in a disorder,
His patience hath so tortur'd me.   Sirrah, villain,
I will dissect thee with my rapier's point,
Rip up each vein and sinew of my stoic,[1]

---

[1] The early editions read *storque* [a misprint, as Mr Gilchrist pointed out, for *stoique*, the old form of *stoic*].

Anatomise him, searching every entrail,
To see if Nature, when she made this ass,
This suffering ass, did not forget to give him
Some gall.
    Col.   Put it up, good Orgylus:
Let him not glory in so brave a death,
As by your hand.   It stands not with your honour
To stain your rapier in a coward's blood.
The Lesbian lions, in their noble rage,
Will prey on bulls, or mate the unicorn ;[1]
But trouble not the painted butterfly :
Ants crawl securely by them.
    Org.   'Tis intolerable !
Would thou wert worth the killing.
    Col.   A good wish,
Savouring as well discretion as bold valour.
Think not of such a baffled ass as this,
More stone than man : Medusa's head has turn'd him.
There is in ants a choler, every fly
Carries a spleen ; poor worms, being trampled on,
Turn tail, as bidding battle to the feet
Of their oppressors.   A dead palsy, sure,
Hath struck a desperate numbness through his soul,
Till it be grown insensible.   Mere stupidity
Hath seiz'd him.   Your more manly soul, I find,
Is capable of wrong, and (like a flint)
Throws forth a fire into the striker's eyes.

---

[1] To *mate* signifies to *oppose* or *contend* with ; as in " Rule a Wife and Have a Wife : " [Dyce's Beaumont and Fletcher, ix. 428 —

> " He stood up to me,
> And *mated* my commands."

And in " Friar Bacon and Friar Bungay," by Greene, 1594—

> " Burden, what, are you *mated* by this frolic friar ? "

—*Reed's note* [corrected].

You bear about you valour's whetstone, anger,
Which sets an edge upon the sword, and makes it
Cut with a spirit.   You conceive fond patience
Is an injustice to ourselves : the suffering
One injury invites a second ; that
Calls on a third, till wrongs do multiply,
And reputation bleed.   How bravely anger
Becomes that martial brow ! A glass within
Will show you, sir, when your great spleen doth rise,
How fury darts a lightning from your eyes.

    Org. Learn anger, sir, against you meet me next.
Never was man like me with patience vex'd.   [*Exit.*

    Aor. I am so far from anger in myself,
That 'tis my grief I can make others so.

    Col. It proves a sweetness in your disposition ;
A gentle, winning carriage.   Dear Aorgus,
O, give me leave to open wide my breast,
And let so rare a friend into my soul !
Enter, and take possession ; such a man
As has no gall, no bitterness, no exceptions,
Whom Nature meant a dove, will keep alive
The flame of amity, where all discourse
Flows innocent, and each free jest is taken.
He's a good friend will pardon his friend's errors,
But he's a better takes no notice of them.
How like a beast with rude and savage rage
Breath'd the distemper'd soul of Orgylus ?
The proneness of this passion is the nurse,
That fosters all confusion, ruins states,
Depopulates cities, lays great kingdoms waste.
'Tis that affection of the mind that wants
The strongest bridle : give it reins, it runs
A desperate course, and drags down reason with it.
It is the whirlwind of the soul, the storm
And tempest of the mind, that raises up
The billows of disturbed passions
To shipwreck judgment.   O, a soul like yours,

Constant in patience ! Let the north wind meet
The south at sea, and Zephyrus breathe opposite
To Eurus : let the two-and-thirty sons
Of Æolus break forth at once, to plough
The ocean, and dispeople all the woods,
Yet here could be a calm. It is not danger
Can make this cheek grow pale, nor injury
Call blood into it. There's a glass within
Will let you see yourself, and tell you now,
How sweet a tameness dwells upon your brow.

Aor. Colax, I must believe, and therefore go :
Who is distrustful, will be angry too.

SCENE IV.

ALAZON, EIRON.

Ros. The next are the extremes of Truth. Alazon, one that arrogates that to himself which is not his; and Eiron, one that, out of an itch to be thought modest, dissembles his qualities : the one erring in defending a falsehood, the other offending in denying a truth.

Alaz. I hear you are wondrous valiant?
Eir.   I ! Alas !
Who told you I was valiant?
Ala.   The world speaks it.
Eir. She is deceiv'd. But does she speak it truly ?
Ala. I am indeed the Hector of the age ;
But she calls you [the] Achilles.
Eir.   I Achilles !
No, I am not Achilles. I confess
I am no coward. That the world should think
That I am an Achilles ! yet the world may
Call me what she please.
Ala.   Next to my valour,

(Which but for yours could never hope a second)
Yours is reported.

    Eir.   I may have my share ;
But the last valour show'd in Christendom
Was in Lepanto.[1]

    Ala.   Valour in Lepanto ?[2]
He might be thought so, sir, by them that knew him
    not ;
But I have found him a poor baffled snake :
Sir, I have writ him, and proclaim'd him coward
On every post i' th' city.

    Eir.   Who ?
    Ala.   Lepanto ;
The valour, sir, that you so much renown.

    Eir. Lepanto was no man, sir, but the place
Made famous by the so-much-mention'd battle
Betwixt the Turks and Christians.

    Ala.   Cry you mercy !
Then the Lepanto that I meant, it seems
Was but that Lepanto's namesake.   I can
Find that you are well-skill'd in history.

    Eir. Not a whit : a novice I.   I could, perchance,
Discourse from Adam downward, but what's that
To history ?   All that I know is only
Th' original, continuance, height, and alteration
Of every commonwealth.   I have read nothing

---

[1] This famous battle, between the Turks and the Venetians, was fought in the year 1571.   It is supposed to have been one of the most bloody engagements which ever was known.   The loss on the part of the Venetians was about 7566 ; and on that of the Turks, more than double the number.   See an account of it in Knolles's "History of the Turks," 1631, p. 878.   In the Venetian fleet, the celebrated Cervantes served, and had the misfortune to lose his left hand by the shot of a harquebus.

[2] This interrogation is omitted in the later impressions.— *Collier.* [Alazon supposes Lepanto to be some person, a rival to him in valour.]

But Plutarch, Livy, Tacitus, Suetonius,
Appian, Dion, Julius,[1] Paterculus,
With Florus, Justin, Sallust, and some few
More of the Latin. For the modern, I
Have all without book. Gallo-Belgicus,[2]
Philip de Comines, Machiavel, Guicciardine,
The Turkish and Egyptian histories,
With those of Spain, France, and the Netherlands,
For England, Polydore Virgil, Camden, Speed,
And a matter of forty more : nothing,
Alas ! to one that's read in histories.
In the Greek I have a smack or so, at
Xenophon, Herodotus, Thucydides, and
Stowe's Chronicle.[3]
   Ala. Believe me, sir, and that
Stowe's Chronicle is very good Greek. You little
Think who writ it. Do you not see him? Are
You blinded ? I am the man.
   Eir. Then I must number
You with my best authors in my library.
   Ala. Sir, the rest too are mine, but that I venture
    'em
With other names to shun the opinion
Of arrogance. So the subtle cardinal
Calls one book Bellarmine, 'nother Tostatus,
Yet one man's labour both. You talk of numb'ring :
You cannot choose but hear how loud Fame speaks
Of my experience in arithmetic :
She says you too grow near perfection.
   Eir. Far from it I ; some insight, but no more.
I count the stars ; can give the total sum,

---

   [1] [All the edits., *Junius.*]
   [2] See Gifford's Ben Jonson, 1816, ii. 530, *note.*
   [3] [It is not very obvious why Eiron, who is not meant to be
a blunderer, places Stowe among Greek authors, unless it be to
entrap Alazon.]

How many sands there be i' th' sea ; but these
Are trifles to the expert, that have studied
Penkethman's [1] president.   Sir, I have no skill
In anything : if I have any, 'tis
In languages ; but yet in sooth I speak
Only my mother tongue.   I have not gain'd
The Hebrew, Chaldee, Syriac, or Arabic ;
Nor know the Greek with all her dialects.
Scaliger and Tom Coriat both excel me.
I have no skill in French, Italian, Spanish,
Turkish, Egyptian, China, Persian tongues.
Indeed the Latin I was whipp'd into ;
But Russian, Sclavonian, and Dalmatian,
With Saxon, Danish, and Albanian speech,
That of the Cossacks, and Hungarian too,
With Biscay's, and the prime of languages.
Dutch, Welsh, and Irish are too hard for me
To be familiar in : and yet some think
(But thought is free) that I do speak all these
As I were born in each, but they may err
That think so ; 'tis not every judgment sits
In the infallible chair.   To confess truth,
All Europe, Asia, and Africa too ; [2]
But in America and the new-found world
I very much fear there be some languages
That would go near to puzzle me.
    Ala.   Very likely.
You have a pretty pittance in the tongues.
But, Eiron, now I am [3] more general ;

---

[1] Probably the additions made by John Penkethman to Hopton's "Concordance of Years, containing a new, easy, and most exact computation of time, according to the English account." London, 8°, 1616.

[2] [There seems to be an ellipsis here, as Eiron apparently is intended to say that he understands the languages of *all Europe*, &c., *but in America*, &c.]

[3] [Old copies, *I am now.*]

I can speak all alike : there is no stranger
Of so remote a nation hears me talk,
But confidently calls me countryman.
The witty world, giving my worth her due,
Surnames me the Confusion.[1] I but want
An orator like you to speak my praise.
    Eir. Am I an orator, Alazon ? no :
Though it hath pleas'd the wiser few to say
Demosthenes was not so eloquent.
But friends will flatter, and I am not bound
To believe all hyperboles : something, sir,
Perchance I have, but 'tis not worth the naming—
Especially, Alazon, in your presence.
    Ala. Your modesty, Eiron, speaks but truth in
      this.
    Col. I need not flatter these, they'll do't them-
      selves,
And cross the proverb that was wont to say,
One mule doth scrub another ; here each ass
Hath learn'd to claw himself.   [*Aside.*
    Ala.   I do surpass
All orators.   How like you my orations ?
Those against Catiline I account them best,
Except my Philippics ; all acknowledge me
Above the three great orators of Rome.
    Eir.   What three, Alazon ?
    Ala. Marcus, Tullius,
And Cicero—the best of all the three.
    Eir. Why, those three names are all the selfsame
      man's.
    Ala. Then all is one : were those three names three
      men,
I should excel them all.   And then for poetry——
    Eir. There is no poetry but Homer's Iliads.

---

[1] [*i.e.,* The confusion of tongues, which is said to have been
in the Tower of Babel.]

Ala. Alas! 'twas writ i' th' nonage of my muses.
You understand th' Italian?
    Eir.   A little, sir;
I have read Tasso.
    Ala.   And Torquato too?
    Eir. They're still the same!
    Ala.   I find you very skilful:
Eiron, I err only to sound your judgment.
You are a poet too?
    Eir.   The world may think so,
But 'tis deceiv'd, and I am sorry for it.
But I will tell you, sir, some excellent verses
Made by a friend of mine. I have not read
A better epigram of a Neoteric.[1]
    Ala. Pray, do my eyes the favour, sir, to let me
    learn 'em.
    Eir. *Strange sights there late were seen, that did affright*
       The multitude; the moon was seen by night,
       And sun appear'd by day—
Is it not good!
    Ala.   Excellent good! proceed.
    Eir.   *Without remorse,*
       Each star and planet kept their wonted course.
       What here could fright them?
Mark the answer now—
                O, sir, ask not that;
       The vulgar know not why they fear, nor what;
       But in their humours too inconstant be;
       Nothing seems strange to them but constancy.
Has not my friend approv'd himself a poet?
    Ala. The verses, sir, are excellent; but your friend
Approves himself a thief.
    Eir.   Why, good Alazon?
    Ala. A plagiary, I mean: the verses, sir,
Were stolen.

---

[1] New, modern.

Eir.   From whom ?

Ala.   From me, believe't ; I made 'em.

Eir. They are, alas ! unworthy, sir, your owning :
Such trifles as my muse had stumbled on
This morning.

Ala. Nay, they may be yours : I told you
That you came near me, sir.   Yours they may be ;
Good wits may jump : but let me tell you, Eiron,
Your friend must steal them, if he have 'em.

Col. What pretty gulls are these ! I'll take them off.
Alazon,[1] you are learned.

Ala.   I know that.

Col.   And virtuous.

Ala. 'Tis confess'd.

Col.   A good historian.

Ala.   Who dares deny it ?

Col. A rare arithmetician.

Ala.   I have heard it often.

Col.   I commend your care,
That know your virtues : why should modesty
Stop good men's mouths from their own praise ? our
    neighbours
Are envious, and will rather blast our memories
With infamy, than immortalise our names.
When Fame hath taken cold, and lost her voice,
We must be our own trumpets : careful men
Will have an inventory of their goods ;
And why not of their virtues ? should you say
You were not wise, it were a sin to truth.
Let Eiron's modesty tell bashful lies,
To cloak and mask his parts : he's a fool for't.
'Twas heavenly counsel bid us *know ourselves.*[2]

---

[1] *Alazon* has been hitherto omitted by Dodsley and Reed,
although found in every copy.   The measure was thus destroyed.
—*Collier.*

[2] *E cælo descendit* γνωθι σεαυτον.—Juvenal, XI. 27.—*Gilchrist.*

You may be confident : chant your own encomiums,
Ring out a panegyric to yourself,
And yourself write the learned commentary
Of your own actions.

    Ala.   So I have.

    Col.   Where is it ?

    Ala. 'Tis stolen.

    Col.   I know the thief ; they call him Cæsar.
Go in, good sir, there is within a glass,
That will present you with the felon's face.

                       [*Exit* ALAZON.

Eiron, you hear the news ?

    Eir.   Not I, what is it ?

    Col. That you are held the only man of art.

    Eir. Is't current, Colax ?

    Col.   Current as the air ;
Every man breathes it for a certainty.

    Eir. This is the first time I heard on't, in truth.
Can it be certain ? so much charity left
In men's opinion ?

    Col.   You call it charity,
Which is their duty.   Virtue, sir, like yours,
Commands men's praises : emptiness and folly,
Such as Alazon is, use their own tongues,
While real worth hears her own praise, not speaks it,
Other men's mouths become your trumpeters,
And winged fame proclaims you loudly forth
From east to west, till either pole admire you.
Self-praise is bragging, and begets the envy
Of them that hear it, while each man therein
Seems undervalued.   You are wisely silent
In your own worth, and therefore 'twere a sin
For others to be so : the fish would loose
Their being mute, ere such a modest worth
Should want a speaker.   Yet, sir, I would have
    you
Know your own virtues, be acquainted with them.

Eir. Why, good sir, bring me but acquainted with
them.

Col. There is a glass within shows you yourself
By a reflection ; go and speak 'em there.

Eir. I should be glad to see 'em anywhere.

[*Exit* EIRON.

Ros. Retire yourselves again ; for these are sights
Made to revive, not burden with delights.

[*Exeunt omnes.*

ACT IV., SCENE I.

MISTRESS FLOWERDEW, BIRD, ROSCIUS.

Bird. My indignation boileth like a pot—
An over-heated pot—still, still it boileth ;
It boileth, and it bubbleth with disdain.

Mis. Flo. My spirit within me too fumeth, I say,
Fumeth and steameth up, and runneth o'er
With holy wrath, at these delights of flesh.

Ros. The actors beg your silence. *The next virtue whose extreme we would present wants a name
both in the Greek and Latin.*

Bird. Wants it a name ? 'tis an unchristian virtue.

Ros. *But they describe it such a modesty as directs
us in the pursuit and refusal of the meaner honours,
and so answers to Magnanimity, as Liberality to Magnificence. But here, that humour of the persons, being
already forestalled, and no pride now so much practised
or countenanced as that of apparel, let me present you
Philotimia, an over-curious lady, too neat in her attire,
and for Aphilotimus, Luparius, a nasty, sordid sloven.*

Mis. Flo. Pride is a vanity worthy the correction.

PHILOTIMIA, LUPARIUS, COLAX.

Phil. What mole dress'd me to-day ?   O patience !

Who would be troubled with these mop-ey'd chamber-
    maids ?
There's a whole hair on this side more than t'other,
I am no lady else ! Come on, you sloven.
Was ever Christian madam so tormented
To wed a swine as I am ? make you ready.
   Lup. I would the tailor had been hang'd, for me,
That first invented clothès. O nature, nature !
More cruel unto man than all thy creatures !
Calves come into the world with doublets on ;
And oxen have no breeches to put off.
The lamb is born with her freeze-coat about her ;
Hogs go to bed in rest,[1] and are not troubled
With pulling on their hose and shoes i' th' morning,
With gartering, girdling, trussing, buttoning,
And a thousand torments that afflict humanity.
   Phil. To see her negligence ! she hath made this
    cheek
By much too pale, and hath forgot to whiten
The natural redness of my nose ; she knows not
What 'tis wants dealbation. O fine memory !
If she has not set me in the selfsame teeth
That I wore yesterday, I am a Jew.
Does she think that I can eat twice with the same,
Or that my mouth stands as the vulgar does ?
What, are you snoring there ? you'll rise, you slug-
    gard,
And make you ready ?
   Lup.   Rise, and make you ready ?
Two works of that your happy birds make one ;
They, when they rise, are ready. Blessed birds !
They (fortunate creatures !) sleep in their own clothes,
And rise with all their feather-beds about them.
Would nakedness were come again in fashion ;

---

   [1] [Pegge suggested *all drest* or *as drest ;* but there seems no
reason to alter the text.]

I had some hope then, when the breasts went bare,[1]
Their bodies, too, would have come to't in time,
   Phil. Beshrew her for't, this wrinkle is not fill'd—
You'll go and wash—you are a pretty husband !
   Lup. Our sow ne'er washes, yet she has a face
Methinks as cleanly, madam, as yours is,
If you durst wear your own.
   Col.   Madam Superbia.
You're studying the lady's library,
The looking-glass : 'tis well ! so great a beauty
Must have her ornaments. Nature adorns
The peacock's tail with stars ; 'tis she attires
The bird of paradise in all her plumes ;
She decks the fields with various flowers ; 'tis she
Spangled the heavens with all those glorious lights ;
She spotted th' ermine's skin, and arm'd the fish
In silver mail. But man she sent forth naked,
Not that he should remain so, but that he,
Endued with reason, should adorn himself
With every one of these. The silkworm is
Only man's spinster, else we might suspect
That she esteem'd the painted butterfly
Above her masterpiece. You are the image
Of that bright goddess, therefore wear the jewels
Of all the East ; let the Red Sea be ransack'd

---

[1] How far the ladies of the times were censurable in this particular may be seen in Hollar's " Ornatus Muliebris Anglicanus." The rigid Puritans discovered almost every evil to be the consequence of this unrestrained freedom of dress, against which they were continually pouring out the most severe invectives.

Many books were published against the licence which ladies allowed themselves in those particulars mentioned in the text. Among others was " A Just and Seasonable Reprehension of Naked Breasts and Shoulders. Written by a grave and learned Papist. Translated by Edward Cooke, Esquire ; with a Preface by Mr Richard Baxter," 8º, 1678. The fashion continued until late in the 17th century. In 1683 John Duncan printed an invective on the same subject.

To make you glitter.　Look on Luparus,
Your husband there, and see how in a sloven
All the best characters of divinity,
Not yet worn out in man, are lost and buried.
　　Phil. I see it to my grief; pray, counsel him.
　　Col. This vanity in your nice lady's humours,
Of being so curious in her toys and dresses,
Makes me suspicious of her honesty.
These cobweb lawns catch spiders, sir, believe:
You know that clothes do not commend the man,
But 'tis the living; though this age prefer
A cloak of plush before a brain of art.
You understand what misery 'tis to have
No worth but that we owe the draper for.
No doubt you spend the time your lady loses
In tricking up her body, to clothe the soul.
　　Lup. To clothe the soul? must the soul too be
　　　cloth'd?
I protest, sir, I had rather have no soul
Than be tormented with the clothing of it.
　　*Ros. To these enter the extremes of Modesty, a near
kinswoman of the virtues, Anaiskyntia or Impudence,
a bawd, and Kataplectus an overbashful scholar; where,
our author hopes, the women will pardon him if, of
four-and-twenty vices, he presents but two* (Pride and
Impudence) *of their sex.*

SCENE II.

ANAISKYNTIA, KATAPLECTUS.

　　Phil. Here comes Anaiskyntia too; O fates!
Acolastus and Asotus have sent for me,
And my breath not perfum'd yet!
　　Kat.　　　　　　　　　　　　O sweet mother,
Are the gentlemen there already?

Anais.   Come away,
Are you not asham'd to be so bashful? well,
If I had thought of this in time, I would
As soon have seen you fairly hang'd, as sent you
To the university.
    Phil.   What gentleman is that?
    Anais. A shamefac'd scholar, madam.   Look upon
      her,
Speak to her, or you lose your exhibition : [1]
You'll speak, I hope : wear not away your buttons.
    Kat. What should I say?
    Anais.   Why, tell her you are glad
To see her ladyship in health : nay, out with it.
    Kat. Gaudeo te bene valere.
    Phil.   A pretty proficient !
What standing is he of i' th' university?
    Anais. He dares not answer to that question, madam.
    Phil. How long have you been in the academy?
    Kat. Profecto Do—Domina sum Bac—Bac—Bac-
    calaureus Artium.
    Phil. What pity 'tis he is not impudent !
    Anais. Nay, all my cost, I see, is spent in vain.
I having, as your ladyship knows full well,
Good practice in the suburbs ; and by reason
That our mortality there is very subject
To an infection of the French disease,
I brought my nephew up i' th' university,
Hoping he might (having attain'd some knowledge)
Save me the charge of keeping a physician ;
But all in vain : he is so bashful, madam,
He dares not look upon a woman's water.
    Col. Sweet gentleman, proceed in bashfulness,
'Tis virtue's best preserver.
    Kat. Recte dicis, sic inquit Aristoteles.

---

[1] *i.e.,* Your stipend, your allowance. See Dyce's " Shakespeare Glossary," 1868, in *v.*

Col.   That being gone,
The rest soon follow, and a swarm of vice
Enters the soul : no colour but a blush
Becomes a young man's cheek.   Pure shamefac'dness
Is porter to the lips and ears, that nothing
Might enter or come out of man but what
Is good and modest : Nature strives to hide
The parts of shame ; let her, the best of guides——
    Kat. Natura dux optima.
    Col. Teach us to do so too in our discourse.
    Kat. Gratias tibi ago.
    Phil. Inure him to speak bawdy.
    Anais. A very good way. Kataplectus, here's a lady
Would hear you speak obscenely.
    Kat. Obscenum est, quod intra scenam agi non oportuit.
    Anais. Off goes your velvet cap ! did I maintain you,
To have you disobedient ? you'll be persuaded ?
    Kat. Liberis operam dare.
    Anais. What's that in English ?
    Kat.   To do an endeavour for children.
    Anais. Some more of this ; it may be something one
    day.
    *Kat. Communis est omnium animantium conjunctionis
appetitus, procreandi causâ.*
    Phil. Construe me that.
    Kat. All creatures have a natural desire or appe-
tite to be joined together in the lawful bonds of matri-
mony, that they may have sons and daughters.
    Anais. Your laundress has bestow'd her time but ill :
Why could not this have been in proper terms ?
If you should catechise my head, and say,
What is your name, would it not say, A head ?
So would my skin confess itself a skin ;
Nor any part about me be asham'd
Of his own name, although I catechis'd
All over.   Come, good nephew, let not me
Have any member of my body nicknam'd.

Col. Our stoic, the gravest of philosophers,
Is just of your opinion, and thus argues :
Is anything obscene, the filthiness
Is either grounded in the things themselves,
Or in the words that signify those things,
Not in the things : that would make Nature guilty,
Who creates nothing filthy and unclean,
But chaste and honest : if not in the things,
How in the words, the shadows of those things,
To manure grounds, is a chaste, honest term ;
Another word that signifies the same
Unlawful : every man endures to hear
He got a child ; speak plainer, and he blushes,
Yet means the same.   The stoic thus disputes :
Who would have men to breathe as freely downward,
As they do upward.
　Anais.　　　　　I commend him, madam,
Unto your ladyship's service ; he may mend
With counsel : let him be your gentleman-usher,
Madam, you may in time bring down his legs
To the just size, now overgrown with playing
Too much at football.
　Phil.　　　　　So he will prove a stoic ;
I long to have a stoic strut before me :
Here, kiss my hand.   Come, what is that in Latin ?
　Kat. Deosculor manum.
　Phil. My lip; nay, sir, you must, if I command you.
　Kat. Osculo te, vel osculor a te.
　Phil. His breath smells strong.
　Anais.　　　　　'Tis but of logic, madam.
　Phil. He will come to it one day ; you shall go
　　with me
To see an exquisite glass to dress me by.
Nay, go ! you must go first ; you are too mannerly.
It is the office of your place ; so, on.　　　[*Exeunt.*
　Col. Slow Luparus, rise, or you'll be metamorphos'd ;
Acteon's fate is imminent.

Lup.   Where's my wife?

Col. She's gone with a young snip and an old
   bawd.

Lup. Then I am cuckolded: if I be, my comfort is,
She's put me on a cap that will not trouble me
With pulling off: yet, madam, I'll prevent you. [*Exit.*

Ros. The next are the extremes of Justice.

SCENE III.

Enter Justice Nimis, Justice Nihil.   Plus *and*
Parum, *their Clerks.*

Nim. Plus!

Plus.   What says your worship?

Nim.   Have my tenants,
That hold their lease of lust here in the suburbs,
By copyhold from me, their lord in chief,
Paid their rent-charge?

Plus.   They have, an't please your worship;
I, receiver-general, gave 'm my acquittance.

Par. Sir, I resign my pen and inkhorn to you;
I shall forget my hand if I stay here.
I have not made a mittimus since I serv'd you.
Were I a reverend justice as you are,
I would not sit a cypher on the bench,
But do as Justice Nimis does, and be
The *Dominus factotum* of the sessions.

Nihil. But I will be a *Dominus fac-misericordiam*,
Instead of your *Totums:* people shall not wish
To see my spurs fil'd off: it does me good
To take a merciful nap upon the bench,
Where I so sweetly dream of being pitiful,
I wake the better for it.

Nim.   The yearly value
Of my fair manor of Clerkenwell is pounds

So many, besides new-year's capons, the lordship
Of Turnbull,[1] so—which, with my Pickt-hatch grange[2]
And Shoreditch farm, and other premises
Adjoining—very good, a pretty maintenance
To keep the justice of peace, and coram too ;
Besides the fines I take of young beginners,
With heriots of all such as die : *quatenus* whores
And ruin'd bawds, with all amercements due
To such as hunt in purlieu ;[3] this is something—
With mine own game reserv'd.

   Plus. Besides a pretty pittance, too, for me,
That am your worship's bailiff.

   Par.   Will it please
Your worship, sir, to hear the catalogue
Of such offenders as are brought before you ?

   Nihil. It does not please me, sir, to hear of any,

---

[1] Turnbull or *Turnmill* street. This street, situated between Clerkenwell Green and Cow Cross, had its name, says Stow, from a river or brook formerly here, whereon stood several mills. This receptacle of thieves and harlots is frequently mentioned by writers of the times.

[2] Pickt-hatch was in Turnbull Street. See notes by Mr Steevens and Mr Warton to " The Merry Wives of Windsor," act ii. sc. 2.

> "Your whore doth live
> In Pickt-hatch, *Turnbole Street.*"

—Field's " Amends for Ladies," sig. D, 1639.—*Gilchrist.*

Taylor the Water-poet, in his piece entitled " A Bawd," celebrates *Turnbull Street*—

> " Here's bawds of state, of high and mighty place :
> Our Turnbull Street poor bawds to these are base."

Davenport has put into three lines nearly all the places in London formerly celebrated for the respectability of their inhabitants—

> " Search all the alleys, Spittle, or *Pickt-hatch*,
> *Turnball*, the Bankside, or the Minories,
> Whitefriars, St Peter's Street, and Mutton Lane."

—" New Trick to Cheat the Devil," sig. B 3.—*Collier.*

[3] [Fines payable by persons found frequenting houses of ill-repute.]

That do offend. I would the world were innocent :
Yet, to express my mercy, you may read them.

Par. First, here is one accus'd for cutting a purse.

Nihil. Accus'd ? is that enough ? If it be guilt
To be accus'd, who shall be innocent?
Discharge him, Parum.

Par.   Here's another brought
For the same fact, taken in the very action.

Nihil. Alas ! it was for need ; bid him take warning,
And so discharge him too : 'tis the first time.

Nim. Plus, say, what hopes of gain brings this day's
    sin ?

Plus. Anaiskyntia, sir, was at the door,
Brought by the constable.

Nim.   Set the constable by the heels :
She's at certain [1] with us.

Plus.   Then there's Intemperance the bawd.

Nim. A tenant too.

Plus. With the young lady, Madam Incontinence.

Nim. Search o'er my Doom's-day Book.[2] Is not
    she, Plus,
One of my last compounders ?

Plus.   I remember it.
Then there is jumping Jude, heroic Doll,
With bouncing Nan, and Cis, your worship's sinner.

Nim. All subsidy-women : go, free 'em all.

Par. Sir, here's a known offender, one that has
Been stock'd and whipp'd innumerable times ;
Has suffer'd Bridewell often ; not a jail
But he's familiar with ; burnt in the hand,
Forehead, and shoulder ; both his ears cut off,
With his nose slit ; what shall I do with him ?

---

[1] [*i.e.,* Has made terms. See just below, where Nimis speaks of his *compounders.*]

[2] [A sort of parody on the word in its original and usual sense.]

Nim. So often punish'd? nay, if no correction
Will serve his turn, e'en let him run his course.

Plus. Here's Mistress Frailty, too, the waiting-woman.

Nim. For what offence?

Plus. A sin of weakness too.

Nim. Let her be strongly whipp'd.

Plus. An't please your worship,
She has a nobleman's letter.

Nim. Tell her, Plus, she must
Have the king's picture too.[1]

Plus. Besides,
She has promised me, I should examine her
Above i' th' garret.

Nim. What's all that to me?

Plus. And she entreats your worship to accept.

Nim. Nay, if she can *entreat in English:* Plus,
Say she is injured.

Par. Sir, here's Snip the tailor,
Charg'd with a riot.

Nihil. Parum, let him go,
He is our neighbour.

Par. Then there is a stranger[2] for quarrelling.

Nihil. A stranger! O, 'tis pity
To hurt a stranger: we may be all strangers,
And would be glad to find some mercy, Parum.

Plus. Sir, here's a gentlewoman of St Joan's is
Charg'd with dishonesty.

Nim. With dishonesty?
Severity will amend her: and yet, Plus,
Ask her a question—if she will be honest?

Plus. And here's a cobbler's wife brought for a
scold.

---

[1] [*i.e.,* A pardon under the royal seal, with the king's effigy on it.]

[2] [A person out of the immediate district or parish was formerly called so.]

Nim. Tell her of cucking-stools : tell her there be
Oyster-queans, with orange-women,
Carts and coaches store, to make a noise ;
Yet, if she can *speak English*,
We may suppose her silent.

Par.   Here's a bachelor
And a citizen's wife for flat adultery ;
What will you do with them ?

Nihil.   A citizen's wife !
Perchance her husband is grown impotent,
And who can blame her then ?

Par. Yet I hope you'll bind o'er the bachelor.

Nihil. No : inquire
First if he have no wife ; for if the bachelor
Have not a wife of his own, 'twas but frailty,
And justice counts it venial.

Plus.   Here's one Adicus
And Sophron, that do mutually accuse
Each other of flat felony.

Nim. Of the two, which is the richer ?

Plus.   Adicus is the richer.

Nim. Then Sophron is the thief.

Plus.   Here is withal
Panourgus come, with one call'd Prodetes,
Lay treason, sir, to one another's charge.
Panourgus is the richer.

Nim.   He's the traitor, then.

Plus. How, sir, the richer ?

Nim.   Thou art ignorant, Plus :
We must do some injustice for our credit,
Not all for gain.

Plus.   Eutrapeles complains, sir,
Bomolochus has abus'd him.

Nim.   Send Eutrapeles to the jail.

Plus. It is Eutrapeles that complains, sir.

Nim. Tell him, we're pleas'd to think 'twas he
   offended.

Will must be law.   Were't not for *Summum Jus*,
How could the land subsist?
  Col.   Ay, or the justices
Maintain themselves : go on.   The land wants such
As dare with rigour execute her laws :
Her fester'd members must be lanc'd and tented.[1]
He's a bad surgeon that for pity spares
The part corrupted till the gangrene spread,
And all the body perish.   He that's merciful
Unto the bad is cruel to the good.
The pillory must cure the ear's diseases ;
The stocks the foot's offences ; let the back
Bear her own sin, and her rank blood purge forth
By the phlebotomy of a whipping-post.
And yet the secret and purse-punishment
Is held the wiser course ; because at once
It helps the virtuous and corrects the vicious.
Let not the sword of justice sleep, and rust
Within her velvet sheath : preserve her edge,
And keep it sharp with cutting; use must whet
    her.
Tame mercy is the breast that suckles vice,
Till, Hydra-like, she multiply her heads.
Tread you on sin, squeeze out the serpent's brains,
All you can find ; for some have lurking-holes
Where they lie hid.   But there's within a glass
Will show you every close offender's face.
  Nim. Come, Plus, let's go in to find out these con-
    cealments ;
We will grow rich, and purchase honour thus—
I mean to be a baron of Summum Jus.
                    [*Exeunt* NIMIS *and* PLUS.
  Par. You are the strangest man ; you will acknow-
    ledge

---

[1] A surgical term.—*Collier.* [To *tent*, to search or probe, as
a wound.]

None for offenders.   Here's one apprehended
For murder.
    Nihil.   How?
    Par.   He kill'd a man last night.
    Nihil. How came't to pass?
    Par.   Upon a falling out.
    Nihil. They shall be friends; I'll reconcile them,
    Parum.
    Par. One of them is dead.
    Nihil.   Is he not buried yet?
    Par. No, sir.
    Nihil.   Why then, I say, they shall shake hands.
    Col. As you have done
With clemency, most reverend Justice Nihil.
A gentle mildness thrones itself within you;
Your worship would have Justice use her balance
More than her sword; nor can you endure to dye
The robe she wears deep scarlet in the blood
Of poor offenders.   How many men hath rigour,
By her too hasty and severe proceeding,
Prevented from amendment, that perchance
Might have turn'd honest, and have prov'd good
    Christians?
Should Jove not spare his thunder, but as often
Discharge at us as we dart sins at him,
Earth would want men, and he himself want arms,
And yet tire Vulcan and Pyracmon too.
You imitate the gods! and he sins less
Strikes not at all than he strikes once amiss.
I would not have Justice too falcon-ey'd;
Sometimes a wilful blindness much becomes her;
As when upon the bench she sleeps and winks
At the transgressions of mortality:
In which most merciful posture I have seen
Your pitiful worship snoring [1] out pardons

---

[1] [Edits., *snorting.*]

To the despairing sinner.   There's within
A mirror, sir.   Like you, go see your face,
How like Astrea's 'tis in her own glass!
    Par. And I'll petition Justice Nimis' clerk,
To admit me for his under-officer.   *[Exeunt.*

SCENE IV.

AGROICUS.

*Ros. This is Agroicus, a rustic, clownish fellow,
whose discourse is all country ; an extreme of Urbanity :
whereby you may observe there is a virtue in jesting.*

    Agro. They talk of witty discourse and fine con-
ceits, and I ken not what a deal of prittle-prattle,
would make a cat piss to hear 'em.   Cannot they be
content with their grandam's English?   They think
they talk learnedly, when I had rather hear our
brindled cur howl, or sow grunt.   They must be
breaking of jests, with a murrain, when I had as lief
hear 'em break wind, sir reverence.   My zon Dick
is a pretty bookish scholar of his age, God bless him :
he can write and read, and make bonds and bills
and hobligations, God save all ; but, by'r Lady, if I
wotted it would make him such a Jack-sauce as to
have more wit than his vorefathers, he should have
learned nothing, for old Agroicus, but to keep a tally.
There is a new trade lately come up to be a vocation,
I wis not what : they call 'em boets : a new name for
beggars, I think, since the statute against gipsies.   I
would not have my zon Dick one of these boets for the
best pig in my sty, by the mackins.   Boets ! heaven
shield him, and zend him to be a good varmer.   If
he can cry, *Hey, ho, ge, heyt, ge, ho !* it is better, I trow,
than being a boet.   Boets ! I had rather zee him

remitted to the jail, and have his twelve godvathers,[1]
good men and true, contemn him to the gallows, and
there see him fairly prosecuted.   There is Bomolochus,
one of the boets ; now a bots[2] take all the red-nose
tribe of 'em for Agroicus !   He does so abuse his
betters !   Well, 'twas a good world when I virst held
the plough !

    Col. They car'd not then so much for speaking
       well,
As to mean honest ; and in you still lives
The good simplicity of the former times,
When to do well was rhetoric, not to talk.
The tongue disease of court spreads her infections
Through the whole kingdom.   Flattery, that was
       wont
To be confin'd within the verge, is now
Grown epidemical ; for all our thoughts
Are born between our lips : the heart is made
A stranger to the tongue, as if it us'd
A language that she never understood.
What is it to be witty in these days,
But to be bawdy or profane ?—at least,
Abusive.   Wit is grown a petulant wasp,
And stings, she knows not whom, or where, or why :
Spues vinegar and gall on all she meets

---

[1] The same vein of humour is found in the "Merchant of
Venice," edit. 1778, iii. 228—

> " In christening thou shalt have two godfathers :
>   Had I been judge, thou shouldst have had ten more,
>   To bring thee to the gallows, not the font."

—*Steevens.*

[2] *i.e.,* pox—a common corruption.   In "The Great Duke o
Florence," by Massinger, act iv. sc. 1, Calandrino says—

> "The *bots* on these jolting jades, I am bruis'd to jelly."

And again, in " Wily Beguiled," 1606, Will Cricket exclaims—

> "A *bots* on you ! "

Without distinction ; buys laughter with the loss
Of reputation, father, kinsman, friend ;
Hunts ordinaries only to deliver
The idle timpanies of a windy brain,
That beats and throbs above the pain of childbed,
Till every care she meets be made a midwife
To her light bastard issue.   How many times
Bomolochus' sides and shoulders ache and groan,
He is so witty.   Here he comes.   Away.

    Agro. His wit is dangerous, and I dare not stay.
                                        [Exit.

SCENE V.

BOMOLOCHUS.

    Ros. This is the other extreme, of Urbanity: Bomolochus, a fellow conceited of his own wit, though indeed it be nothing but the base dregs of scandal, and a lump of most vile and loathsome scurrility.

    Bird. Ay, this is he we look'd for all the while !
Scurrility, here she hath her impious throne,
Here lies her heathenish dominion,
In this most impious cell of corruption ;
For 'tis a purgatory, a mere limbo,
Where the black devil and his dam Scurrility
Do rule the roost, foul princes of the air !
Scurrility !   That is he that throweth scandals—
Soweth and throweth scandals, as 'twere dirt,
Even in the face of holiness and devotion.
His presence is contagious ; like a dragon
He belches poison forth, poison of the pit,
Brimstone, hellish and sulphureous poison.
I will not stay, but fly as far as zeal
Can hurry me ; the roof will fall and brain me,
If I endure to hear his blasphemies,
His graceless blasphemies.

Ros.   He shall vent none here ;
But stay, and see how justly we have us'd him.

 Mis. Flo. Stay, brother, I do find the spirit grow
  strong.

 Col. Hail, sacred wit! Earth breeds not bays enough
To crown thy spacious merit.

 Bom.   O, O, O !

 Col. Cratinus, Eupolis, Aristophanes,
Or whatsoever other wit did give
Old comedies the reins, and let her loose
To stigmatise what brow she pleas'd with slander
Of people, prince, nobility, all must yield
To this triumphant brain.

 Bom.   O, O, O !

 Col. They say you'll lose a friend before a jest ; [1]
'Tis true, there's not a jest that comes from you,
That is the true Minerva of this brain,
But is of greater value than a world
Of friends, were every pair of men we meet
A Pylades and Orestes.

 Bom.   O, O, O !

 Col. Some say you will abuse your father too,
Rather than lose the opinion of your wit :
Who would not, that has such a wit as yours ?
'Twere better twenty parents were expos'd
To scorn and laughter, than the simplest thought
Or least conceit of yours should die abortive,
Or perish a brain-embryo.

 Bom.   O, O, O !

 Col. How's this ? that tongue grown silent, that
  Syrens
Stood still to admire ?

 Bom. O, O, O !

---

[1] Boileau makes the sacrifice greater—

  " *Et pour un bon mot va perdre vingt amis.*"
 —*Collier.*

Col. 'Twere better that the spheres should lose their
    harmony,
And all the choristers of the wood grow hoarse.
What wolf hath spied you first?[1]
    Bom.   O, O, O !
    Col. Sure, Hermes, envying that there was on earth
An eloquence more than his, has struck you dumb !
Malicious deity !
    Bom.   O, O, O !
    Col. Go in, sir, there's a glass that will restore
That tongue, whose sweetness angels might adore.
    Bom. O, O, O, O, O, O, O !   [*Exit.*
    Ros. Thus, sir, you see how we have put a gag
In the licentious mouth of base scurrility ;
He shall not, Ibis-like, purge upward here,[2]
T' infect the place with pestilential breath.
We'll keep him tongue-tied, you and all I promise,
By Phœbus and his daughters, whose chaste zones
Were never yet by impure hands untied.
Our language shall flow chaste ; nothing sound here,
That can give just offence to a strict ear.
    Bird. This gag hath wrought my good opinion of
    you.
    Mis. Flo. I begin to think them lawful recreations.
    Col. Now, there's none left here, whereon to practise,
I'll flatter my dear self.   O, that my skill
Had but a body, that I might embrace it !
Kiss it, and hug it, and beget a brood—
Another brood of pretty skills upon it !
Were I divided, I would hate all beauties,
And grow enamour'd with my other half !
Self-love, Narcissus, had not been a fault,

---

[1] [See " Popular Antiquities of Great Britain," iii. 192.]
[2] This bird is said to give himself a clyster with his beak, to
live on serpents, and to void himself in the manner here alluded
to.—See Pliny's " Natural History," bk. viii. c. 27.

Hadst thou, instead of such a beauteous face,
Had but a brain like mine! I can gild vice,
And praise it into alchemy, till it go
For perfect gold, and cosen almost the touchstone.
I can persuade a toad into an ox,
'Till swelled too big with my hyperboles,
She burst asunder ; and 'tis virtue's name
Lends me a mask to scandalise herself.
Vice, if it be no more, can nothing do :
That art is great makes virtue guilty too.
I have such strange varieties of colours,
Such shifts of shapes, blue Proteus sure begot me
On a cameleon ; and I change so quick,
That I suspect my mother did conceive me,
As they say mares do,[1] on some wind or other.
I'll peep to see, how many fools I made,
With a report of a miraculous glass.
Heaven bless me, I'm ruin'd ! O my brain,
Witty to my undoing ! I have jested
Myself to an eternal misery.
I see lean hunger with her meagre face
Ride post to overtake me : I do prophesy
A Lent immortal. Phœbus, I could curse
Thee and thy brittle gifts ; Pandora's box,
Compared with this, might be esteem'd a blessing.
The glass, which I conceiv'd a fabulous humour,
Is to the height of wonder prov'd a truth ;
The two extremes of every virtue there,
Beholding how they either did exceed
Or want of just proportion, join'd together,

---

1 "*Ora omnes versæ in Zephyrum stant rupibus altis,*
   Exceptantque leves auras : et sæpe sine ullis
   Conjugiis vento gravidæ (mirabile dictu)
   Saxa per et scopulos et depressas convalles
   Diffugiunt ; non, Eure, tuos, neque solis ad ortus,
   In Boream Caurumque, aut unde nigerrimus Auster
   Nascitur, et pluvio contristat frigore cœlum."
—Virgil's " Georgica," [lib. iii. l. 278, *et seq.*, edit. Keightley.]

And are reduced into a perfect mean :
As when the skilful and deep-learn'd physician
Does take two different poisons, one that's cold,
The other in the same degree of heat,
And blends them both to make an antidote ;
Or as the lutenist takes flats and sharps,
And out of those so dissonant notes does strike
A ravishing harmony.   Now there is no vice—
'Tis a hard world for Colax: what shift now?
Dyscolus doth expect me.   Since this age
Is grown too wise to entertain a parasite.
I'll to the glass, and there turn virtuous too,
Still strive to please, though not to flatter you.

   Bird. There is good use indeed, la, to be made
From their conversion.

   Mis. Flo.   Very good in sooth, la,
And edifying.

   Ros.   Give your eyes some respite.
You know already what your vices be,
In the next act you shall your[1] virtues see.   [*Exeunt.*

ACT V., SCENE I.

Roscius, Mistress Flowerdew, Bird.

   Mis. Flo. Now verily I find the devout bee
May suck the honey of good doctrine thence,
And bear it to the hive of her pure family,
Whence the profane and irreligious spider
Gathers her impious venom !   I have pick'd
Out of the garden of this play a good
And wholesome salad of instruction !
What do you next present ?

   Ros.   The several virtues.

---

[1] [Edits., *our.*]

Bird. I hope there be no cardinal-virtues there !
Ros. There be not.
Bird.   Then I'll stay.   I hate a virtue
That will be made a cardinal : cardinal-virtues,
Next to pope-virtues, are most impious.
Bishop-virtues are unwarrantable.
I hate a virtue in a morrice-dance.
I will allow of none but deacon-virtues
Or elder virtues.
Ros.   These are moral virtues.
Bird. Are they lay-virtues ?
Ros.   Yes.
Bird.   Then they are lawful :
Virtues in orders are unsanctified.
Ros. We do present them royal, as they are
In all their state in a full dance.
Bird.   What dance ?
No wanton jig, I hope : no dance is lawful
But prinkum-prankum !
Mis. Flo.   Will virtues dance ?
O vile, absurd, maypole, maid-marian virtue !
Ros. Dancing is lawful, &c.   [*Flourish.*

Enter MEDIOCRITY.

Mis. Flo. Who's this ?
Ros.   It is the mother of virtues.
Mis. Flo. Mother of pearl, I think ; she is so gaudy.
Ros. It is the golden Mediocrity.
Mis. Flo. She looketh like the idol of Cheapside.[1]

---

[1] This was the cross which stood there.   It was erected by
Edward the First at one of the places where the body of his
deceased queen rested in its progress from Herdeby, where she
died, to Westminster Abbey, where she was buried.   This cross
was afterwards frequently repaired, and was ornamented with a
statue of the Virgin Mary ; which being held in great reverence
by the Papists, consequently very highly offended the Puritans

Med. I am that even course, that must be kept
To shun two dangerous gulfs : the middle tract
'Twixt Scylla and Charybdis : the small isthmus,
That suffers not the Ægean tide to meet
The violent rage of the Ionian wave.[1]
I am a bridge o'er an impetuous sea ;
Free and safe passage to the wary step :
But he, whose wantonness or folly dares
Decline to either side, falls desperate
Into a certain ruin.   Dwell with me,
Whose mansion is not plac'd so near the sun,
As to complain of's neighbourhood, and be scorch'd
With his directer beams : nor so remote
From his bright rays as to be situate
Under the icy pole of the cold Bear ;
But in a temperate zone.   'Tis I am she,
I am the golden Mediocrity :
The labour of whose womb are all the virtues,
And every passion too commendable ;
Sisters so like themselves, as if they were
All but one birth ; no difference to distinguish them,
But a respect they bear to several objects :
Else had their names been one, as are their features.
So when eleven fair virgins of a blood,
All sisters, and alike grown ripe of years,
Match into several houses, from each family
Each makes a name distinct, and all are different.
They are not of complexion red or pale,
But a sweet mixture of the flesh and blood,

---

of the times.   When these last obtained the ascendancy in the
State, it cannot be wondered at that what displeased them
should be removed.   One of their first acts of power was an
order for destroying the several crosses, which was executed on
the 2d of May 1643, on that which is the subject of this note.

[1] *" Si terra recedat*
         Ionium Ægeo franget mare."
—Lucan, bk. i.—*Collier.*

As if both roses were confounded there.
Their stature neither dwarf nor giantish.
But in a comely well-dispos'd proportion ;
And all so like their mother, that indeed
They are all mine, and I am each of them.
When in the midst of dangers I stand up,
A wary confidence betwixt fear and daring,
Not so ungodly bold, as not to be
Fearful of Heaven's just anger, when she speaks
In prodigies, and tremble at the hazard
Of my religion, shake to see my country
Threat'ned with fire and sword, be a stark coward
To anything may blast my reputation ;
But I can scorn the worst of poverty,
Sickness, captivity, banishment, grim death,
If she dare meet me in the bed of honour ;
Where, with my country's cause upon my sword—
Not edg'd with hope or anger, nor made bold
With civil blood or customary danger,
Nor the fool's whetstone, inexperience,
I can throw valour as a lightning from me,
And then I am the Amazon Fortitude !
Give me the moderate cup of lawful pleasures,
And I am Temperance. Make me Wealth's just steward,
And call me Liberality : with one hand
I'll gather riches home, and with the other
Rightly distribute 'em, and there observe
The persons, quantity, quality, time and place.
And if in great expenses I be set
Chief arbitress, I can in glorious works,
As raising temples, statues, altars, shrines,
Vestures and ornaments to religion, be
Neither too thrifty nor too prodigal.
And to my country the like mean observe,
In building ships and bulwarks, castles, walls,
Conduits, theatres, and what else may serve her
For use or ornament ; and at home be royal

In buildings, gardens, costly furniture,
In entertainments free and hospitable,
With a respect to my estate and means,
And then I may be nam'd Magnificence;
As Magnanimity, when I wisely aim
At greatest honours, if I may deserve 'em,
Not for ambition, but for my country's good;
And in that virtue all the rest do dwell.
In lesser dignities I want a name;
And when I am not over-patient,
To put up such gross wrongs as call me coward,
But can be angry, yet in that observe,
What cause hath mov'd my anger, and with whom;
Look that it be not sudden, nor too thirsty
Of a revenge, nor violent, nor greater
Than the offence; know my time when [and] where
I must be angry, and how long remain so;
Then, then you may surname me Mansuetude.
When in my carriage and discourse I keep
The mean, that neither flatters nor offends;
I am that virtue the well-nurtur'd court
Gives name, and should do, being Courtesy.
'Twixt sly dissembling and proud arrogance,
I am the virtue Time calls daughter—Truth.
Give me my sword and balance rightly sway'd,
And Justice is the title I deserve.
When on this stage I come with innocent wit,
And jests that have more of the salt than gall;
That move the laughter and delight of all,
Without the grief of one; free, chaste conceits,
Not scurrile, base, obscene, illiberal,
Or contumelious slanders, I am then
The virtue they have term'd Urbanity:
To whom, if your least countenance may appear
She vows to make her constant dwelling here.
My daughters now are come.—

THE SONG.

SCENE II.

The Masque, wherein all the Virtues dance together.

Med. You have seen all my daughters, gentlemen.
Choose your wives hence. You that are bachelors
Can find no better ; and the married too
May wed 'em, yet not wrong their former wives.
Two may have the same wife, and the same man
May wed two virtues, yet no bigamy :
He that weds most, is chastest. These are all
The daughters of my womb : I have five more,
The happy issue of my intellect,
And thence sirnam'd the intellectual virtues.
They now attend not on their mother's train,
We hope they act in each spectator's brain.
I have a niece besides, a beauteous one.
My daughter's dear companion, lovely Friendship,
A royal nymph : her we present not too ;
It is a virtue we expect from you.

       [Exit cum Choro contantium.

SCENE III.

Bird. O sister, what a glorious train they be !
Mis. Flo. They seem to me the Family of Love ;
But is there such a glass, good Roscius ?
Ros. There is, sent hither by the great Apollo
Who, in the world's bright eye and every day
Set in his car of light, surveys the earth
From east to west ; who, finding every place
Fruitful in nothing but fantastic follies
And most ridiculous humours, as he is
The god of physic, thought it appertain'd
To him to find a cure to purge the earth

Of ignorance and sin, two grand diseases,
And now grown epidemical : many receipts
He thought upon, as to have planted hellebore
In every garden : but none pleas'd like this.
He takes out water from the muses' spring,
And sends it to the north, there to be freez'd
Into a crystal : that being done, he makes
A mirror with it, and instils this virtue ;
That it should by reflection show each man
All his deformities, both of soul and body,
And cure 'em both——

 Mis. Flo.   Good brother, let's go see it !
Saints may want something of perfection.

 Ros. The glass is but of one day's continuance ;
For Pluto, thinking if it should cure all,
His kingdom would grow empty (for 'tis sin
That peoples hell), went to the Fates, and bid 'em
Spin it too short a thread (for everything,
As well as man, is measur'd by their spindle) ;
They, as they must obey, gave it a thread
No longer than the beast's of Hypanis,
That in one day is spun, drawn out, and cut.
But Phœbus, to requite the black god's envy,
Will, when the glass is broke, transfuse her virtue
To live in comedy. If you mean to see it,
Make haste.

 Mis. Flo.   We will go post to reformation.
             [*Exeunt.*

 Ros. Nor is the glass of so short life, I fear,
As this poor labour : our distrustful author
Thinks the same sun that rose upon her cradle
Will hardly set before her funeral.
Your gracious and kind acceptance may
Keep her alive from death, or, when she's dead,
Raise her again, and spin her a new thread.

SCENE IV.

Enter MISTRESS FLOWERDEW *and* BIRD.

Mis. Flo. This ignorance even makes religion sin ;
Sets zeal upon the rack, and stretches her
Beyond her length.   Most blessed looking-glass,
That didst instruct my blinded eyes to-day !
I might have gone to hell the narrow way !
   Bird. Hereafter I will visit comedies,
And see them oft ; they are good exercises !
I'll teach devotion now a milder temper ;
Not that it shall lose any of her heat
Or purity, but henceforth shall be such
As shall burn bright, although not blaze so much.
                                                  [*Exeunt.*

EPILOGUE.

ROSCIUS *solus.*

You've seen The Muses' Looking-Glass, ladies fair
And gentle youths : and others too whoe'er
Have fill'd this orb : it is the end we meant :
Yourselves unto yourselves still to present.
A soldier shall himself in Hector see ;
Grave councillors, Nestor, view themselves in thee.
When Lucrece' part shall on our stage appear,
Every chaste lady sees her shadow there.
Nay, come who will, for our indifferent glasses
Will show both fools and knaves, and all their faces,
To vex and cure them : but we need not fear,
We do not doubt but each one now that's here,
That has a fair soul and a beauteous face,
Will visit oft The Muses' Looking-Glass.

AMYNTAS

OR

THE IMPOSSIBLE DOWRY.

EDITIONS.

Amyntas or The Impossible Dowry. A Pastorall Acted before the King & Queene at Whitehall. Written by Thomas Randolph.

Pastorem, Tityre, pingues
Pascere oportet oves, diductum dicere Carmen.

Oxford, Printed by Leonard Lichfield, for Francis Bordman.
1638.

For the other editions, see the account of the "Poems."

"Randolph's 'Amyntas,'" Mr Halliwell remarks ("Dictionary of Old Plays," 1860, in *v.*), "is one of the finest specimens of pastoral poetry in our language, partaking of the best properties of Guarini's and Tasso's poetry, without being a servile imitation of either." The "Amyntas" is, beyond doubt, a fascinating production, and a drama of unusual beauty and power.

Specimens of the piece are given in "Fairy Tales, Legends, and Romances," 1875, 12⁰. It seems not unlikely that the scenes between Damon and Amaryllis were suggested by the somewhat parallel passages found in the "Midsummer Night's Dream."

PROLOGUS.

——o——

NYMPH, SHEPHERD.

Nymph. I'll speak the prologue.

Shep.   Then you do me wrong.

Nymph. Why, dare your sex compete with ours for
   tongue?

Shep. A female prologue!

Nymph.   Yes, as well as male !

Shep. That's a new trick.

Nymph.   And t'other is as stale.

Shep. Men are more eloquent than women made.

Nymph. But women are more powerful to persuade.

Shep. It seems so ; for I dare no more contend.

Nymph. Then best give o'er the strife, and make
   an end.

Shep. I will not yield.

Nymph.   Shall we divide it, then?

Shep. You to the women speak?

Nymph.   You to the men?

  Shep. Gentlemen, look not from us rural swains
For polish'd speech, high lines, or courtly strains :
Expect not we should bring a labour'd scene,
Or compliments ; we ken not what they mean.

  Nymph. And ladies, we poor country girls do come
With such behaviour as we learn'd at home.
How shall we talk to nymphs so trim and gay,
That ne'er saw lady yet but at a *May?*

Shep. His muse is very bashful, should you throw
A snake into her cradle, I do know
She is no Hercules to outlive your ire.

Nymph. One hiss would make the fearful fool
expire,
Without a sting.

Shep.   Gentlemen, do but you
Like this, no matter what the women do.

Nymph. It was a saucy swain thus to conclude !
Ladies, the gentlemen are not so rude,
If they were ever school'd by powerful love,
As to dislike the things you shall approve.
If you but like him, 'twill be greater praise
Than if each muse of nine had fetch'd him bays.

DRAMATIS PERSONÆ.

———0———

PILUMNUS, the high-priest of Ceres: father to Damon and
  Urania.
MEDORUS, father to Laurinda.
CLAIUS, a wild Sylvian, father to Amyntas and Amaryllis.
CHORYMBUS, an under-priest.
DAMON, ⎫
ALEXIS, ⎬ two rivals in Laurinda's love.
AMYNTAS, a man-shepherd.
LAURINDA, a wavering nymph.
URANIA, a sad nymph, enamoured on Amyntas.
AMARYLLIS, a distressed shepherdess, in love with Damon.
THESTYLIS, an old nymph, sister to Claius.
JOCASTUS, a fantastic shepherd and a fairy knight.
BROMIUS, his man, a blunt clown.
MOPSUS, a foolish augur, enamoured on Thestylis.
DORYLAS, a knavish boy.
ECHO.
Chorus of Priests, Shepherds, Nymphs.
Quorum fit mentio, PHILÆBUS, LALAGE, MYCON.

The scene, SICILY, in the Holy Vale.   The time, an astrological
day from noon to noon.

Amyntas.

———o———

ACT I., SCENE I.

LAURINDA, DORYLAS.

Dor. 'TIS news, Laurinda, that will ravish you?
    Lau. How, ravish me? if't be such desperate news,
I pray conceal it.

    Dor.   So I will.

    Lau. Nay, Dorylas, pray tell it, though.

    Dor. 'Tis desperate news: I dare not.

    Lau. But prythee do.

    Dor.   I must conceal it.

    Lau.   Do not.

    Dor. Mistress, you have prevail'd: I will relate it.

    Lau. No matter, though, whether you do or no.

    Dor. No? then I will not tell you.

    Lau. Yet I care not much if I hear it.

    Dor. And I care. not much whether I tell't or no.

    Lau. What is it?

    Dor.   Nothing.

    Lau.   Sweet Dorylas, let me know,

    Dor. What pretty weathercocks these women are!
I serve a mistress here

Fit to have made a planet : she'll wax and wane
Twice in a minute.

    Lau. But, good Dorylas, your news?

    Dor. Why, excellent news!

    Lau. But what?

    Dor. Rare news! news fit——

    Lau. For what?

    Dor. To be concealed : why, mistress,
The rivals, those on whom this powerful face
Doth play the tyrant.

    Lau. Dorylas, what of them?

    Dor. Now, now she wanes : O, for a dainty hus-
    band
To make her a full moon! The amorous couple,
Your brace of sweethearts, Damon and Alexis,
Desire your audience.

    Lau. Is this all your news?
You may conceal it.

    Dor. Now you have heard it told,
I may conceal it! Well, I thank thee, nature,
Thou didst create me man, for I want wit
Enough to make up woman; but, good mistress,
What do you think of Damon?

    Lau. As a man worthy the best of nymphs.

    Dor. What of Alexis?

    Lau. As one that may
Deserve the fairest virgin in Sicilia.

    Dor. What virgin?

    Lau. Proserpine, were she yet Ceres' daughter.

    Dor. And what Damon?

    Lau. He? Ceres' self,
Were she not yet a mother.

    Dor. Crete, Crete!
There is no labyrinth but a woman!
Laurinda, gentle mistress, tell me which
Of these you love?

    Lau. Why, Damon best of any.

Dor. Why so, that's well and plain.
Lau.   Except Alexis.
Dor. Why, then, you love Alexis best?
Lau.   Of any.
Dor. I am glad on't.
Lau.   But my Damon.
Dor.   Be this true,
And I'll be sworn Cupid is turn'd a juggler;
Presto! you love Alexis best, but Damon;
And Damon, but Alexis! Love you Damon?
Lau. I do.
Dor.   And not Alexis?
Lau.   And Alexis.
Dor. She would ha' both, I think.
Lau.   Not I, by Ceres.
Dor. Then you love neither?
Lau.   Yes, I do love either.
Dor. Either, and yet not both! both best, yet
    neither!
Why do you torture those with equal racks,
That both vow service to you. If your love
Have preferr'd Damon, tell Alexis of it;
Or if Alexis, let poor Damon know it,
That he which is refus'd, smothering his flame,
May make another choice. Now doubtful hope
Kindles desire in both.
Lau.   Ah, Dorylas!
Thy years are yet uncapable of love.
Thou hast not learn'd the mysteries of Cupid!
Dost thou not see through all Sicilia,
From gentlest shepherds to the meanest swains,
What inauspicious torches Hymen lights
At every wedding: what unfortunate hands
Link in the wedding ring? Nothing but fears,
Jars, discontents, suspicions, jealousies,
These many years meet in the bridal sheets;
Or if all these be missing, yet a barrenness—

A curse as cruel, or abortive births
Are all the blessings crown the genial bed.
Till the success prove happier, and I find
A blessed change, I'll temper my affection,
Conceal my flames, dissemble all my fires,
And spend those years I owe to love and beauty
Only in choosing on whose love to fix
My love and beauty.

    Dor.   Rare feminine wisdom!
Will you admit 'em?

    Lau.   Yes, go call them hither.
Yet do not, now I think on't : yet, you may too ;
And yet come back again.

    Dor.   Nay, I will go.

    Lau. Why, Dorylas?

    Dor.   What news?

    Lau.   Come back, I say.

    Dor. Yes, to be sent again!

    Lau.   You'll stay, I hope.

    Dor. Not I, by Ceres.

    Lau.   Dorylas.

    Dor.   No, good mistress ;
Farewell, for I at length have learn'd to know
You call me back only to bid me go.   [*Exit.*

    Lau. 'Tis no great matter, sirrah : when they come,
I'll bear myself so equal unto both,
As both shall think I love him best ; this way
I keep both fires alive, that when I please
I may take which I please. But who comes here?

SCENE II.

Enter THESTYLIS.

O Thestylis, y' are welcome !

    Thes.   If, Laurinda,

My too abrupt intrusion come so rudely
As to disturb your private meditations,
I beg your pardon.

Lau.   How now, Thestylis?
Grown orator of late? has learned Mopsus
Read rhetoric unto you, that you come
To see me with exordiums?

Thes.   No, Laurinda;
But if there be a charm call'd rhetoric,
An art, that woods and forests cannot skill,
That with persuasive magic could command
A pity in your soul, I would my tongue
Had learn'd that powerful art!

Lau.   Why, Thestylis,
Thou know'st the breasts I suck'd were neither wolf's
Nor tiger's; and I have a heart of wax,
Soft and soon melting; try this amorous heart, 'tis not
Of flint or marble.

Thes.   If it were, Laurinda,
The tears of her, whose orator I come,
Have power to soften it.   Beauteous Amaryllis—
She that in this unfortunate age of love,
This hapless time of Cupid's tyranny,
Plac'd her affection on a scornful shepherd,
One that disdains her love——

Lau.   Disdains her love!
I tell thee, Thestylis, in my poor judgment
(And women, if no envy blind their eyes,
Best judge of women's beauties), Amaryllis
May make a bride worthy the proudest shepherd
In all Sicilia: but wherein can I
Pity this injur'd nymph?

Thes.   Thus she desires you:
As you desire to thrive in him you love;
As you do love him whom you most desire,
Not to love Damon: Damon, alas! repays
Her love with scorn; 'tis a request she says

She knows you cannot grant ; but if you do not,
She will not live to ask again.
    Lau.   Poor nymph !
My Amaryllis knows my fidelity.
How often have we sported on the lawns,
And danc'd a roundelay to Jocastus' pipe !
If I can do her service, Thestylis,
Be sure I will. Good wench, I dare not stay,
Lest I displease my father who, in this age
Of hapless lovers, watches me as close
As did the dragon the Hesperian fruit.
Farewell !
    Thes. Farewell, Laurinda ! Thus, poor fool,
I toil for others like the painful bee,
From every flower cull honey-drops of love
To bring to others' hives : Cupid does this,
'Cause I am Claius' sister. Other nymphs
Have their variety of loves for every gown,
Nay, every petticoat ; I have only one,
The poor fool Mopsus ! Yet no matter, wench,
Fools never were in more request than now.
I'll make much of him ; for that woman lies
In weary sheets whose husband is too wise.

SCENE III.

THESTYLIS, MOPSUS, JOCASTUS.

    Mop. Jocastus, I love Thestylis abominably,
The mouth of my affection waters at her.
    Joc. Be wary, Mopsus ; learn of me to scorn
The mortals ; choose a better match : go love
Some fairy lady ! Princely Oberon
Shall stand thy friend : and beauteous Mab, his queen,
Give thee a maid-of-honour.
    Mop.   How, Jocastus,

Marry a puppet? wed a mote i' th' sun?
Go look a wife in nutshells? woo a gnat,
That's nothing but a voice?　No, no, Jocastus,
I must have flesh and blood, and will have Thestylis.
A fig for fairies!
　　Thes.　　　　'Tis my sweetheart Mopsus
And his wise brother.　O, the twins of folly!
These do I entertain only to season
The poor Amyntas' madness.
　　Mop.　　　　　　Sacred red and white!
How fares thy reverend beauty?
　　Thes.　　　　　　Very ill.
Since you were absent, Mopsus! where have you
Been all this livelong hour?
　　Mop.　　　　　I have been
Discoursing with the birds.
　　Thes.　　　　　Why, can birds speak?
　　Joc. In fairyland they can: I have heard 'em
　　chirp
Very good Greek and Latin.
　　Mop.　　　　　And our birds
Talk better far than they: a new-laid egg
Of Sicilia shall out-talk the bravest parrot
In Oberon's Utopia.
　　Thes.　　　　But what languages
Do they speak, servant?
　　Mop.　　　　　Several languages,
As Cawation, Chirpation, Hootation,
Whistleation, Crowation, Cackleation,
Shriekation, Hissation——
　　Thes.　　　　　And Foolation?
　　Mop. No, that's our language: we ourselves speak
　　that,
That are the learned augurs.
　　Thes.　　　　　What success
Does your art promise?
　　Mop.　　　　Very good.

Thes.　　　　　　　　　　　What birds
Met you then first?
　　Mop.　　　　　　A woodcock and a goose.
　　Thes. Well met.
　　Mop.　　　　I told 'm so.
　　Thes.　　　　　　　And what might this portend?
　　Mop. Why thus—and first the woodcock—wood
　　　and cock—
Both very good signs.　For first the wood doth signify
The fire of our love shall never go out,
Because it has more fuel (wood doth signify
More fuel).
　　Thes.　　What the cock?
　　Mop.　　　　　　　　　Better than t'other:
That I shall crow o'er those that are my rivals,
And roost myself with thee.
　　Thes.　　　　　　　　But now the goose?
　　Mop. Ay, ay; the goose—that likes me best of all,
Th' hast heard our greybeard shepherds talk of
　　　Rome,
And what the geese did there?　The goose doth
　　　signify
That I shall keep thy capitol.
　　Thes.　　　　　　　Good gander!
　　Joc. It cannot choose but strangely please his
　　　highness!
　　Thes. What are you studying of, Jocastus, ha?
　　Joc. A rare device, a masque to entertain
His grace of fairy with.
　　Thes.　　　　　　A masque! what is't?
　　Joc. An anti-masque of fleas, which I have taught
To dance corantoes on a spider's thread.
　　Mop. An anti-masque of fleas? brother, methinks
A masque of birds were better, that could dance
The morrice in the air, wrens and robin-redbreasts,
Linnets and titmice.
　　Joc.　　　　　So! and why not rather

Your geese and woodcocks? Mortal, hold thy tongue,
Thou dost not know the mystery.
    Thes.   'Tis true.
He tells you, Mopsus, leave your augury;
Follow his counsel, and be wise.
    Mop.   Be wise?
I scorn the motion! follow his counsel, and be
    wise?
That's a fine trick, i' faith! Is this an age
For to be wise in?
    Thes.   Then you mean, I see,
T' expound the oracle.
    Mop.   I do mean to be
Th' interpreter.
    Joc.   —And then a jig of pismires
Is excellent.
    Mop.   What, to interpret oracles?
A fool must be th' interpreter.
    Thes.   Then no doubt
But you will have the honour.
    Mop.   Nay, I hope
I am as fair for't as another man.
If I should now grow wise against my will,
And catch this wisdom!
    Thes.   Never fear it, Mopsus.
    Mop. 'Twere dangerous vent'ring. Now I think
    on't too,
Pray heaven this air be wholesome! is there not
An antidote against it? What do you think
Of garlic every morning?
    Thes.   Fie upon't,
'Twill spoil our kissing! and besides, I tell you
Garlic's a dangerous dish; eating of garlic
May breed the sickness; for, as I remember,
'Tis the philosopher's diet.
    Mop.   Certainly
I am infected, now the fit's upon me!

'Tis something like an ague : sure, I caught it
With talking with a scholar next my heart.
   Thes.   How sad a life live I,
Betwixt their folly and Amyntas' madness !   [*Aside.*
For Mopsus, I'll prescribe you such a diet
As shall secure you.
   Mop.   Excellent she-doctor !
Your women are the best physicians,
And have the better practice.
   Thes.   First, my Mopsus,
Take heed of fasting, for your hungry meals
Nurse wisdom.
   Mop.   True ! O, what a stomach have I,
To be her patient !
   Thes.   Besides, take special care
You wear not threadbare clothes : 'twill breed at least
Suspicion you are wise.
   Joc.   Ay, marry, will it.
   Thes. And walk not much alone ; or if you walk
With company, be sure you walk with fools—
None of the wise.
   Mop.   No, no, I warrant you,
I'll walk with nobody but my brother here,
Or you, or mad Amyntas.
   Thes.   By all means
Take heed of travel; your beyond-sea wit
Is to be fear'd.
   Mop.   If e'er I travel, hang me.
   Joc. Not to the fairyland ?
   Thes.   Thither he may.
But, above all things, wear no beard : long beards
Are signs the brains are full, because the excrements
Come out so plentifully.
   Joc.   Rather, empty !
Because they have sent so much out, as if
Their brains were sunk into their beards. King Oberon

Has ne'er a beard, yet for his wit I am sure
He might have been a giant.   Who comes here?

Enter DORYLAS.

Dor. All hail unto the fam'd interpreter
Of fowls and oracles !
Mop.   Thanks, good Dorylas.
Dor. How fares the winged cattle? are the wood-
    cocks,
The jays, the daws, the cuckoos, and the owls
In health?
Mop.   I thank the gracious stars they are.
Dor. Like health unto the president of the jigs,
I hope King Oberon and his royal Mab
Are well.
Joc.   They are : I never saw their graces
Eat such a meal before.
Dor.   E'en much good do 't 'em !
Joc. They're rid a-hunting.
Dor.   Hare or deer, my lord?
Joc. Neither : a brace of snails of the first head.
Thes. But, Dorylas, there is a mighty quarrel
    here,
And you are chosen umpire.
Dor.   About what?
Thes. The exposition of the oracle.
Which of these two you think the verier fool.
Dor. It is a difficult cause ; first let me pose 'em.
You, Mopsus, 'cause you are a learned augur,
How many are the seven liberal sciences?
Mop. Why, much about a dozen.
Dor.   You, Jocastus,
When Oberon shav'd himself, who was his barber?
Joc. I knew him well, a little dapper youth :
They call him Periwinkle.

Dor.   Thestylis,
A weighty cause, and asks a longer time.
Thes. We'll in the while to comfort sad Amyntas.
[*Exeunt* Thestylis, Mopsus, Jocastus.

SCENE IV.

Laurinda; *to her* Dorylas.

Lau. I wonder much that Dorylas stays so long;
Fain would I hear whether they'll come or no.
Dor. Ha! would you so?
Lau.   I see in your messages
You can go fast enough.
Dor.   Indeed, forsooth,
I loiter'd by the way.
Lau.   What, will they come?
Dor. Which of them?
Lau.   Damon.
Dor.   No.
Lau. Alexis will?
Dor.   Nor he.
Lau. How, neither? am I then neglected?
Dor. Damon will come.
Lau.   And not Alexis too?
Dor. Only Alexis comes.
Lau.   Let him not come.
I wonder who sent for him; unless both,
I'll speak with none.
Dor.   Why, both will visit you.
Lau. Both? one had been too many. Was e'er nymph
So vex'd as I? you saucy rascal, you,
How do you strive to cross me?
Dor.   And, sweet mistress,
Still I will cross you: 'tis the only way
Truly to please you.

SCENE V.

Enter MEDORUS.

Med. So, you'll all please her!
I wonder who'll please me? you all for her
Can run on errands, carry lovesick letters
And amorous eclogues from her howling suitors.
To her and back again; be Cupid's heralds,
And point out meetings for her.
    Dor. Truly, sir,
Not I: pray ask my mistress.
Your sweethearts—speak—nay, speak it, if you can;
Do I?
    Lau. Why, no.
    Dor. Nay, say your worst, I care not,
Did I go ever?
    Lau. Never.
    Dor. La you now!
We were devising nothing but a snare
To catch the polecat.
    Med. Sirrah, get you in;
Take heed I do not find your haunts.
    Dor. What haunts?
    Med. You'll in?
    Dor. I know no haunts I have but to the dairy,
To skim the milk-bowls like a liquorish fairy.
                 [*Exit* DORYLAS.
    Med. He that's a woman's keeper should have eyes
A hundred more than Argus, and his ears
Double the number. Now the news? what letters?
What posy, ring, or bracelet woos to-day?
What grove to-night is conscious of your whispers?
Come, tell me; for I fear your trusty squire—
Your little closet blabs into your ear
Some secret—let me know it.

Lau.   Then you fear
Lest I should be in love.
    Med.   Indeed I do,
Cupid's a dangerous boy, and often wounds
The wanton roving eye.
    Lau.   Were I in love
(Not that I am! for yet, by Diana's bow,
I have not made my choice), and yet suppose—
Suppose I say I were in love, what then?
    Med. So I would have thee, but not yet, my girl,
Till loves prove happier, till the wretched Claius
Hath satisfied the gods.
    Lau.   Why Claius, father?
    Med. Hast thou not heard it?
    Lau.   Never.
    Med.   'Tis impossible.
    Lau. How should I, sir? you know that my
      discourse
Is all with walls and pictures, I ne'er meet
The virgins on the downs.
    Med.   Why, I will tell thee.
Thou knowest Pilumnus?
    Lau.   The high-priest of Ceres?
    Med. Yes.   This Pilumnus had a son Philæbus,
Who was, while yet he was, the only joy,
The staff and comfort of his father's age,
And might have still been so, had not fond love
Undone him.
    Lau.   How did love undo Philæbus?
    Med. Why, thus: one Lalage, a beauteous nymph
As ever eye admired, Alphestus' daughter,
Was by her father promis'd him in marriage.
    Lau. Why, hitherto his love had good success.
    Med. But only promis'd; for the shepherd Claius
(A man accursed in Sicilian fields),
Being rich, obtained the beauteous Lalage
From sweet Philæbus: he (sad heart), being robb'd

Of all his comfort—having lost the beauty
Which gave him life and motion—seeing Claius
Enjoy those lips whose cherries were the food
That nurs'd his soul, spent all his time in sorrow,
In melancholy sighs and discontents ;
Look'd like a wither'd tree o'ergrown with moss ;
His eyes were ever dropping icicles :
Disdain and sorrow made Pilumnus rage,
And in this rage he makes his moan to Ceres
(Ceres, most sacred of Sicilian powers),
And in those moans he prosecutes revenge,
And that revenge to fall on Lalage.
    Lau. Would Ceres hear his prayers ?
    Med.   Silly maid !
His passions were not causeless ; and with what justice
Could she deny Pilumnus ? how oft hath he sprinkled
The finest flower of wheat and sweetest myrrh
Upon her altars ? Lalage ru'd the time
She flouted brave Philæbus. Now she was great
With two sweet twins, the fair, chaste Amaryllis
And mad Amyntas (an unlucky pair) ;
These she brought forth, but never liv'd to see
    them.
Lucina caus'd her sorrows stop her breath,
Leaving this matchless pair of beauteous infants,
In whom till now she lives.
    Lau.   After her death,
How far'd the sorrowful Philæbus ?
    Med.   Worse
Than ever. She being dead whose life was his,
Whose looks did hold his eyes from shutting up,
He pin'd away in sorrows ; grief it was
To see she was not his, but greater far
That she was not at all. Her exequies being past,
He casts him down upon that turf of earth,
Under whose roof his Lalage was hous'd,
And parleyed with her ashes, till his own lamp

Was quite extinguish'd with a fatal damp.
Here ended th' noble shepherd.
    Lau.   Unhappy lover!
'Tis pity, but the virgins once a year
Should wash his tomb with maiden tears! but now,
Both Lalage being dead and her Philæbus,
How comes it other loves should prove unfortunate?
    Med. Pilumnus having lost his hopeful son,
Though he had two more children, fair Urania
And noble Damon; yet the death of Lalage
Suffic'd not his revenge, but he anew implores
His goddess' wrath 'gainst Claius.—Doth Ceres prize
    me thus?
Shall Claius tread upon the flow'ry plain,
And walk upon the ashes of my body?
Will I be archflamen, where the gods
Are so remiss? let wolves approach their shrines,
Their howlings are as powerful as the prayers
Of sad Pilumnus! Such disgusts at last
Awaken'd Ceres: with hollow murmuring noise
Her Ompha like a thunder 'gins to roar
(The Ompha, if it menace, speaks at large
In copious language, but perplexed terms),
And laid this curse on all Trinacria:

> *Sicilian swains, ill-luck shall long betide*
> *To every bridegroom and to every bride;*
> *No sacrifice, no vow shall still mine ire,*
> *Till Claius' blood both quench and kindle fire;*
> *The wise shall misconceive me, and the wit,*
> *Scorn'd and neglected, shall my meaning hit.*

    Lau. Angry and intricate! Alas for love!
What then became of Claius?
    Med.   Why, the Ompha
Having denounc'd against him, and he knowing
The hate of old Pilumnus, fled away;
I think he's sail'd to the Antipodes;

No tidings can be brought what ground receives him ;
Unless Chorymbus make a happy voyage—
Chorymbus, that will search both east and occident,
And when he finds him, spill his captive blood.
Which Ceres grant he may, tender Laurinda.
Now dost thou see the reason of my care,
And why my watchful eyes so close observe
Thy steps and actions.
  Lau.   And I promise, father,
To temper my affections till the goddess
Do mitigate her anger.
  Med.   Do so, then ;
For now you see with what unfortunate choice
Pilumnus' daughter, delicate Urania, loves
The mad Amyntas ; for the angry goddess,
Though she repaid the wrong done to Philæbus,
Yet, not approving the revengeful mind
Of great Pilumnus, scourg'd him with his own asking,
By threat'ning an unhappy marriage
To his Urania, unless he that woos her
Pay an impossible dowry ; for as others
Give portions with their daughters, Ceres' priests
Use to receive for theirs. The words are these—

> *That which thou hast not, may'st not, canst not have,*
> *Amyntas, is the dowry that I crave.*
> *Rest hopeless in thy love, or else divine*
> *To give Urania this, and she is thine.*

Which, while the poor Amyntas would interpret,
He lost his wits. Take heed of love, Laurinda,
You see th' unhappiness of it in others ;
Let not experience in thyself instruct thee ;
Be wise, my girl, so come and follow me. [*Exit.*
  Lau. I'll make a garland for my kid, and follow you.
What a sad tale was here ! how full of sorrow !
Happy that heart that never felt the shaft
Of angry Cupid !

SCENE VI.

Enter DAMON *and* ALEXIS.

Damon and Alexis!
Their presence quickly puts these cogitations
Out of my mind. Poor souls'! I fain would pity
    them,
And yet I cannot; for to pity one
Were not to pity t'other, and to pity
Both were to pity neither. Mine old temper
Is all the shift I have—some dew of comfort
To either of them. [*Aside.*] How now, bold in-
    truders,
How dare you venture on my privacy?
If you must needs have this walk, be it so,
I'll seek another. What, you'll let me go?
    Damon. Cruel Laurinda (if a word so foul
Can have so fair a dwelling), seal not up
Thy ears, but let a pity enter there
And find a passage to thy heart.
    Alexis.   Laurinda
(The name which but to speak I would not wish
For life or breath), let not thy powerful beauty
Torment us longer: tell us which of us
You value most.
    Damon.   ——and t'other, for old friendship,
Strangling his bitter corrosive in his heart,
Hath promis'd to desist from further suit.
    Alexis. ——or if he cannot so (as, sure, he cannot),
Yet he will rather choose to die than live
Once to oppose your liking.
    Lau.   Since you are
Grown so importunate, and will not be answer'd
With modest silence, know, I wish you well.
    Alexis. How? me, Laurinda?

Lau.   Why, I wish, Alexis,
I were thy wife.
 Damon.   Then most unhappy me!
 Alexis. That word doth relish immortality.
 Lau. And I do wish thou wert my husband, Damon.
 Alexis. Still more perplex'd! What do you think
  I am?
 Lau. My head, Alexis.
 Damon.   And what I?
 Lau.   My heart.
 Damon. Which hand am I?
 Lau.   Damon, my right.
 Alexis.   Which I?
 Lau. My left, Alexis.
 Alexis.   Thus you scorn my love?
 Lau. Not I, Alexis : th' art my only hope.
 Damon. Then I am all despair : no hope for me.
 Lau. Why so, my Damon? thou art my desire.
Alexis is my flame, Damon my fire.
Alexis doth deserve my nuptial-bed,
And Damon's worthy of my maidenhead!
       [*Exit* LAURINDA.
 Alexis. Damon, desist thy suit, or lose thy life.
Thou heardst Laurinda wish she were my wife.
 Damon. Thy wife, Alexis? But how can it be
Without a husband? and I must be he.
 Alexis. I am her head: that word doth seem t' impart
She means me [1] marriage.
 Damon.   How without her heart?
For that am I : besides, you heard her say
I was the right hand, you the left. Away,
Desist, Alexis ; mine's the upper hand.
 Alexis. But, Damon, I next to her heart do stand,
I am her hope ; in that you plainly see,
The end of her intents doth aim at me.

---

[1] Old copies, *my.*

Damon. But I am her desire, in that 'tis shown
Her only wish is to make me her own.
Alexis. I am her flame.
Damon.   'Tis true ; but I her fire.
Alexis. The flame's the hotter, therefore her desire
Most aims at me.
Damon.   Yet when the flame is spent,
The fire continues ; therefore me she meant.
Alexis. She promis'd now I should enjoy her bed.
Damon. Alexis, do ; so I her maidenhead.
Alexis. I see she still conceals it, and with speeches
Perplex'd and doubtful masks her secret thoughts.
Damon. Let's have another meeting, since her
   words
Delude us thus ; we'll have a pregnant sign
To show her mind.
Alexis.   I go that way a-hunting,
And will call for her.
Damon.   I'll the while retire
Into the temple ; if I linger here,
I'm afraid of meeting Amaryllis,
Who with unwelcome love solicits me.
Alexis.   And would she might prevail ! [*Aside.*
Damon. Till then, farewell.
Alexis.   All happiness to Damon be,
Except Laurinda.
Damon.   All but hers to thee.
Alexis. Thus we in love and courtesy contend.
Damon. The name of rival should not lose the
   friend.   [*Exeunt.*

ACT II., SCENE I.

Pilumnus, Urania.

Ura. Father, persuade me not ! The power of
   heaven

Can never force me from Amyntas' love ;
'Tis rooted here so deep within my heart,
That he which pulls it out, pulls out at once
That and my soul together.
  Pil.   Fond Urania !
Can ignorant love make thee affect the seed,
The hateful seed of cursed Lalage ?
Did I for this beget thee.
  Ura.   Father, you know
Divinity is powerful ; Cupid's will
Must not be question'd. When love means to sport
(I have heard yourself relate it), he can make
The wolf and lamb kiss kindly ; force the lion
T' forget his majesty, and in amorous dalliance
Sport with the frisking kid. When Venus rides,
She'll link the ravenous kite and milder swan
To the same chariot, and will yoke together
The necks of doves and eagles ; whenas she
Commands, all things lose their antipathy,
Even contrarieties. Can I alone
Resist her will ? I cannot ; my Amyntas
Shall witness that !
  Pil.   I blame thee not so much
For loving him while yet he was Amyntas ;
But being mad, and having lost himself,
Why shouldst not thou lose thy affection too ?
  Ura. I love him now the rather he hath lost
Himself for me ; and should he lose me too ?
It were a sin he should !
  Pil.   What canst thou love
In his distemper'd wildness ?
  Ura.   Only that—
His wildness ; 'tis the comfort I have left
To make my tears keep time to his distractions,
To think as wildly as he talks ; to marry
Our griefs together, since ourselves we cannot.
The oracle doth ask so strange a dowry,

That now his company is the only bliss
My love can aim at.   But I stay too long,
I'll in to comfort him.
    Pil.   Do not, Urania.
    Ura.   Do not?
I must and will ; nature commands me no,
But love more powerful says it shall be so.   [*Exit.*
    Pil. The gods did well to make their destinies
Of women, that their wills might stand for law
Fix'd and unchang'd.   Who's this ?   Chorymbus.

SCENE II.

Enter CHORYMBUS.

    Pil. Chorymbus, welcome.
    Chor.   Sacred Pilumnus, hail !
And, fruitful Sicily, I kiss thy dust.
    Pil. What news, Chorymbus ? is our country's mis-
    chief
Fetter'd in chains ?
    Chor.   Thrice the sun hath past
Through the twelve inns of heaven since my diligence
Has been employ'd in quest of him whose death
Must give poor lovers life, the hateful Claius ;
Yet could I ne'er hear of him.   The meanwhile,
How fare the poor Sicilians ?   Does awful Ceres
Still bend her angry brow ?   Find the sad lovers
No rest, no quiet yet ?
    Pil.   Chorymbus, none !
The goddess has not yet deign'd to accept
One sacrifice ; no favourable Echo
Resounded from her Ompha ; all her answers
Are dull and doubtful.
    Chor.   The true sign, Pilumnus,
Her wrath is not appeas'd.

Pil. Appeas'd, say you?
Rather again incens'd so far, Chorymbus,
As that myself am plagu'd; my poor Urania
Doats on Amyntas.
 Chor. First shall our hives swarm in the venomous
  yew,
And goats shall browse upon our myrtle wands!
One of our blood, Pilumnus (is it possible?)
Love Lalage's and Claius' brood?
 Pil. The chain of fate
Will have it so! And he lov'd her as much
 Chor. That makes it something better.
 Pil. Ah! thou knowest not
What sting this waspish fortune pricks me with.
I, seeing their loves so constant, so inflexible,
Chid with Dame Ceres, 'cause she us'd me thus.
My words were inconsiderate; and the heavens
Punish'd my rough expostulations.
Being Archiflamen of Trinacria,
I did demand a dowry of that shepherd
That asks my daughter. Set the price, said I,
Thou goddess, that dost cause such hateful loves;
If that Amyntas be thy darling swain,
Ask thou, and set a dowry for Urania.
With that the altar groan'd; my hair grew stiff,
Amyntas look'd aghast, Urania quiver'd,
And the Ompha answer'd.
 Chor. With an Echo?
 Pil. No.
 Chor. Then I presage some ill!
 Pil. This dark demand.

That which thou hast not, may'st not, canst not have,
Amyntas, is the dowry that I crave.
Rest hopeless in thy love, or else divine
To give Urania this, and she is thine.

And so he did; but the perplexed sense

Troubled his brains so far he lost his wits ;
Yet still he loves, and she—— My grief, Chorymbus,
Will not permit me to relate the rest.
I'll in into the temple, and express.
What's yet behind in tears.   [*Exit.*
   Chor.   Sad, sad Pilumnus !
And most distress'd Sicilians ! other nations
Are happy in their loves ; you only are unfortunate !
In all my travels ne'er a spring but had
Her pair of lovers, singing to that music.
The gentle bubbling of her waters made.
Never a walk unstor'd with amorous couples
Twin'd with so close embraces, as if both
Meant to grow one together ! every shade
Shelter'd some happy loves that, counting daisies,
Scor'd up the sums on one another's lips
That met so oft and close, as if they had
Chang'd souls at every kiss.   The married sort
As sweet and kind as they : at every evening
The loving husband and full-breasted wife
Walk'd on the downs so friendly, as if that
Had been their wedding-day.   The boys of five
And girls of four, e'er that their lisping tongues
Had learn'd to prattle plain, would prate of love,
Court one another, and in wanton dalliance
Return such innocent kisses, you'd have thought
You had seen turtles billing.

SCENE III.

Enter MOPSUS.

   Mop. What air is that ?   *The voice of turtles billing ?*
Of turtles ! a good omen ! she is chaste—
And *billing, billing,* O delicious *billing !*
That word presages kissing.

Chor.   Who is this?
Mopsus, my learned augur?
  Mop.   Stand aside—
The other side. I will not talk to thee,
Unless I have the wind.
    Chor.   Why, what's the matter, Mopsus?
    Mop. Th' art infected.
    Chor.   What, with the plague?
    Mop. Worse than the plague, the wisdom!
You have been in travel; and that's dangerous
For getting wisdom.
    Chor.   Then ne'er fear it, Mopsus,
For *I* come home a fool just as I went.
    Mop. By Ceres?
    Chor.   Yes.
    Mop.   By Ceres, welcome then.
    Chor. But, Mopsus, why do you walk here alone?
That's dangerous too.
    Mop.   Ay; but I come to meet
The citizens of the air; you have heard my skill
In augury?
    Chor.   Why, I have heard your name
Not mention'd anywhere in all my travels.
  Mop. How? not mention'd?
    Chor.   Y' are too hasty, Mopsus,
Not without admiration.
    Mop.   I know that.
    Chor. How should you know it?
    Mop.   Why, some birds or other
Fly from all countries hither, and they tell me.
    Chor. But how dare you converse with birds that
      travel?
    Mop. With an antidote I may; but, my Chorymbus,
What strange birds have you seen beyond seas?
    Chor.   Brave ones:
Ladies with fans and feathers! dainty fowls!
There were brave taking augury!

Mop.   But, Chorymbus,
Are those fine ladybirds such pretty things?
   Chor. As tame as sparrows, and as sweet as
      nightingales.
   Mop. Is the cock ladybird or the hen ladybird
The better?
   Chor.   All are hens.
   Mop.   O, admirable!
Would you had brought me one! But what's the fan?
   Chor. A fan's a—wing of one side.
   Mop.   Delicate!
And what's their feather?
   Chor.   Like the copple crown
The lapwing has.
   Mop.   The lapwing? then they'll lie.
   Chor. With men they will.
   Mop.   Delicious ladybirds!
But have they such brave trains, such curious tails
As our birds have?
   Chor.   Like peacocks; there's the head
Of all their pride.
   Mop.   Nay, 'tis the tail, Chorymbus,
Surely these things you call the ladybirds
Are the true birds of Paradise?

            Enter CHORYMBUS' *carriage.*

   Chor.   Very right.
Mopsus, I cannot stay, I must attend
My carriage to the temple: gentle Mopsus,
Farewell.
   Mop.   Farewell, Chorymbus! By my troth,
I never long'd for anything in my life
So much as ladybirds—dainty ladybirds!
I would fetch one of them, but I dare not travel
For fear I catch the wisdom. O sweet ladybirds!
With copple crowns, and wings but on one side!
And tails like peacocks! Curious ladybirds!

SCENE IV.

AMYNTAS, URANIA, AMARYLLIS. *Manet* MOPSUS.

Amyn. *That which I have not, may not, cannot have!*
It is the moon! Urania, thou shalt wear
The horned goddess at thy beauteous ear.
Come hither, Pegasus, I will mount thy back,
And spur thee to her orb.

Mop.   O good Amyntas!

Amyn. Why, art thou foundered, Pegasus?
    Amaryllis,
Fetch him a peck of provender.

Ura.   Sweet Amyntas!

Amyn. What says my Cytherea? wouldst thou eat
A golden apple? If thou wilt, by Venus,
I'll rob the Hesperian orchard.

Mop.   Ha, ha, he!

Amyn. Ha? dost thou laugh, old Charon? sirrah
    sculler,
Prepare thy boat.

Ama.   For what? dear brother, speak!

Amyn. Art thou my sister Helen? were we hatch'd
In the same egg-shell?—Is your cock-boat ready?

Mop. It is, an't please your worship.

Amyn.   Very well!
Row me to hell!—no faster! I will have thee
Chain'd unto Pluto's galleys.

Ura.   Why to hell,
My dear Amyntas?

Amyn.   Why? to borrow money!

Ama. Borrow there?

Amyn. Ay, there! they say there be more usurers
    there
Than all the world besides. See how the winds
Rise! Puff, puff, Boreas, what a cloud comes yonder,
Take heed of that wave, Charon! ha! give me

The oars!—so, so; the boat is overthrown,
Now Charon's drowned, but I will swim to shore.

    Ura. O Ceres, now behold him! can thy eyes
Look on so sad an object, and not melt
Them and thy heart to pity?

    Ama.   How this grief
Racks my tormented soul! but the neglect
Of Damon more afflicts me: the whole senate
Of heaven decrees my ruin.

    Ura.   And mine too.
Come, Amaryllis, let's weep both together,
Contending in our sorrows!

    Ama.   Would to Ceres
That I were dead!

    Ura.   And I had ne'er been born!

    Amyn. Then had not I been wretched!

    Ura.   Then Amyntas
Might have been happy.

    Mop.   Nay, if you begin
Once to talk wisely, 'tis above high time
That I were gone: farewell, Bellerophon.
I must go seek my Thestylis. She's not here. [*Exit.*

    Amyn. My arms are weary; now I sink, I sink!
Farewell, Urania.

    Ama.   Alas! what strange distractions
Toss his distempered brain!

    Ura.   Yet still his love to me
Lives constant.

    Amyn.   Styx, I thank thee! that curl'd wave
Hath toss'd me on the shore—come, Sisyphus,
I'll roll thy stone awhile: methinks this labour
Doth look like love! does it not, Tisiphone?

    Ama. Mine is that restless toil.

    Amyn.   Is't so, Erynnis?
You are an idle huswife; go and spin
At poor Ixion's wheel.

    Ura.   Amyntas!

Amyn. Ha?
Am I known here?
   Ura.   Amyntas, dear Amyntas!
   Amyn. Who calls Amyntas? beauteous Proserpine?
'Tis she.—Fair empress of the Elysian shades,
Ceres' bright daughter, intercede for me
To thy incensed mother: prythee, bid her
Leave talking riddles, wilt thou?
   Ura.   How shall I
Apply myself to his wild passions?
   Ama.   Seem to be
What he conceives you.
   Amyn.   Queen of darkness,
Thou supreme lady of eternal night.
Grant my petitions! wilt thou beg of Ceres
That I may have Urania?
   Ura.   'Tis my prayer,
And shall be ever, I will promise thee
She shall have none but him.
   Amyn.   Thanks, Proserpine.
   Ura. Come, sweet Amyntas, rest thy troubled head
Here in my lap.—Now here I hold at once
My sorrow and my comfort. Nay, lie still.
   Amyn. I will, but Proserpine——
   Ura.   Nay, good Amyntas——
   Amyn. Should Pluto chance to spy me, would
    not he
Be jealous of me?
   Ura.   No.
   Amyn.   Tisiphone,
Tell not Urania of it, lest she fear
I am in love with Proserpine: do not, fury.
   Ama.   I will not.
   Ura. Pray, lie still!
   Amyn.   [Know] you, Proserpine,
There is in Sicily the fairest virgin
That ever blest the land, that ever breath'd:

Sweeter than Zephyrus! didst thou never hear
Of one Urania?
   Ura.   Yes.
   Amyn.   This poor Urania
Loves an unfortunate shepherd, one that's mad,
    Tisiphone,
Canst thou believe it? Elegant Urania
(I cannot speak it without tears) still loves
Amyntas, the distracted mad Amyntas.
Is't not a constant nymph?—But I will go
And carry all Elysium on my back,
And that shall be her jointure.
   Ura.   Good Amyntas,
Rest here awhile.
   Amyn.   Why weep you, Proserpine?
   Ura. Because Urania weeps to see Amyntas
So restless and unquiet.
   Amyn.   Does she so?
Then will I lie as calm as doth the sea
When all the winds are lock'd in Æolus' jail;
I will not move a hair, nor let a nerve
Or pulse to beat, lest I disturb her. Hush!
She sleeps!
   Ura.   And so do you.
   Amyn. You talk too loud,
You'll waken my Urania.
   Ura.   If Amyntas—
Her dear Amyntas, would but take his rest,
Urania could not want it.
   Amyn.   Not so loud.
   Ama. What a sad pair are we?
   Ura.   How miserable!
He that I love is not!
   Ama.   And he that I
Do love, loves not; or, if he love, not me.
   Ura. I have undone Amyntas!
   Ama.   And my Damon
Has undone me.

Ura.   My kindness ruin'd him.

Ama. But his unkindness me, unhappy me !

Ura. More wretched I ; for Damon has his reason,
And he may love.

Ama.   But does not thy Amyntas
Return thee mutual love ?

Ura.   True, Amaryllis ;
But he has lost his reason.   Mine has love,
No reason.

Ama.   Mine has reason, but no love.
O me !

Ura. My Amaryllis, how thy griefs
Meet full with mine to make the truest story
Of perfect sorrow that e'er eye bedew'd
With tears of pity !

Ama.   Come, Urania ;
Let's sit together like to marble monuments
Of ever-weeping misery.

Enter DAMON.

Damon.   Minds in love
Do count their days by minutes : measure hours
By every sand that drops through the slow glass,
And for each vie a tear.

Ama.   If so, my Damon,
How many times hath thy unkindness ruin'd
Sad Amaryllis ? every frown is mortal.

Damon. Ill luck, to seek my love and find my hate.

Ama. Be not so cruel to me !   Gentle Damon,
Accept this witness of my love : it is
The story of poor Echo, that for love
Of her Narcissus pin'd into a voice.

Damon. Do thou so too.

Ama.   Damon, suppose I should,
And then the gods for thy contempt of me
Should plague thee like Narcissus.

Damon. Amaryllis,
They cannot do it; I have fix'd my love
So firm on my Laurinda, that for her
I e'er shall hate myself.

  Ama. Prythee, love, accept it,
'Twas wrought by mine own hand.

  Damon. For that I hate it!

  Ura. Fie, brother! can you be of the same stock,
Issue, and blood with me, and yet so cruel?

  Damon. Nor can I, sister, doat like you on any,
That is the cursed brat of Lalage.

  Amyn. Sayest thou so, Centaur?

  Ura. Good Amyntas, hold,
This is the Sacred Valley: here 'tis death
For to shed human blood.

  Damon. Still idly you complain
To cross me, Amaryllis, but in vain!   [*Exit.*

  Ama. O, I am sick to death!

  Amyn. What a brave show
The monster's brains would make!

SCENE V.

Thestylis, Mopsus, Amyntas, Amaryllis, Urania.

  Ama. My grief o'erweighs me!

  Thes. How fares my Amaryllis?

  Ama. Like a taper
Almost burnt out: sometimes all a' darkness,
And now and then a flash or two of comfort,
But soon blown out again. Ah, Thestylis!
I cannot long subsist; for thee, vain labour,
Away! I hate thee, 'cause my Damon does;
And for that reason too I hate myself,
And everything but him!

Ura. Come, my sad partner;
Poor rival of my sorrows. Go with me
Into the temple, I'll entreat my brother
To use thee kindly; if in me it lie,
I'll help thee.

  Ama.   Do, Urania, or I die.

   [*Exeunt* URANIA, AMARYLLIS. *Manet* AMYNTAS,
     THESTYLIS, MOPSUS.

  Thes. What a strange thing is love !

  Amyn.   It is a madness.
See how it stares ! Have at thee, thou blind archer !
O, I have miss'd him ! Now I'll stand thee, Cupid !
Look how the rascal winks a one eye, Thestylis !
Nay, draw your arrow home, boy, just i' th' heart !
O, I am slain !

  Thes.   Amyntas !

  Amyn.   Dost not see ?
My blood runs round about me ; I lie soaking
In a red sea. Take heed ! See, Thestylis.
What a fine crimson 'tis ?

  Mop.   Where ?

  Amyn.   Here, you puppet !
Dost thou not see it ?

  Mop.   Yes, I see it plain,
But I spy nothing.

  Amyn.   Then thou art a mole.

  Mop. Now I look better on't, I see it plain ;
Does it not hurt you ?

  Amyn.   Strangely. Have at thee !
How think you now ?

  Thes.   Be quiet, good Amyntas.

  Mop. You'll fright away the birds else, and clean spoil
My augury.

  Amyn.   Go about it ; I am quiet.

  Mop. Now for some happy omen ! [*A cuckoo cries.*

  Amyn.   Ha, ha, he !

  Mop. Why laughs the madman ?

Amyn.　　　　　　　Who can choose but laugh?
The bird cried *Horns.*
　　Thes.　　　　　　　What happiness portends it,
Sweet Mopsus?
　　Mop.　　　　Constancy in love, my Thestylis:
This bird is always in a note.
　　Thes.　　　　　　　　Most excellent!
　　Mop. Bird of the spring, I thank thee—Mopsus
　　thanks thee.
　　Amyn. This is a man of skill, an Œdipus,
Apollo, Reverend Phœbus, Don of Delphos.
　　Mop. What a brave man am I?
　　Amyn.　　　　　　　　Thou canst resolve
By thy great art all questions: what is that,
That which I have not, may not, cannot have?
　　Mop. That which you have not, may not, cannot
　　have?
It is my skill—you cannot have my skill.
　　Amyn. Where lies that skill?
　　Mop.　　　　　　Lies here within this noddle.
　　Amyn. Fetch me my woodknife, I will cut it off,
And send it to Urania for a dowry.
　　Mop. No, no, I am deceiv'd: it is not that.
　　Amyn. You dolt, you ass, you cuckoo!
　　Mop.　　　　　　　　Good Amyntas.

SCENE VI.

Dorylas, Mopsus, Jocastus, Thestylis, Amyntas.

　　Joc. Is't not a brave fight, Dorylas? can the mortals
Caper so nimbly?
　　Dor.　　　　Verily they cannot!
　　Joc. Does not King Oberon bear a stately pre-
　　sence?
Mab is a beauteous empress.

Dor.   Yet you kiss'd her
With admirable courtship.

Joc.   I do think
There will be of Jocastus' brood in Faëry.

Mop. You cuckold-maker, I will tell King Oberon
You lie with Mab his wife.

Joc.   Do not, good brother,
And I'll woo Thestylis for thee.

Mop.   Do so, then.

Joc. Canst thou love Mopsus, mortal?

Thes.   Why, suppose
I can, sir, what of that?

Joc.   Why, then, be wise,
And love him quickly.

Mop. Wise? then I'll have none of her; that's the
     way
To get wise children; troth, and I had rather
They should be bastards.

Amyn.   No, the children may
Be like the father.

Joc.   True, distracted mortal:
Thestylis, I say, love him; he's a fool.

Dor. But we will make him rich, then 'tis no
     matter.

Thes. But what estate shall he assure upon me?

Joc. A royal jointure, all in faëryland.

Amyn. Such will I make Urania.

Joc.   Dorylas knows it—
A curious park.

Dor.   Pal'd round about with pick-teeth.

Joc. Besides a house made all of mother-of-pearl,
An ivory tenniscourt.

Dor.   A nutmeg parlour.

Joc. A sapphire dairy-room.

Dor.   A ginger hall.

Joc. Chambers of agate.

Dor.   Kitchens all of crystal.

Amyn. O, admirable ! This is it for certain !

Joc. The jacks are gold.

Dor. The spits are Spanish needles.

Joc. Then there be walks.

Dor. Of amber.

Joc. Curious orchards.

Dor. That bear as well in winter as in summer.

Joc. 'Bove all, the fish-ponds : every pond is full——

Dor. Of nectar. Will this please you ? Every grove
Stor'd with delightful birds.

Mop. But be there any
Ladybirds there?

Joc. Abundance.

Mop. And cuckoos too,
To presage constancy ?

Dor. Yes.

Thes. Nay, then let's in
To seal the writings.

Amyn. There, boy, so-ho-ho-ho !

[*Exeunt.*

Dor. What pretty things are these both to be born
To lands and livings ! we poor witty knaves
Have no inheritance but brains. Who's this?

Enter ALEXIS.

One of my mistress's beagles.

Alexis. Dorylas,
I have had the bravest sport.

Dor. In what, Alexis ?

Alexis. In hunting, Dorylas : a brace of greyhounds
cours'd a stag
With equal swiftness, till the wearied deer
Stood bay at both alike : the fearful dogs
Durst neither fasten.

Dor. So ; and did not you

Compare the stag to my fair mistress, ha !
Pursued by you and Damon, caught by neither ?
 Alexis. By Cupid, th' art i' th' right.
 Dor.   Alas, poor whelps !
In troth I pity you. Why, such a hunting
Have we had here ! Two puppies of a litter,
Mopsus and wise Jocastus, hunting folly
With a full mouth.
 Alexis.   I much wonder, Dorylas,
Amyntas can be sad, having such follies
To provoke mirth.
 Dor.   And to that end his sister
Keeps them about him ; but in vain—his melancholy
Has took so deep impression.

Enter DAMON.

 Damon.   My Alexis !
Well met, I've been at your cottage to seek you.
 Alexis. But I am ne'er at home. Thou and I,
  Damon,
Are absent from ourselves.
 Dor.   Excellent application !
To see the wit of love !
 Damon.   Let us go seek her,
To have a final judgment.
 Alexis.   That may end
One of our miseries and the other's life.
 Damon. O, lamentable ! who would be in love ?
 Damon. Content.

SCENE VII.

Enter LAURINDA.

 Damon.   Here comes my joy or death.
 Dor.   O, pitiful !

Alexis. My sweet affliction.

Dor.   Pitifully sweet :
Ne'er fear your father, mistress, kiss securely ;
I'll be your Mercury, and charm asleep
Old Argus.

Lau.   Do.

Dor.   But if he chance to spy
You and your sweethearts here, I know not of it ?

Lau. You do not.

Dor.   Nay, you know if I had seen them,
I should have told him.

Lau.   Y' are a trusty servant.

Dor. Poor Dorylas is blind, he sees not here.

Damon. No, nor Alexis.

Lau.   No, not he !

Dor. Alack ! I am innocent : if the belly swell,
I did not fetch the poison.

Lau.   No ; begone.   [*Exit* DORYLAS.

Damon. Laurinda, now for mercy sake give period
To our long miseries.

Alexis.   Now you are [a]like cruel
To both, and play the tyrant equally
On him you hate as much as him you love.

Damon. Depriving one the comfort of his joy.

Alexis. The other the sure remedy of his death.

Lau. Damon, you have a love, fair Amaryllis :
Content yourself with her.

Damon.   I'll rather kiss
An Ethiop's crisped lip : embrace a viper.
Deformity itself to her is fair.

Alexis. Damon, thou hast thy answer.

Lau.   And Alexis,
There be in Sicily many virgins more
Worthy your choice : why did you place 't on me ?
Go seek some other.

Alexis.   O, those words to me
Are poison.

Damon.   But to me an antidote.

Alexis. Thus she gave life to me to take't away.

Damon. And me she slew to raise me up again :
You shall not slight us thus : what do you think
Of me ?

Lau. Thou art the glory of the woods.

Alexis. And what am I ?

Lau.   The pride of all the plains.

Alexis. These your ambiguous terms have now too
   oft
Deluded us.

Damon.   Show by some sign which of us
You have design'd for happiness.

Lau.   So I will.

   [*She takes* DAMON'S *garland, and wears it on her*
        own head, and puts her own on ALEXIS.

Damon, as I affect thee, so I vow
To wear this garland that adorns thy brow :
This wreath of flow'rs, Alexis, which was mine,
Because thou lov'st me truly, shall be thine.
This is plain dealing; let not Cupid's wars
Drive your affections to uncivil jars !   [*Exit.*

Damon. Now, happy Damon, she thy garland wears,
That holds thy heart chain'd in her golden hairs.

Alexis. Most blessed I ! this garland once did twine
About her head that now embraces mine.*

Damon. Desist, Alexis, for she designs to have
The garland that was mine.

Alexis.   But me she gave
That which was hers.

Damon.   'Tis more to take than give.

Alexis. I think 'tis greater kindness to receive.

Damon. By this your share's the less; you but
   receive.

Alexis. And by your argument, yours you did but
   give ;
Love is the garland.

Damon.   Then she did approve
Of my affection best : she took my love.

Alexis. Fond Damon, she accepted love from thee,
But (what is more) she gave her love to me ;
In giving that to me, she proves my right.

Damon. Why took she mine, but meaning to requite?

Alexis. I will dispute no more.

Damon.   Then let our spears
Plead for us.

Alexis.   And determine of our fears.
Come, Damon, by this argument let us prove,
Which 'tis of us Laurinda best doth love.

Damon. Yet 'tis, Alexis, clean against our oath.

Alexis. True, Damon, and perchance may ruin both.

Damon. So neither shall enjoy her.

Alexis.   Cruel breath !
Besides, this is the sacred vale, 'tis death
To stain the hallowed grass but with one drop
Of human blood.

Damon.   So both should lose their hope.

Alexis. And (which is more) 'tis against her commands.

Damon. Whose very[1] breath has power to stay
our hands.

Alexis. We'll have her answer make a certain end.

Damon. Till then, Alexis, let me be thy friend.

Alexis. Come, Damon, let's together seek relief.

Damon. 'Tis fit, being rivals both in love and grief.

ACT III., SCENE I.

Enter to them LAURINDA.

Damon. Laurinda, by thyself—the sweetest oath
That can be sworn——

---

[1] [Old copies, *every.*]

Alexis. By those fair eyes, whose light
Comforts my soul !
    Damon.   Whose heat inflameth mine.
    Alexis. Unless you deign at length to end our strife,
    Damon. We both have vow'd to sacrifice our life,
    Alexis. On one another's spear.
    Lau.   What shall I do ?
I find an equal war within my soul—
Myself divided ; now I would say Damon,
Another time Alexis ; then again
Damon, and then Alexis, like a shepherd,
That sees on either hand a ravenous wolf,
One snatching from his ewe a tender lamb,
The other watching for a gentle kid,
Knows not (poor soul) which hand to turn to first.
Now he would save his lamb, but seeing his kid
Half in the jaw of death, turns back in haste
To rescue that, where viewing then his lamb
In greater danger, runs to that again ;
As doubtful which to save as which to lose :
So fares it now with me.   But, love, instruct me !
    Damon. Resolve.
    Alexis.   Or we'll resolve.
    Lau.   No trick left yet ?   [*Aside.*

Enter DORYLAS.

    Dor. If ever one was pepper'd, look on me !
    Lau. Why, what's the matter ?
    Dor.   You talk of love and Cupid,
I have been plagu'd with a whole swarm of Cupids.
    Alexis. What should this mean ?
    Dor.   I know not ; but I am sure
I have a thousand natural rapiers
Stick in my flesh.
    Damon.   The meaning of the riddle ?
    Alexis. The moral ?

Dor.   In plain terms, I have been driving
One of your swarms of bees, gentle Laurinda.

Lau. The purest wax give Damon: and, good swain,
The honey to Alexis : this is plain.

Dor. Now will the honey and the wax fall together
    by th' ears.

Damon. Alexis, this plain sign confirms her grant,
She gave me wax to seal the covenant.

Dor. Well argu'd for the wax : now for the honey !

Alexis. To me she gave the honey, that must be
The sweetest, and the sweetest sweet is she.

Dor. The honey is the sweetest argument.

Damon. But by the wax she says that she from none
But me will take true love's impression.

Dor. The wax is very forward to the bargain ;
He would be sealing of her.

Alexis. But plain the honey speaks ; no other guest
But I shall taste in her a lover's feast.

Dor. Delicious reason ! my mouth waters at it.

Damon. The wax must make the taper that must
    light
The wedded pair to bed on Hymen's night.
Besides, 'tis virgin's wax ; by that you see
To me she destines her virginity.

Dor. Two excellent twin-arguments born at a
    birth.

Alexis. And honey shows a wedding, that must
    knead
A cake for Hymen ere we go to bed.
Take you the wax, the honey is for me ;
There is no honey in the world but she.

Dor. His disputation still has some good relish in't.

Damon. I see, Alexis, all Laurinda's bees
Serve but to sting us both.

Dor.   Now, what's the matter?
The moral?

Lau.   See what it is to live a maid !

Now two at once do serve us and adore;
She that weds one, serves him serv'd her before.
   Damon. Alexis, come!
   Alexis.   Come, Damon!
   Damon.   Cure my fear.
   Alexis. There's no help left but in a Pelian spear.
   Lau. O, stay your hands, for, by my maidenhead——
   Dor. Happy the man that shall quit her of that
     oath!
   Alexis. Most happy Dorylas!
   Dor.   I knew that before.
   Lau. I have protested never to disclose
Which 'tis that best I love; but the first nymph,
As soon as Titan gilds the eastern hills,
And chirping birds, the saunce-bell of the day,
Ring in our ears a warning to devotion—
That lucky damsel, whatsoe'er she be,
Shall be the goddess to appoint my love:
To say, Laurinda, this shall be your choice;
And both shall swear to stand on her award.
   Both. By fair Laurinda's hand we swear.
   Lau.   Till then
Be friends, and for this night it is my pleasure
You sleep, like friendly rivals, arm in arm.
   Both. Thanks to the fair Laurinda.
   Alexis. Come, Damon, you this night with me shall
     rest.
   Damon. Wert thou but my Laurinda, I were blest.
              [*Exeunt* DAMON *and* ALEXIS.
   Dor. Mistress, if they should dream now——
   Lau.   And they should!

SCENE II.

Enter AMARYLLIS (*her hair dishevelled*) *and* URANIA.

   Ura. Sweet Amaryllis.
   Ama.   Stay me not, Urania.

Dor. More Cupids, more bees, more stinging yet!

Ama. Dishevell'd hair, poor ornament of the head,

I'll tear you from my crown! what dost thou here?
Weak chains! my pride presum'd you had a power
To fetter heroes, and in amorous gyves
Lead any shepherd captive!

Ura. Amaryllis!

Ama. But Damon breaks thee like a spider's loom!
And thou, poor face, that wert so oft belied
For fair and beauteous by my flattering glass,
I'll tear those crimson roses from my cheeks,
That but myself ne'er yet enchanted any,
My will is fixed!

Lau. Where go you, Amaryllis?

Ama. Since Damon hates my life, I'll go and see
If I can please him in my death: if he'll but deign
To kiss me, and accept my latest breath,
I shall salute the gods a happy soul.
This dart I'll give him; and upon my knees
Beg till I have obtain'd to die by him—
Death from that hand is welcome.

Lau. I will show you
A way most probable to redeem his love.

Ama. I shall wrong you, Laurinda. No, enjoy him,
The treasure of the earth: my latest words
Shall be prayers for you. Mild Urania,
Sister in blood to Damon, not in affection—
Nymph, take this whistle—'twas a Triton's once—
With which I call my lambkins when they stray;
'Tis Amaryllis' last bequeathment to you.

Ura. Live happy, shepherdess, and wear it still.

Ama. Laurinda, my great legacy is yours,
Gentle-ungentle Damon.

Lau. I re-bequeath him to my Amaryllis;
Come, therefore, amorous maid, be rul'd by me;
This night we'll sleep together.

Dor.   And she too
Should dream of Damon?
    Lau.   Dorylas, go to Thestylis
T' excuse her this night's absence.   Amaryllis,
Wenches are ne'er so witty as abed,
And two together make a statesman's head.
Begone to Thestylis.
    Dor.   So I am, sure,
Still Cupid's factor: well, ere long, I see,
There will be many an heir the more for me.
    Ura. My Bellamore, y' are under good protection;
The temple gates will close unless I haste.
    Lau. Urania, a happy night unto you.
    Ura. The like to her that pities the distressed
        Amaryllis.

                [Exeunt LAURINDA, AMARYLLIS, URANIA.

    Dor. So, so this honey with the very thought
Has made my mouth so liquorish, that I must
Have something to appease the appetite.
Have at Jocastus' orchard! dainty apples,
How lovely they look! Why, these are Dorylas'
    sweethearts.
Now must I be the princely Oberon,
And in a royal humour, with the rest
Of royal fairies attendant, go in state
To rob an orchard: I have hid my robes
On purpose in a hollow tree.   Heaven bless me!

                Enter CLAIUS.

What Puck, what goblin's this?
    Cla.   Thrice-sacred valley,
I kiss thy hallow'd earth!
    Dor.   Another lover:
Enamour'd of the ground!
    Cla.   Fain would I speak,

And ask for Amaryllis, but my fear
Will not permit me.
 Dor.   'Slid! I think he takes me
For Oberon already.
 Cla.   Youth, can you tell me
How I may speak to-night with Amaryllis?
 Dor. Age, by no means to-night: this night she
  lodges
With fair Laurinda, old Medorus' daughter.
 Cla. Can you instruct me then how I may meet
Amyntas?
 Dor. Who, the madman? Every evening
He walks abroad into the valley here
With Thestylis. Farewell, old walking ivy-bush!
         [*Exit* DORYLAS.

CLAIUS *solus.*

 Cla. I see the smoke stream from the cottage tops;
The fearful huswife rakes the embers up;
All hush to bed. Sure, no man will disturb me.
O blessed valley! I, the wretched Claius,
Salute thy happy soil, I that have liv'd
Pelted with angry curses in a place
As horrid as my griefs, the Lylibean mountain.
These sixteen frozen winters there have I
Been with rude outlaws, living by such sins
As run o' th' score with justice 'gainst my prayers and
  wishes;
And when I would have tumbled down a rock,
Some secret power restrained me. There I lately
  heard,
By a disconsolate pilgrim that sought death,
That my Amyntas' wits (ah me!) were marr'd.
'Twas not a time to think to save myself,
When my poor boy was lost. Lost, said I? O
  Phœbus!
If there be sovereign power in juice of herbs,

And that the teeming earth yield medicinal flowers
To cure all maladies, I have sought the skill,
No leaf, no root hath 'scap'd me—I may boast it—
I have been nature's diligent apothecary.
Be lucky, my emplaister ! I have temper'd
The surest receipt the world's garden yields ;
'Twould put Orestes in his wits again.
I know I step upon my death : the oracle
Desires my blood for sacrifice, and Pilumnus
For his old hate still seeks it ; make long stay
I dare not, only I desire t' apply
My medicine and be gone.   Who's this I spy ?

SCENE III.

THESTYLIS, AMYNTAS, MOPSUS.

I do remember now that countenance,
It is my sister Thestylis ; I'll stand close
T' observe their actions.   [*Retires.*
   Thes.   Would to Ceres,
She would be pleas'd at length to end her anger,
And pity poor Amyntas !
   Cla.   So pray I.
   Amyn. I have the bravest spaniel in the world,
Of a sharp scent and quick ; so-ho-ho ! so-ho-ho-ho !
Ringwood, Jowler, Whitefoot, so-ho-ho ! so-ho-ho !
   Mop. I shall be a whole kennel of dogs anon.
   Amyn. Juno, Vulcan, Venus ! so-ho-ho ! so-ho-ho !
   Mop. Lord, what a heavenly puppy he makes me
     now ?
   Amyn. There, lady, there !
   Mop. Ha ! be there ladydogs as well as ladybirds
     too ?
   Amyn. Beauty, Beauty !
   Mop. 'Slid ! I was never call'd that name before.

Thestylis, Amyntas calls me Beauty,
I prythee, come kiss me.
    Thes.   Thus I spend my life
Laughing amidst my tears.
    Amyn.   Now, Virtue, Virtue.
    Mop. Is that a dog's name too? would I were
      hang'd
If I'll have anything of it for that trick.
    Amyn. Dost thou not scent it yet? Close, close,
      you rogue!
By Pan, the cur hunts counter.
    Mop. O good master! Bow-wow, bow-wow-wow!
    Amyn. So, now he has't again.
What, at a fault, you mongrel? will you never
Start me this oracle?
    Mop.   Start an oracle?
As if an oracle were a hare?
    Amyn.   So 'tis,
And scuds away so swift we cannot take it.
Start me this oracle.
    Mop.   Start it whoso will for me,
For I'll not start it.
    Amyn.   Then unkennel it.
    Mop. Unkennel it?
    Amyn.   Ay, 'tis a fox, a fox!
A cunning, crafty rogue; nobody knows
Which way to find him. Ha! what scent is this?
Dost thou not smell?
    Mop.   What?
    Amyn.   The meaning of the oracle.
Unkennel it, or I will leash thee.
    Mop.   Good sir,
I have no skill in starting or unkennelling,
But if you'll have me spring an oracle——
    Amyn. And wilt thou do it? spring me, then, this
      oracle.
    Mop. Ay, that I will; my skill lies all in birds,

Whose flight I fear I have observ'd so long
That I am metamorphos'd to a spaniel.

   Amyn. Look, how my hawk of understanding soars
About the partridge oracle !—Ill luck !
'Tis a retreat again.

   Mop.   O, shall I never
Rid me of this misfortune ! Thanks, good omen !
                      [*A crow caws.*
Cras, cras, she says, to-morrow 'twill be better,
Blackbird, I thank thee !

   Thes. Little thinks the wretched Claius now
How sad a life his poor Amyntas lives !

CLAIUS comes forward.

   Cla. Too well, unto his grief. I'll go unto him,
And follow him in his humour. [*Aside.*] You have got
A dainty spaniel, sir ?

   Amyn.   I think the world
Cannot afford his equal.

   Cla.   What breed is he ?

   Amyn. True Spartan, I'll assure you.

   Cla.   Was the sire
Of the same country ?

   Amyn.   No, as I remember
He was an Irish greyhound; but the dam
Came of Acteon's brood.

   Cla.   As how, I pray ?

   Amyn. Why, thus: Melampus was the sire of
      Lelaps,
Lelaps to Lagon, Lagon to Ichnobates,
Ichnobates to Pamphagus, and Pamphagus
To Dorceus, he to Labros, that was sire
To Oresitrophus, Oresitrophus
To fleet Theridamas, Theridamas
To swift Nebrophonos, Nebrophonos
To the quick-nos'd Aellus, he to Dromas,

Dromas to Tigris, Tigris to Orybasus,
Orybasus to Peterelas, he to Nape,
The dam of Mopsus.
    Mop.   So, then, Orybasus
Was my great-grandfather. Though I be a dog,
I come of a good house. My ancestors
Were all of noble names past understanding.
What a brave man's my master! where learn'd he
All this mystery.[1] Now I could find in my heart
To leave my augury and study heraldry.
A man, I think, may learn't as well as t'other,
Yet never fear of growing too wise upon't.
And then will I record the pedigree
Of all the dogs i' th' world. O, that I had
The arms of all our house by th' mother's side!
    Cla. Sir, I have brave things in a basket for you.
Give me your dog, and you shall have 'em all.
    Amyn.   Take him.
    Mop. O heaven! and shall I change my master,
One madman for another?
    Amyn.   Cur, be quiet,
I have said it, and my will shall be a law.
    Mop. O good sir, for Melampus' sake, and Dorceus,
Lelaps, Ichnobates, Lagon, Melanchetes,
Labros, Nebrophonos, Oresitrophus,
Tigris, Orybasus, Theridamas,
Aellus, Dromas, Nape, and the rest
Of all my noble ancestors deceas'd:
Be merciful unto me! Pity, pity,
The only hope of all our family.
    Cla. Sir, can he fetch and carry?
    Amyn.   You shall see him.
Fetch, sirrah—there—the cur is run away,
Help me to catch my dog: you'll bring, you mongrel?

---

[1] Old copies, *this? Ne'er stirre.*

Mop. Yes, much! the birds will not advise me to it.
[*Exit.*

Thes. Sylvan, why gaze you on us? would you frolic
With poor Amyntas' madness? 'twould ill beseem
    you
To make our grief your pastime.

Cla.   Not I, by heaven!
My joys are counterfeit, my sorrows real
(I cannot hold from weeping). Ah! you know not
What grief lies here within. (Tears, you'll betray me.)
Give me my eyeful of this noble shepherd!
Who hath not heard how he hath chas'd the boar?
And how his spear hath torn the paunch of wolves.
On the bark of every tree his name's engraven.
Now planet-struck, and all that virtue vanish'd.

    Thes. Thy looks are fierce, thy words bespeak thee
        gentle.

    Amyn. Why, wept he, Thestylis?

    Thes.   I did not mark him.

    Amyn. It was a mote in's eyes, I'll kiss it out;
I'll curl thy shackled locks, and crisp thy hair
Like the straight-growing cypress; come, let's put
Our heads together. Thou art more than mortal,
And shalt expound to Ceres what she asks.
It is a gallant Sylvan, Thestylis.

    Cla. I am not skill'd in riddles, no interpreter
Of divinations, but dare contend
With any empiric to do a cure,
Whether the body or the mind be sick.
That is my study: I but crave the leave
To try the power of art upon this shepherd.
If Esculapius be propitious to him,
After the dew of one night's softer slumbers,
I dare be bold to say he shall recover.

    Amyn. My dog again? dost read it in the stars?
What a strange man is this?

    Cla.   Thy wits, Amyntas,

I mean ; O, cast thy arms in my embraces.
Speak, careful nymph, how came he thus distracted ?
   Amyn. I, do you mean ? with a very, very, very
    mad trick—
By making verses.
   Cla.   Rest, rest, deluded fancy !
   Thes. There was a time (alas, that e'er it was !)
When my poor shepherd fell in love.
   Cla.   With whom ?
   Thes. The star of beauty, Pilumnus' much-admir'd
    Urania.
   Cla. O the cross darts of fate !
   Thes.   She (sweet nymph) enlodged
The casket of his love in her own bosom,
But Ceres set a dowry. Out, alas !
Would she had asked our flocks, our kids, our groves :
Would she had bid us quench the flames of Ætna
In Arethusa's streams, it had been easy—
We fight with words, and cannot conquer them ;
This her imperious Ompha ask'd and thunder'd—
That which thou hast not, may'st not, canst not have,
Amyntas, is the dowry that I crave.
To find out her commands he lost himself.
   Cla. Your story's pitiful. 'Tis my profession
To wander through the earth, and in my travel
I am inquisitive after the sick to heal 'em ;
Their cure and kind acceptance is my pay.
You will not fear to lodge me for a night ?
   Thes. We have but homely hospitality.
   Amyn. I'll feast thee with some venison, brave
    Montano.
   Cla. Thy restitution is my feast, Amyntas ;
Your curds and chestnuts, and your country fare,
Is bounteous for so mean a guest as I :
But send for that Urania ; her sweet voice
Must sing a lullaby to drown his senses,
And charm soft sleep upon his troubled fancy.

And 'fore the grey-ey'd morn do peep, be confident,
I'll put the music of his brains in tune.
You'll call Urania?
  Thes.   Doubt not, sir, I will.
Or send my servant Mycon by the Vale.
  Amyn. Come, Sylvan, if the dogs do bark, I'll brain
  'em.
We'll sleep to-night together, and to-morrow——
  Cla. Will end (I hope) thy madness, not my sor-
  row.
  Amyn. We'll go a-hunting, so-ho-ho! so-ho-ho!
               [*Exeunt.*

Enter MOPSUS *from the orchard.*

  Mop. Are the mad dogs gone yet?
A little more would have persuaded me
Into a spaniel; and I may be one,
For anything I know. Yet, sure, I am not,
Because (methinks) I speak; but an this speaking
Should be but barking now? if I be a dog,
Heaven send me a better master than the former!
Ceres defend me, what strange elves are there?

SCENE IV.

Enter DORYLAS *with a bevy of Fairies.*

  Dor. How like you now my grace? is not my
  countenance
Royal, and full of majesty? Walk not I
Like the young Prince of Pigmies? Ha! my knaves,
We'll fill our pockets. Look, look yonder, elves,
Would not yon apples tempt a better conscience
Than any we have, to rob an orchard, ha?
Fairies, like nymphs with child, must have the things

They long for. You sing here a fairy catch
In that strange tongue I taught you, while ourself
Do climb the trees. Thus princely Oberon
Ascends his throne of state.

Elves. *Nos Beata Fauni Proles,*
Quibus non est magna moles,
Quamvis Lunam incolamus,
Hortos sæpe frequentamus.
Furto cuncta magis bella,
Furto Dulcior Puella
Furto omnia decora.
Furto poma dulciora.
Cum mortales lecto jacent,
Nobis poma noctu placent,
Illa tamen sunt ingrata,
Nisi furto sint parata.

JOCASTUS, BROMIUS.

Joc. What divine noise, fraught with immortal har-
mony,
Salutes mine ear?
Bro. Why, this immortal harmony
Rather salutes your orchard; these young rascals—
These pescod-shellers, do so cheat my master,
We cannot have an apple in the orchard,
But straight some fairy longs for't. Well, if I
Might have my will, a whip again should jerk 'em
Into their old mortality.
Joc. Dar'st thou, screech-owl,
With thy rude croaking interrupt their music,
Whose melody hath made the spheres to lay
Their heavenly lutes aside, only to listen
To their more charming notes?
Bro. Say what you will,
I say a cudgel now were excellent music.

Elves.   *Oberon, descende citus,*
        Ne cogaris hinc invitus.
        Canes audio latrantes.
        Et mortales vigilantes.

Joc. Prince Oberon? I heard his grace's name.
  Bro.   O, spy his grace! Most noble prince,
Come down, or I will pelt your grace with stones,
That I believe your grace was ne'er so pelted
Since 'twas a grace.
  Dor.   Bold mortal, hold thy hand.
  Bro. Immortal thief, come down, or I will fetch
    you.
Methinks it should impair his grace's honour
To steal poor mortals' apples. Now have at you!
  Dor. Jocastus, we are Oberon, and we thought
That one so near to us as you in favour
Would not have suffered this profane, rude groom,
Thus to impair our royalty.
  Joc.   Gracious prince,
The fellow is a fool, and not yet purged
From his mortality.
  Dor.   Did we out of love,
And our entire affection, of all orchards
Choose yours, to make it happy by our dances,
Light airy measures and fantastic rings,
And you, ingrateful mortal, thus requite us—
All for one apple!
  Joc.   Villain, th' hast undone me!
His grace is much incens'd.
  Dor.   You know, Jocastus,
Our grace have orchards of our own more precious
Than mortals can have any, and we sent you
A present of them t'other day.
  Joc.   'Tis right,
Your grace's humble servant must acknowledge it.
  Bro. Some of his own, I am sure.

Dor.   I must confess
Their outside looked something like yours indeed ;
But then the taste more relish'd of eternity,
The same with Nectar.
  Joc.   Your good grace is welcome
To any things I have.   Nay, gentlemen,
Pray do not you spare neither.
    Elves.   Ti-ti-ta-tie.
  Joc. What say these mighty peers, great Oberon?
  Dor. They cannot speak this language, but in ours
They thank you, and they say they will have none.
    Elves. Ti-ti-ta-ti, Tititatie.
  Joc.   What say they now?
  Dor.   They do request you now
To grant them leave to dance a fairy ring
About your servant, and for his offence
Pinch him : do you the while command the traitor
Not dare to stir, not once presume to mutter.
    Joc. Traitor (for so Prince Oberon deigns to call
      thee),
Stir not, nor mutter.
    Bro.   To be thus abus'd !
  Joc.   Ha? mutter'st thou?
  Bro. I have deserved better.
  Joc.   Still mutter'st thou?
  Bro.   I see I must endure it.
  Joc. Yet mutter'st thou?   Now, noble lords, begin
When it shall please your honours.
    Elves.   Tititatie.
Our noble friend permits.
    Elves.   Tititatie.
Do you not, sir?
    Joc.   How, should I say I do?
    Dor. Tititatie.
    Joc.   Tititatie, my noble lords.
    Elves.   *Quoniam per te violamur*
              Ungues hic experiamur.

> *Statim dices tibi datam*
> *Cutem valde variatam.*   [*They dance.*

Joc. Tititatie to your lordship for this excellent
  music.

Bro. This 'tis to have a coxcomb to one's master.

Joc.   Still mutter'st thou? [*Exit* BROMIUS.

DORYLAS *from the tree.* JOCASTUS *falls on his knees.*

Dor. And rise up, Sir Jocastus, our dear knight.
Now hang the hallowed bell about his neck—
We call it a mellisonant tingle-tangle :
Indeed a sheep-bell stolen from's own fat wether—
                                        [*Aside.*
The ensign of his knighthood.   Sir Jocastus,
We call to mind we promis'd you long since
The president of our dance's place ; we are now
Pleas'd to confirm it on you.   Give him there
His staff of dignity.

Joc.   Your grace is pleas'd
To honour your poor liegeman.

Dor.   Now begone.

Joc.   Farewell unto your grace, and eke to you :
Tititatie, my noble lords, farewell.   [*Exit* JOCASTUS.

Dor.   Tititatie, my noble fool, farewell :
Now my nobility and honoured lords,
Our grace is pleas'd for to part stakes ; here, Jocalo,
These are your share ; these his, and these our grace's,
Have we not gull'd him bravely ! see, you rascals,
These are the fruits of witty knavery.

MOPSUS *enters barking.*

Dor. Heaven shield Prince Oberon and his honoured
  lords !
We are betrayed.

Mop. Bow-wow-wow !

Nay, nay, since you have made a sheep of my brother,
I'll be a dog to keep him.

   Dor.   O good Mopsus !

   Mop. Does not your grace, most low and mighty
     Dorylas,
Fear whipping now?

   Dor.   Good Mopsus, but conceal us,
And I will promise by to-morrow night
To get thee Thestylis.

   Mop.   I will ask leave
Of the birds first.   An owl? the bird of night;

                              [*An owl shrieks.*
That plainly shows that by to-morrow night,
He may perform his office.

   Dor.   And I will.

   Mop. Why, then, I will conceal you.   But your
     grace
Must think your grace beholding to me.

   Dor.   Well, we do.

   Mop. And thank the owl, she stood your friend—
And for this time, my witty grace, farewell.

   Dor. Nay, be not so discourteous.   Stay and take
An apple first : you, Jocalo, give him one,
And you another, and our grace a third.

   Mop. Your grace is liberal : but now I fear
I am not he that must interpret th' oracle.
My brother will prevent me, to my grief.
I much suspect it, for this Dorylas
A scarecrow cosen'd him most shamefully,
Which makes me fear he's a more fool than I.

                         [*Exit* Mopsus.

   Dor. So, we are clean got off : come, noble
     peers
Of faëry, come attend our royal grace.
Let's go and share our fruit with our Queen Mab
And th' other dairymaids, where of this theme
We will discourse amîdst our cakes and cream.

Elves.   *Cum tot poma habeamus,*
Triumphos læti jam canamus.
Faunos ego credam ortos
Tantum ut frequentent hortos.

I domum, Oberon, ad illas
Quæ nos manent nunc ancillas.
Quarum osculemur sinum,
Inter poma, lac, et vinum.

ACT IV., SCENE I.

MOPSUS, THESTYLIS.

Mop. I would have you to know, Thestylis, so I
would,
I am no dog, but mortal flesh and blood,
As you are.
    Thes.   O, be patient, gentle Mopsus.
Mop. 'Slid, fetch and carry !
    Thes.   Nay, good sweetheart
Be not angry.
    Mop.   Angry ? why, 'twould anger
A dog indeed to be so us'd.   A dog !
I would not use a dog so : bid a dog
That comes of a good house to fetch and carry !
Discourteous ! let him get dogs of his own,
For I have got my neck out of the collar.
Let him unkennel 's oracles himself
For Mopsus : if I start or spring him one,
I'll die the dog's death, and be hang'd.   Mad fool !
    Thes. But, Mopsus, you may now securely visit
Me and my house : Amyntas (heaven be prais'd !),
Is now recover'd of his wits again.
    Mop. How ? and grown wise !
    Thes.   Ceres be prais'd ! as ever.

Mop. Shut up your doors, then ; *Carduus Benedictus*,
Or dragon water may do good upon him.

Thes. What mean you, Mopsus?

Mop. Mean I? what mean you
To invite me to your house, when 'tis infected?

Thes. Infected!

Mop. Ay ; Amyntas has the wits,
And do you think I'll keep him company?
Though, as I told you still, I am suspicious
Jocastus is the man that must——

Thes. Do what?

Mop. It grieves me to think of it.

Thes. Out with't, man.

Mop. That must interpret. I have cause to think
(With sorrow be it spoken) he will prove
The verier fool, but let him ; yet now my augury
That never fails me, tells me certainly,
That I shall have thee, Thestylis, yet ere night.
It was an owl—

SCENE II.

Enter to them CLAIUS *and* AMYNTAS.

And see, see, Thestylis!
Here comes the ivy-bush ; I'll stand aside,
For I am most bodily afraid.

Amyn. What deity lives here? the soul of Phœbus
Breathes in this powerful man : sure, Esculapius
Revisits earth again, and in this shape
Deals health amongst us! I before was nothing
But a brute [1] beast. O, tell me by what relic
Of heavenly fire have you inspir'd me with
This better soul of reason! worthy sir,
If y' are some god (as less I cannot deem you),

---

[1] Old copies, *bruit and.*

That, pitying of my miseries, came down
From heaven to cure me—tell me, that I may
With sacrifice adore you.
 Mop.   Adore him?
Are there such ruffian gods in heaven as he,
Such beggarly deities?   [*Aside.*
 Amyn.   If you will conceal it,
And I by ignorance omit to pay
Those sacred duties that I ought, be pleas'd
To pardon me.
 Mop.   Heyday! well, Thestylis,
You may be glad your house is not infected;
He's ten times madder now than e'er he was,
To deify this rude ill-favour'd Sylvan,
This fellow with the beard all over. Thestylis,
I dare not stay; unless my heels maintain
My safety, I shall turn a dog again.
       [*Aside. Exit* MOPSUS.
 Cla. I am as you are, mortal; 'tis my skill
In physic, and experience in the rare
Virtue of herbs, that wrought this miracle:
No divinity or power in me.
 Thes. Amyntas, when shall we requite this kindness?
 Amyn. Never; I would willingly
Have sacrific'd unto him; but his modesty
Will not permit it. Though he will not suffer us
T' adore him as a god, yet we may pay
A reverence to him as a father.
 Cla. O, those words do touch the quick! [*Aside.*
 Amyn.   For, if he be
A father that begot this flesh, this clay,
What's he to whom we owe our second birth
Of soul and reason? Father, I must call you
By that name Father.
 Cla.   Now the floodgate's open, [*Aside.*
And the full stream of tears will issue out:
Traitors, you will betray me: [*To his eyes.*

Thes.　　　　　　　　　Sir, why weep you?
Cla. To think of this man's father. O, I lov'd
　him
As dearly as myself (my words and all
Break out suspicious), has he not a daughter?
As I remember well, he said her name was——
　Thes. Amaryllis.
　Cla.　　　　　　　　Yes, I had almost
Forgot it; I would fain have seen her too.
　Thes. You cannot now, because to-night she lodgeth[1]
With one Laurinda.

SCENE III.

Enter URANIA.

　Amyn.　　　　　　　O my Urania, welcome!
Amyntas bids thee so—I, that till now
Was not Amyntas: come, my joy, and meet me,
Full of our happiness!
　Ura.　　　　　　　Grant, Ceres, now
My hopes be faithful to me. My Amyntas,
How come your thoughts so settled?
　Amyn.　　　　　　　　　　O Urania!
Here, here he stands to whom I owe myself,
And thou owest me: we reverence in our temples
Marble and brass, whose statues serve for nothing
But to hang cobwebs on: O, how much rather
Should we adore this deity, that bestowed
Such happiness upon us!
　Ura.　　　　　　　Would we knew
How to deserve it!

---

[1] Old copies, *lodg'd.*

Cla.   So you may, Urania,
If you will grant me one request.
     Ura.   Command it.
     Cla. I would entreat you presently to vow
Virginity to Ceres, that Amyntas
No more may toil his brain in thinking what
To give you for a dowry.
     Ura.   Sir, I will
Presently about it : I'll only first
Get some unknown disguise.
     Cla.   I dare stay here
No longer; for I must be gone, ere yet
The light betray me.   [*Aside.*
     Ura.   Happiness attend you.
     Cla. Remember it, Urania.
     Amyn.   Farewell, father.
          [*Exeunt* URANIA, AMYNTAS, THESTYLIS.

CLAIUS *solus.*

     Cla. Thus, like a bat or owl, I spend my age
In night or darkness, as asham'd of day,
And fearful of the light : the sun and I
Dare never be acquainted.   O guilt, guilt !
Thou and thy daughter Fear are punishments
Perpetual; every whistling of the wind
Doth seem the noise of apprehenders; shadows
Affright me more than men.   Each step I tread
Is danger.   Life ! why to live longer should we
Not live at all?   I hear a noise; false timorous-
     ness,
Deceive me not.   My eyes, instruct me too.
Heaven shield me !

SCENE IV.

Enter to him ALEXIS *and* DAMON.

Fain I would inquire of them
For Amaryllis, but if one of these
Be Damon, I am lost.   [*Aside.*
   Alexis.   How early, Damon, do lovers rise?
   Cla. 'Tis he! I hear his name: good mole, away!
                          [*Exit.*
   Damon. No larks so soon, Alexis.
   Alexis. He that of us shall have Laurinda, Damon,
Will not be up so soon: ha! would you, Damon?
   Damon. Alexis, no; but if I miss Laurinda,
My sleep shall be eternal.
   Alexis. I much wonder the sun so soon can rise!
   Damon. Did he lay his head in fair Laurinda's lap,
We should have but short days.
   Alexis.   No summer, Damon.
   Damon. Thetis to her is brown.
   Alexis.   And he doth rise
From her to gaze on fair Laurinda's eyes.
   Damon. O, now I long to meet our arbitress.
   Alexis. On whom depends our only happiness.
   Damon. It must be the first virgin that we greet
From Ceres' temple.
   Alexis.   Yes, the first we meet.
   Damon. I hear no noise of any yet that move.
   Alexis. Devotion's not so early up as love.
   Damon. See how Aurora blushes! we suppose
Where Tithon lay to-night.
   Alexis.   That modest rose
He grafted there.
   Damon.   O heaven! 'tis all I seek,
To make that colour in Laurinda's cheek.
   Alexis. The virgins now come·from the temple.
   Damon. Appeal unto the first.

SCENE V.

The Virgins pass over the stage with wax candles in their hands. AMARYLLIS *goes the first; but she is stayed by* DAMON, *as unknown to be* AMARYLLIS, *she being veiled, and having on her head the garland that* LAURINDA *took from* DAMON.

         Chaste, beauteous nymph !
Ceres so grant your prayers, as you determine
Justly our cause !
 Ama.   Ceres has heard my prayers,
For all my morning orisons begg'd no more
Than one kind word from Damon.
 Damon.   Amaryllis !
 Alexis. That name breathes life and soul to poor
  Alexis.
 Ama. The same,—why startle you? you have not
  met
A poison, Damon.
 Damon.   Yes, a thousand vipers
Have stung my soul.
 Alexis.   As many joys crown mine
With happiness.
 Damon.   Would I had met this morning
Infectious vapours, cursing[1] plagues, not thee !
No curse but that had power to ruin me !
 Alexis. No other blessing hath preserved me.
 Ama. What should this mean, my Damon? how
  have I
Displeas'd you, sweet ? heaven knows it is my prayer,
More than for heaven, to please you.
 Damon.   O my torture !
Fly hence as far as hell, and hide thy head
Lower than darkness ; would thou hadst been acting

---

[1] Old copy, *nursing.*

Incest or murder when thou cam'st to pray,
Thou hadst in anything sinn'd less than this :
Unseasonable devotion !

Ama.   Can it be
A sin to pray for Damon ?

Damon.   Thou hadst blest me,
Hadst thou sat all this while in some dark cell,
Loading my head with curses.

Ama.   Innocence
Let[s] me not understand you.

Damon.   I'll not stand
To her award ; she is a partial judge,
And will decree unjustly.

Ama.   How ? to Damon ?
To him she loves so dearly ?

Damon.   That's the reason ;
She does confess, Alexis, that she loves me,
That's argument enough against her.

Ama. Ceres, these obscure passions move me.

Alexis.   I'll instruct you,
Take here the paper, pen, and ink.

Ama.   Why yet, sir,
I know no more.

Alexis.   You are to pass your censure,
Being the first nymph that we have met this morning,
Which of us two must have the fair Laurinda.
Write your award ; our mutual oaths do bind us
Not to deny't.

Damon.   'Tis a mere plot contriv'd
Betwixt this cursed nymph and you, Alexis.

Alexis. Damon, you wrong us both.

Damon.   Where did you steal
This garland ? it was mine.

Ama.   For that I love it,
Because it once was thine.

Damon.   For that I hate it,
Cause it is thine ; had it been true to me,

Methinks, as soon as it had touch'd thy head
It should have withered.
    Ama.   So it would have done,
Had it not first touch'd yours.   Laurinda gave me
This garland, but ne'er told me of this accident.
    Damon. Alexis, you deal false : 'tis a conspiracy
'Twixt you and her.
    Alexis.   How can it ? you know, Damon,
I have not been one moment from your presence.
    Damon. You took your time while I was sleeping.
    Alexis. Neither,
Nor I nor you could sleep one wink this night ;
The expectation of this morning trial
Did keep us both awake.
    Damon.   I do not know,
But there is some trick in't, and I'll appeal
From her too partial sentence.
    Alexis.   I'll the while
Go fetch Laurinda : she shall force you stand
Unto her trial.   *[Exit.*
    Ama.   Damon, thy harsh language
Is more than death unto me.
    Damon. I do charge you to tear the paper,
And refuse to judge between us.
    Ama. No, I am resolved to write what I determine.
    Damon. Now thou hast indeed a time wherein
Thou may'st revenge my scorn.   Take it,
But I'll prevent thee.   *[He strikes her.*
    Ama.   Welcome, death !
From him all things are so.   Damon, fly hence,
Thou hast shed blood here in the Sacred Valley ;
Make haste away, or thou art lost for ever !
    Damon. Thy counsel's good ; no matter whose the
      guilt.   *[Exit* DAMON.
    Ama. What was it he said last ?—Thou hast
      indeed
A time wherein thou may'st revenge my scorn !

With love, no otherwise : and there thou shalt not
Prevent me, Damon ; I will write.   This ink
Deserves not to record the name of Damon :
'Tis black and ugly : thou thyself hath furnish'd me
With that of better colour.   'Tis my blood—
That's truly Cupid's ink.   Love ought to write
Only with that.   This paper is too coarse ;
O, that I had my heart to write it there.
But so it is already.   Would I had
A parchment made of my own skin, in that
To write the truth of my affection—
A wonder to posterity !   Hand, make haste
As my blood does, or I shall faint, I fear,
Ere I have done my story.   [*Swoons.*

SCENE VI.

Enter DORYLAS.

Dor. These milkmaids are the daintiest rogues ;
    they kiss
As sweet as sillibubs ; surely Oberon
Lives a delicious life :—ha ! who lies here ?
A nymph ?   If 'twere but now in Oberon's power
To steal away her maidenhead as she sleeps ;
O, 'twould be excellent sport, to see how she
Would miss it when she wakes ; what misery it is
To be a boy !   why could not my good father
Have got me five years sooner ? here had been
A purchase.   Well, 'tis but five years longer,
And I shall hope to see a merrier world.
Nobody near, too !   'Slid, the very thought's
Enough to make me man o' the sudden.   Well,
I'll kiss her, though.
    Ama.   O, I faint.
    Dor.   She dreams.
Now shall I know all secrets.   These same women

Are given so much to talk when they are awake,
That they prate sleeping too.
 Ama.   My blood congeals
Within my quill, and I can write no more.
 Dor. Love-letters? she was troubled yesternight
About inditing; and she dreams on't now.
Poor sleepy secretary!
 Ama.   I will fold it up
And send it—who's that's here? my eyes
Are dim—ha! Dorylas.
 Dor. Now she dreams she gives it me to carry;
I half fear I use to carry letters in my sleep,
Wearying myself all night, and that's the reason
I am so loth to rise in the morning.
 Ama. Dorylas, carry this letter for me.
 Dor.   I thought so.
That's all that I can do : carry their letters
Or run of errands! well, come five years hence,
They may employ me better. [*Aside.*] Unto whom is it?
 Ama. Unto Laurinda take it.
 Dor.   How, a red letter?
 Ama. Say I wish all health to her and Damon ;
And being not able for to bear my griefs,
I sought a remedy from mine own spear,
And died.
 Dor.   How, dead?   O me!
See how her blood hath stain'd the holy valley!
Well, you have done me wrong to kill yourself,
Only to have me sacrific'd on the altar.
I ne'er deserv'd it.
 Ama.   Fear not, Dorylas.
 Dor. Fear not to die so like a calf?   O Dorylas! O!
 Ama. Good Dorylas, begone, whilst yet my breath
Will give me leave to say it was not you.
 Dor. See that you do, and so farewell.   [*Exit.*
 Ama.   Farewell!
How fearful death is unto them whose life

Has[1] any sweetness in it! My days have all
Been so o'erworn with sorrow, that this wound
Is unto me rather a salve than sore,
More physic than disease. Whither my journey
Shall lead me now: through what dark, hideous place:
Among what monsters, hags, and snake-hair'd furies
Am I to go, I know not: but my life
Hath been so spotless, chaste, and innocent,
My death so undeserv'd, I have no reason
(If there be gods) but to expect the best;
Yet what doth most torment me is the thought
How long 'twill be ere I again enjoy
My Damon's presence. Until then, Elysium
Will be no place of pleasure; and perchance,
When he comes thither too, he then may slight me
As much as now. That very fear doth make thee
Die, wretched Amaryllis!

SCENE VII.

Enter CLAIUS.

Cla.   Now[2] no fear
Can make me lose the father. Death or danger,
Threat what you can: I have no heart to go
Back to the mountains, till my eyes have seen
My Amaryllis.
Ama.   O, was ever love
So cross'd as mine! was ever nymph so wretched
As Amaryllis?
Cla.   Ha! I heard the sound
Of Amaryllis; where's that blessed creature,
That owes the name? are you the virgin?
Ama.   Yes.
That fatal name is mine; I shall anon
Be nothing but the name.

---

[1] Old copies, *Had.*   [2] Old copies, *How.*

Cla.   O, speak : what hand,
What barbarous tiger's issue, what curst whelp
Of bears or lions had the marble heart
To wound so sweet a nymph ?
    Ama.   O, sir, my blood
Calls none but fortune guilty : I by chance
Stumbled on mine own dart, and hurt myself.
    Cla. Then I have herbs to cure it.   Heaven, I
        thank thee,
That didst instruct me hither !   Still the blood
Flows like a scarlet torrent, whose quick stream
Will not be check'd : speak, Amaryllis, quickly !
What hand this skin[1] hath stain'd, upon whose soul
This blood writes murther ; till you see the man
Before your eyes, that gave the hurt, all hope
In physic is despair.   She will not speak,
And now the cure grows to the last.   Yet here
I have a receipt will revive her spirits,
            [*Applies a medicine, and rubs her temples.*
And till the last drop of her blood be clean
Exhausted from those azure veins, preserve her ;
But then she's lost for ever !   Then, O Ceres,
If there be any in these groves—men, virgins,
Beast, bird, or trees, or anything detesting
This horrid fact, reveal it !   Sacred grass,
Whose hallowed green this bloody deed hath stain'd,
Ask nature for a tongue to name the murtherer !
I'll to the temple.   If this place contain
Any divinity, piety, or religion :
If there be any god at home, or priest,
Ompha or oracle, shrine or altar, speak
Who did it : who is guilty of this sin,
That dyes the earth with blood, and makes the heavens
Asham'd to stand a witness?

---

[1] Old copy, *sinne.*

SCENE VIII.

Enter PILUMNUS *and* CHORYMBUS.

Pil.　　　　　　　　What sad voice
Disturbs our pious orgies?
　Chor.　　　　　　　See, Pilumnus,
A virgin all in gore.
　Pil.　　　　　Ceres defend us!
The Sacred Valley is profan'd.
　Chor.　　　　　　　The place
So dear to Ceres all defil'd with blood.
　Pil. By Ceres and her holy Ompha, he
That did it with his blood shall satisfy
The goddess' anger; who by blood offends,
By his own (sacrific'd) must make amends.
　Cla. I durst presume upon the power of art,
Did I but know the murtherer.
　Pil.　　　　　　　Howsoever,
'Tis death to him that did it.
　Chor.　　　　　　Speak his name,
Fair virgin.
　Amyn.　　　O, if it be death to him
That did it, I have not the power to live
Behind him.
　Chor.　　　Who was it, then?
　Amyn.　　　　　　　Myself,
And therefore in my death your law is satisfied,
The blood and act both mine.
　Chor.　　　　　　　It is not so,
For had it been by her own hand, my skill
Could have preserv'd her life.
　Amyn.　　　　　　It was myself,
Or one as dear.
　Cla.　　　Who's that?
　Amyn.　　　　　　I'll rather die

Than name him, though it be a name I use
Oft to repeat, and every repetition
Is a new soul unto me : 'tis a name
I have taught the birds to carol ; every
Laurel and cedar bears it registered
Upon his tender bark : it is a name,
In which is all the life I yet have left,
A name I long to speak ; yet I had rather
Die all the several sorts of death twice over
Than speak it once.
 Cla.   I charge thee by that duty
Thou ow'st to me, Amaryllis—that thou ow'st to me,
Who gave thee life !
 Pil. What should this mean, Chorymbus ? [*Aside.*
 Cla. And by the womb that bare thee, by the breasts
Of thy dead mother Lalage—
 Chor.   This is strange.
 Cla. Conceal him not ! in plain, I am thy father—
Thy father, Amaryllis, that commands thee
By these grey hairs to tell me. I am Claius.
 Pil. How, Claius, and so fortunately found ?
 Cla. Ay, glut your hate. Pilumnus, let your soul,
That has so long thirsted to drink my blood,
Swill till my veins are empty, and carouse
Deep in my heart, till you grow drunk and reel,
And vomit up the surfeit, that your cruelty
Quaff'd off with so much pleasure. I have stood
Long like a fatal oak, at which great Jove
Levels his thunder, all my boughs long since
Blasted and wither'd ; now the trunk falls too !
Heaven end thy wrath in me !
 Pil.   Blessed be Ceres !
What unexpected happiness is here ?
Rejoice, Sicilia's [1] miserable lovers,
Crown all your brows with roses, and adore

---

[1] Old copies, *Sicilians.*

The deity that sent him : he is come
Whose blood must quench the fire of Ceres' wrath,
And kindle more auspicious flames of love
In every breast.
  Cla.   Ay, do : I fear not death.
Let every virgin's hand, when I am slain,
Ring me a knell of plaudits : let my dirges
Be amorous ditties, and instead of weeping
Dance at my funeral !   'Tis no grief for me
To die, to make my countrymen some sport.
Here's one in whom I only wish to live
Another age.
  Ama. What joy have I to live,
That ne'er liv'd yet ? the time that I have spent
Since first I wept, then when I first had entrance
Into this world, this cold and sorrowful world,
Was but a scene of sorrow.   Wretched I,
Fatal to both my parents !   For my birth
Ruin'd my mother, and her [1] death my father.
O tragic life ! I either should have been
Ne'er born, or ne'er have died.   When I began
To be, my sin began ; why should it then
Outlive me ? for, though now I cease to be,
That still continues.   Eyes, flow forth apace,
And be asham'd to see my wound run blood
Faster than you drop tears.

Enter DAMON.

See, here he comes,
His absence never until now I wished.
  Damon. My conscience brings me back ; the feet
   of guilt
Go slow and dull ; 'tis hard to run away
From that we bear about us !

---

[1] Old copies, *my.*

Cla. The murtherer
Is in this place ; the issue of her blood
Is stopped o' th' sudden.   Cruel man, 'tis thou
Hast done this bloody act that will disgrace
The story of our nation, and imprint
So deep a blemish in the age we live in
For savage barbarism, that eternity
Shall ne'er wear out.   Pilumnus, on my knees
I beg the justice of Sicilian laws
Against this monster.
Pil. Claius, 'tis your hate
And old revenge instructs you to accuse
My son—you would have fellows in your death,
And to that purpose you pretend, I know not
What mysteries of art !
Cla. Speak, Amaryllis
Is't not this wolf?
Pil. Say, virgin, was it he ?
Ama. O, I am angry with my blood for stopping.
This coward ebb against my will betrays me,
The stream is turn'd ; my eyes run faster now.
Pil. Can you accuse my son ?
Ama. By Ceres, no.
I have no heart to do it : does that face
Look cruel ? do those eyes sparkle with hate
Or malice ?   Tell me, father, looks that brow,
As if it could but frown ?   Say, can you think
'Tis possible Damon should have the heart
To wound a virgin? surely barbarous cruelty
Dwells not in such a breast.   Mercy and mildness :
Courtesy, love and sweetness breathe in him :
Not anger, wrath, or murther ; Damon was not
Fed at a Thracian teat ; Venus did send
Her doves to nurse him ; and can he be cruel?
Whence should he learn so much of barbarism
As thus to wrong a virgin ?   If he wound me,
'Tis only from his eyes, where love's blind god

Whets his pil'd arrows ; he besides, you know,
Had never cause to wrong me ; for he knows
Always I lov'd him.　Father, do not wrong
An innocent ; his soul is white and pure.
'Tis sin to think there lives a sin in him—
Impiety to accuse him.
　　Pil.　　　　　　　　In his looks
He carries guilt, whose horror breeds this strange
And obstinate silence.　Shame and his conscience,
Will not permit him to deny it.
　　Ama.　　　　　　　　'Tis, alas !
His modest, bashful nature and pure innocence
That makes him silent : think you that bright rose
That buds within his cheeks was planted there
By guilt or shame ?　No, he has always been
So unacquainted with all act of sin,
That but to be suspected strikes him dumb
With wonder and amazement.　For, by Ceres
(I think my oath be lawful), I myself
Was cause of this.
　　Cla.　　　　　Still I am confident
'Twas he.
　　Pil.　　It is your envy makes you so.

SCENE IX.

Enter ALEXIS *and* LAURINDA *conversing.*

　　Lau.　　　　　　　　　　I will, Alexis.
And so he must, if oaths be any tie.
　　Alexis. To lovers they are none : we break those
　　　bonds
As easily as threads of silk.　A bracelet
Made of you [1] maidens' hair's a stronger chain

---

[1] Old copies, *your.*

Than twenty cobweb oaths, which while we break,
Venus but laughs : it must be your persuasion
That works him to it.

 Lau.   Alexis,[1] you must stand
To what you promis'd ; how shall I believe
Those other oaths you swear, if you respect
This one no better ? It was my device
To have her judge, was it not. Amaryllis ?
How, all in blood !

 Cla.   Yes, this unmerciful man
(If he be man, that can do such a crime)
Has wounded her.

 Ama.   Indeed it was not he.

 Pil. You see herself frees him.

 Lau.   When last we left her,
She was with Damon.

 Ama.   Pray believe her not,
She speaks it out of anger. I ne'er saw
Damon to-day before.

 Alexis.   And when we left 'em,
He was incens'd.

 Ama.   You are no competent witness ;
You are his rival in Laurinda's love
And speak not truth, but malice. 'Tis a plot
To ruin innocence.

 Lau.   O ungrateful man !
The wolf that does devour the breast that nurst it
Is not so bad as thou. Hear, hear this letter,
Th' eternal chronicle of affection,
That ought with golden characters to be writ
In Cupid's annals, will (false man) convince thee
Of foul ingratitude : you shall hear me read it.

The Letter.

Laurinda, you have put it unto me
To choose a husband for you. I will be

---

[1] Old copies, *Damon.*

> *A judge impartial, upright, just, and true,*
> *Yet not so much unto myself as you.*

Alexis. Now I expect to hear my blessed doom.
Lau. *Alexis well deserves, but Damon more:*
> *I wish you him I wish'd myself before.*

Alexis. O, I am ruin'd in the height of hope!
How like the herb celestial is a lover!
Now born, now dead again, he buds, sprouts forth,
Flourishes, ripens, withers in a minute.
Lau. *Take him, the best of men that ever eye*
> *Beheld, and live with him for whom I die.*
> > > > *Amaryllis.*

Here look on't.
Damon.   Writ with blood? O, let me kiss
My bill of accusation! here my name
Looks, like my soul, all crimson: every line,
Word, syllable, and letter, wear the livery
Of my unnatural action.   Amaryllis,
That name of all is black, which was alone
Worthy so precious ink; as if disdaining
The character of cruelty, which the rest
Were cloth'd in: for as if that word alóne
Did wear this mourning colour, to bewail
The funeral of my virtue, that lies buried
Here in this living tomb, this moving sepulchre.
Lau. Know, murtherer, I hate thy bed and thee,
Unkind, unthankful villain!
Ama.   Nay, Laurinda,
You have bound yourself to stand to my award;
The sentence now is past, and you must love him;
It cannot be revers'd.   You are deceiv'd;
He is not guilty of this sin, his love
To me; for mine makes him against his conscience
Seem to confess it, but believe him not.
Lau. Nor will I, he is all falsehood and ingratitude.
Damon. Laurinda, you may spare in this harsh
    language

To utter your dislike.   Had you a beauty
More than immortal, and a face whose glory
Far outshin'd angels, I would make my choice
Here, and nowhere but here.   Her virtue now
Moves a more noble flame within my breast
Than e'er your beauty did ; I am enamour'd
More of her soul than ever yet I doated
Upon your face.   I do confess the fact.
Pardon me, virtuous maid ; for though the action
Be worthy death, the object most condemns me !
Take me to death, Chorymbus.   Amaryllis,
I go to write my story of repentance
With the same ink wherewith thou wrote before
The legend of thy love.   Farewell, farewell !
                    [*Exeunt* CHORYMBUS, DAMON.
  Pil. Laurinda and Alexis, do you call
The shepherds and the virgins of Sicilia
To see him sacrific'd whose death must make
Their loves more fortunate.   This day shall be
Happy to all Sicilians but to me.
Yet come, thou cursed Claius, the sweet comfort,
Which I shall take when my revenge is done,
Will something ease the sorrow for my son.
  Cla. Amaryllis, prythee, call Amyntas to me,
And Thestyllis ; I fain would have mine eye
Behold them once again before I die.
                    [*Exeunt* PILUMNUS, CLAIUS.
  Alexis. Come, my Laurinda, through how many
        chances,
Suspicions, errors, sorrows, doubts, and fears
Love leads us to our pleasures ! many storms
Have we sail'd through, my sweet ; but who could fear
A tempest that had hope to harbour here ?
                    [*Exeunt* ALEXIS, LAURINDA.

Amaryllis *sola.*

Ama. All, all but the distressed Amaryllis
Are happy or less wretched.   Fair Laurinda
Is ready for a wedding ; old Pilumnus
Hath lost a son, yet mitigates his grief
In Claius' death ; my father Claius dies,
Yet joys to have the son of his old enemy
A partner of his sorrows ; my father loses
Only himself, and Damon, too, no more ;
Amyntas but a father.   Only I
Have lost all these : I have lost Claius, Damon,
And myself too ; a father with Amyntas,
And all the rest in Damon, and (which more
Affects me) I am cause of all.   Pilumnus
Had not else lost his son, nor had Amyntas
Wept for a father ; nor poor Thestylis
Bewail'd a brother.   Damon might have liv'd,
And Claius, but for me.   All circumstances
Concur to make my miseries complete
And sorrows perfect ; for I lost my father
As soon as I had found him, and my Damon
As soon as I had found he lov'd me : thus
All I can find is loss !   O too-too wretched,
Distressed virgin !   When they both are dead,
Visit their ashes, and first weep an hour
On Claius' urn, then go and spend another
At Damon's, thence again go wet the tomb
Of thy dead father, and from thence return
Back to thy lover's grave : thus spend thy age
In sorrow ; and, till death do end thy cares,
Betwixt these two equally share thy tears.

ACT V., SCENE I.

The Place of Execution.

Enter DORYLAS, *and a Chorus of swains.*

Dor. Come, neighbours, let's go see the sacrifice
Must make you happy lovers : O, 'twill be
A fortunate season ; Father Corydon,
You and old mother Baucis shall be friends.
The sheep-hook and the distaff shall shake hands.
You lovely freeze-coats, nothing now but kissing,
Kissing and culling, culling and kissing.   Heyday !
In hope it will be one day so with me
I am content to live.   Now let's ascend.
[They take their places.

SCENE II.

ALEXIS, LAURINDA, MEDORUS.

Alexis. Now, my Laurinda, now (O happy now !)
All lets that stood between my joy and me
Are gone and fled.
Lau.   Long, O, too long, Alexis,
My doubtful fancy wavered whom to love—
Damon or you ; in both was happiness,
But double happiness was my single misery.
So far'd it once, Alexis (for I well
Remember it), with one of my poor ewes,
Equally mov'd between two tufts of grass :
This tempting one way, that enticing t'other ;
Now she would this, then that, then this again,
Until, poor fool (true emblem of her mistress),
She almost starv'd in choosing which to feed on ;
At last (so heaven pitied the innocent fool)

A western gale nipp'd one, which being blasted
She fed upon the other.

    Alexis.   Pretty fool.
Let's now no more defer our nuptial joys.

    Med. How sweet a folly is this love! But rash
       youth, Alexis,
(As youth is rash) runs indiscreetly on,
While mature judgment, ripened by experience,
Stays for love's season.

    Alexis.   Season? why, can love
Be ever out of season?

    Med.   Yes, Alexis,
Nothing's born ripe; all things at first are green.

    Alexis. Lau. And such shall our affection still be seen.

    Med. You are too hasty reapers, that do call
For sickles in the spring.

    Alexis.   Love's harvest shall;
(Lovers, you know) this harvest ought to be
All the year long.

    Lau.   In Cupid's husbandry,
Who reaps not in the spring reaps not at all.

    Med. Women indeed too soon begin their fall.
Yet, till curst Claius die, as now he must,
Alexis and Laurinda, let my counsel
Assuage the heat of youth; pray, be persuaded
Awhile for to defer your nuptial bliss.
'Tis but a while.

    Alexis.   A while in love's an age.

    Lau. Maids in a while grow old.

    Med.   Temper loves fire.

    Alexis. 'Tis but cold love that's temperate in
       desire.

    Med. Yet, loving pair, stay till a fairer gale;
He deserves shipwreck ('tis the mariner's flout)
And justly too, that in a storm sets out.

    Lau. I will suppress my flame (O, still it glows!)

    Alexis. And I, but how unwilling, Cupid knows!

Med. 'Tis well; now let's go take our place, to
   see
For our sad griefs a sadder remedy.   [*Exeunt.*

SCENE III.

AMYNTAS, AMARYLLIS.

Ama. Yes, it was he: he's in the temple, brother;
A place wherein he doth deserve a shrine,
Yet 'tis [1] to him a prison.   Can you gods
Suffer the place that's reared unto your honours
Be made so vile a thing?
    Amyn.   Pray, give me entrance;
I am not mad (and yet I would I were).
Am I not mad to wish so?   Let me come
And see him; sure, you had yourself a father,
Did you not wish to see him, ere he died?
If he be dead, we'll only pray awhile,
And weep; will tears pollute the hallowed Ompha?
For we must shed them; yes, we cannot choose:
Come, sister, he will let us; for though Lalage
Was our sad mother, yet the gods will let us
Weep for her.   Come, come, Amaryllis, come.
           [*Exeunt.   They take their places,*

SCENE IV.

MOPSUS, JOCASTUS.

Joc. Brother, areed, what means his gracious
   favour?
   Mop. It signifies you bear the bell away
From all his grace's nobles.

---

[1] Old copies, *is.*

Joc.   Divinely augur'd !
For this I'll make thee augur to his grace.
  Mop. Bellwether of knighthood, you shall bind me
    to you.
  Joc. I'll have't no more a sheep-bell; I am knight
Of the mellisonant tingle-tangle.
  Mop. Sure, one of my progeny ; tell me, gracious
    brother,
Was this mellisonant tingle-tangle none
Of old Actæon's hounds ?
  Joc.   Ignorant mortal !
Thou dost not understand the terms of honour.
  Mop. How should I, sir ? my trees bear no such
    apples.
  Joc. As mine ? th' Hesperian fruit are crabs to
    mine.
Hence came the knighthood, hence.
  Mop. The fame whereof rings loud.
  Joc.   We know it.
  Mop. Four such knighthoods more
Would make an excellent peal.
  Joc.   I'll have 'em so.
  Mop. But you must get a squirrel, too.
  Joc.   For what ?
  Mop. To ring your knighthoods.
  Joc.   I'll have anything.
His grace will not deny me.   O sweet orchard !
  Mop. To see the fruit that came of such an
    orchard !
  Joc. But shall we not see Claius sacrific'd ?
  Mop. O, by all means.
  Joc.   But how deserv'd he death ?
  Mop. No matter for deserving it or no ;
'Tis fit he suffer for example's sake.
  Joc.   And not offend ?
  Mop. 'Tis fit he should offend.
                                    [*They take their places.*

SCENE V.

PILUMNUS *with a sacrificing knife, fire laid on the altar; a Priest holding a taper ready to kindle it; another Priest pouring water on* CLAIUS' *head, who was bound:* CHORYMBUS *leading out* DAMON *bound.*

Pil. Sicilians, nature and religion
Are at contention in me : my sad soul
Divided 'twixt my goddess and my son,
Would (in her strange distractions) either have me
Turn parricide or apostate.   Awful Ceres,
For whom I feed the fattest of my lambs,
To whom I send the holiest of my prayers,
Upon the smoky wings of sweetest myrrh,
Instruct my doubtful flamen ! as I cannot
Forget I am thy priest ; (for sooner shall
Our lambs forget to feed, our swains to sing,
Our bees forget first from the fruitful thyme
To cull them bags of nectar : everything
Forget his nature, ere I can forget
I am thy priest) ; nor can I but remember
That Damon is my son, yet take him, Ceres !
You need not pour water upon his head,
I'll do it with my tears.   Ceres, I hope
Thy anger will not bind the father's eye
To look into the bowels of his son.
I'll therefore first spill on thy hallowed altar
This captive's blood, and then retire myself
Not to be present at my Damon's death,
Lest nature might turn rebel to devotion.

Song.

Ceres, to whom we owe that yet
We do not mast and acorns eat :

That didst provide us better meat,
The purest flour of finest wheat.
This blood we spill at thy desire,
To kindle and to quench a fire.
O, let it quench thy flame of ire,
And kindle mercy more entire.
O, let this guilty blood atone
For every poor unlucky one,
Nymph or swain, whoe'er do groan
Under sad love's imperious throne.
That love a happier age may see
In thy long-tortur'd Sicily.
That blood which must th' atonement be,
Thus, goddess, thus we pay to thee.

Enter AMYNTAS, *with* AMARYLLIS.

Amyn. Stay, stay that impious hand, whose hasty
    zeal
Thinks murther can appease the goddess' wrath !
If it be murther must appease her wrath,
What is't can move her anger ?   Do not then,
Do not pollute her altar, lest it keep
The crimson stain of blood, and blush for ever
At this too cruel, ignorant devotion.
    Pil.   Avoid the madman.
    Amyn. Why, Pilumnus, why ?
By the dread Ompha, spare this guilty blood,
And I'll expound the oracle.
What fire has yet his blood or quench'd or kindled ?
    Pil. Why, it hath quenched the sadder flames of
    love,
And more auspicious fires begin to move.
    Amyn. Where ? in what breast ?   No love in ali
    Trinacria
But under Cupid's sceptre faints and groans
More now than ever.   Thy unfortunate Damon,

And more unfortunate Amaryllis stand
A sad example.   Thy Urania
(O sad, sweet name !) may with her poor Amyntas
Witness his tyrannous reign here in Sicilia.
Turtles grow jealous ; doves are turn'd unchaste ;
The very pelicans of Trinacrian woods
Are found unnatural, and thirst the blood
Of their young brood : alas ! who can believe it ?
Whom they were wont to suckle with their own.
O wretched season ! bitter fruits of love !
The very storks with us are parricides !
Nay, even the senseless trees are sensible
Of this imperious rage.   The gentle vine
(The happy emblem once of happier lovers),
That with such amorous twines and close embraces
Did cling about the loved-loving elm,
With slacker branches now falls down, and withers.
If then, to add more fuel to the flame,
To pour in oil and sulphur, be to quench it,
The flame is quench'd.   Nor are you he, Pilumnus,
That must expound the oracle : 'tis a wit,
Such as mine is (neglected), that must hit
The goddess' meaning.   You the living oracle
Of Sicilia, the breathing Ompha of the kingdom,
Will misconceive the goddess ; you are wise,
Skill'd in the virtues of all herbs and flowers,
What makes our ewes ean best, what keeps them sound:
Can tell us all the mysteries of heaven :
The number, height, and motion of the stars,
'Tis a mad brain,[1] an intellect you scorn,
That must unite this riddle.
    Pil.   But, I know,
The wrath of Ceres cannot be appeas'd
But by the blood of Claius.

---

[1] This reminds us of Dryden—
        " Great wits are, sure, to madness near allied."

Amyn. So it is.

Pil. How can that be ? yet his accurs'd gore
Hath not imbru'd the altar.

Amyn. But his blood
Hath been already shed in Amaryllis.
She is his blood ; so is Urania yours,
And Damon is your blood—that is the blood
The goddess aims at—that must still her ire,
For her blood hath both quench'd and kindled fire.

Pil. What hath it quench'd or kindled ?

Amyn. Love : the fire
That must be quench'd and kindled—Damon's love
To his Laurinda, in that blood extinguish'd,
Is by that powerful blood kindled anew
To Amaryllis, now grown his desire :
Thus Claius' blood hath quench'd and kindled fire.

All. Amyntas, Amyntas, Amyntas, Amyntas !

Pil. And is the fire of Damon kindled
But to be quench'd again ? Ceres, a frost
Dwell on thy altars, ere my zeal renew
Religious fires to warm 'em.

Amyn. Spare these blasphemies ;
For Damon is acquitted and assoil'd
Of any trespass.

Pil. How, Amyntas ? speak !
Thou that hast sav'd a father, save a son !

Amyn. Thus. Amaryllis is the sacrifice
The goddess aim'd at ; and the blood of sacrifice
(As you all know) may lawfully be spilt
Even in the Holy Vale, and so it was ;
Besides, your Damon is a priest by birth,
And therefore, by that title, he may spill
The sacrificed Amaryllis' blood.
If this interpretation be not true,
Speak you, Sicilians ; I'll be judg'd by you.

All. Amyntas, Amyntas, Amyntas, Amyntas !

Pil. Amyntas, thou hast now made full amends

For my Philebus' death.   Claius, all envy—
Envy, the viper of a venomous soul,
Shall quit my breast.   This is the man, Sicilians—
The man to whom you owe your liberties.
Go, virgins, and with roses strow his way,
Crown him with violets and lily wreaths;
Cut off your golden tresses, and from them
Weave him a robe of love.   Damon, pay here
The debt of duty that thou ow'st to me;
Hence was thy second birth.
 Damon.   Or hither, rather:
The balsam of Sicilia flowed from hence;
Hence from this scarlet torrent, whose each drop
Might ransom Cupid, were he captive ta'en.
 Ama. How much owe I my Damon, whose blest
  hand
Made me the public sacrifice: could I shed
As many drops of blood, even from the heart,
As Arethusa drops of water can,
I would outvy her at the fullest tide:
That other virgins' loves might happy be,
And mine, my Damon, be as blest in thee.
 Cla. O, what a shower of joy falls from mine eyes,
The now too fortunate Claius ! my Amyntas,
My Amaryllis, how shall I divide
My tears and joys betwixt you?
 Pil.   Lovers, come;
Come all with flow'ry chaplets on your brows,
And singing hymns to Ceres, walk around
This happy village, to express our glee;
This day each year shall Cupid's triumphs be.
 Amyn. Still my impossible dowry for Urania
Leaves me unfortunate in the midst of joy;
Yet out of piety I will here awhile
(Though blest I am not, till she be my bride)
In public joys lay private griefs aside.
      [*Exeunt, cum Choro cantantium.*

Joc. And I'll go fetch the youngsters of the town,
The mortal fairies and the lasses brown,
To bring spic'd cakes and ale, to dance and play ;
Queen Mab herself shall keep it holiday.　　　[*Exit.*

Mop. Ah, Dorylas ! that I could not have th' wit
To have been a madman rather than a fool,
I have lost the credit.

Dor.　　　　　　　　'Tis no matter,
You shall have Thestylis.

Mop.　　　　　　　　Shall I, Dorylas ?
I had as lief interpret her as oracles.

Dor. And here she comes ; give me your quail-
　　pipe,
Hark you——　　[*He whispers in his ear, and retires.*

Enter THESTYLIS.

Mop. Now, Thestylis, thou shalt mine oracle be,
Henceforth I will interpret none but thee.

Thes. Why, have the birds (my Mopsus) counsell'd so.

Mop. They say I must, whether you will or no.

Thes. How know I that ?

Mop.　　　　　　　　The birds do speak it plain.
　　　　　　　　[*Dorylas with a quail-pipe.*
Hark, Thestylis, the birds say so again.

Thes. I understand them not.

Mop.　　　　　　　　Will you be judg'd
By th' next we meet ?

Thes.　　　　　　　　Mopsus, I am content,
So you will stand unto it as well as I.

Mop. By Ceres, Thestylis, most willingly.

Enter DORYLAS.

Mop. Ah, Dorylas ! heard you what the birds did
　　say ?

Dor. Ay, Mopsus, you are a happy man to-day.

Mop. What said they, boy?
Dor.   As if you did not know!
Mop. But, Thestylis——
Dor.   Why, sure, she understands it;
Have you to her this language never read?
   Mop. No, Dorylas, I can teach her best in bed.
   Dor. The birds said twice (as you full well do
    know),
You must have Thestylis, whether she will or no.
   Thes. And I am caught? 'Tis no great matter,
    though.
For this time, Mopsus, I will marry thee;
The next I wed, by Pan, shall wiser be!
   Mop. And have I got thee? thanks, my witty boy.
   Dor. Hark, Thestylis, the birds do bid you joy.
   Thes. For fooling, Mopsus: now 'tis time, give
    o'er.
   Mop. Madam, I may; but will be fool no more.
   Thes. Mad after marriage as a fool before.
For he's a fool that weds, all wives being bad;
And she's a fool makes not her husband mad.

SCENE VI.

JOCASTUS *with a morrice, himself Maid-marian;*
BROMIUS *the clown.*

   Dor. See, Mopsus, see! here comes your fairy
    brother,
Hark you, for one good turn deserves another.
               [*Exeunt* DORYLAS, MOPSUS.
   Joc. I did not think there had been such delight
In any mortal morrice; they do caper
Like quarter-fairies at the least: by my knighthood,
And by this sweet mellisonant tingle-tangle,

The ensign of my glory, you shall be
Of Oberon's revels.
　Bro.　　　　　　What to do, I pray?
To dance away our apples?
　Joc.　　　　　　　　Surely, mortal,
Thou art not fit for any office there.

　　　Enter DORYLAS, *like the King of Fairies, with*
　　　　　　　　MOPSUS.

　Joc. See, blind mortal, see,
With what a port, what grace, what majesty
This princely Oberon comes ! Your grace is welcome.
　Dor. A beauteous lady, bright and rare.
Queen Mab herself is not so fair.
　Joc. Does your grace take me for a woman, then?
　Dor. Yes, beauteous virgin ; thy each part
Has shot an arrow through my heart ;
Thy blazing eye, thy lip so thin :
Thy azure cheek and crystal chin :
Thy rainbow brow, with many a rose :
Thy sapphire ears and ruby nose :
All wound my soul. O, gentle be,
Or, lady, you will ruin me.
　Joc. Bromius, what shall I do ? I am no woman :
If gelding of me will preserve your grace,
With all my heart.
　Bro.　　　　　No, master, let him rather
Steal away all your orchard apples.
　Joc. Ay, and [he] shall,
Beauteous Queen Mab may lose her longing else.
　Dor. How's this ? are you no woman, then ?
Can such bright beauty live with men ?
　Joc. An't please your grace, I am your knight
　　Jocastus.
　Dor. Indeed I thought no man but he
Could of such perfect beauty be.

Joc. Cannot your grace distil me to a woman?

Dor. I have an herb, they moly call,[1]
Can change thy shape (my sweet) and shall.
To taste this moly but agree,
And thou shalt perfect woman be.

Joc. With all my heart. Ne'er let me move,
But I am up to the ears in love.
But what if I do marry thee?

Dor. My Queen Jocasta thou shalt be.

Joc. Sweet moly!
Pray, let Bromius have some moly too,
He'll make a very pretty waiting-maid.

Bro. No, indeed,
Forsooth; you have ladies enough already.

Dor. Half your estate then give to me;
Else, you being gone, there none will be,
Whose orchard I dare here frequent.

Joc. Sweet Oberon, I am content.

Dor. The other half let Mopsus take.

Joc. And Thestylis a jointure make.

Bro. Why, master, are you mad?

Joc. Your mistress, sirrah.
Our grace has said it, and it shall be so.

Bro. What, will you give away all your estate?

Joc. We have enough beside in fairyland.
You, Thestylis, shall be our maid-of-honour.

Thes. I humbly thank your grace.

Joc. Come, princely Oberon,
I long to taste this moly: pray, bestow
The knighthood of the mellisonant tingle-tangle
Upon our brother Mopsus; we will raise
All of our house to honours.

Mop. Gracious sister!

Joc. I always thought I was born to be a queen.

Dor. Come, let us walk, majestic queen,

---

[1] The same employed by Ullysses in the "Odyssey."

Of fairy mortals to be seen.
In chairs of pearl thou plac'd shalt be,
And empresses shall envy thee,
When they behold upon our throne
Jocasta with her—Dorylas.
 All.   Ha, ha, ha !
 Joc. Am I deceiv'd and cheated, gull'd and fool'd ?
 Mop. Alas, sir ! you were born to be a queen.
 Joc. My lands, my livings, and my orchard gone ?
 Dor. Your grace hath said it, and it must be so !
 Bro. You have enough beside in fairyland !
 Thes. What would your grace command your maid-
   of-honour ?
 Dor. Well, I restore your lands : only the orchard
I will reserve for fear Queen Mab should long.
 Mop. Part I'll restore unto my liberal sister
In lieu of my great knighthood.
 Thes.   Part give I.
 Joc. I am beholding to your liberality.
 Bro. I'll something give as well as do the rest.
Take my fool's coat ; for you deserve it best.
 Joc. I shall grow wiser.
 Dor.   Oberon will be glad on't.
 Thes. I must go call Urania, that she may
Come vow virginity.   [*Exit.*

SCENE VII.

PILUMNUS, AMYNTAS, &c.

 Amyn.   Ceres, I do thank thee,
That I am author of this public joy,
But is it justice (goddess) I alone
Should have no share in't ? Every one, I see,
Is happy but myself, that made them so ;
And my Urania, that should most be so.

I thirst amidst the bowls ; when others sit
Quaffing off nectar, I but hold the cup,
And stand a sadder Tantalus of love,
Starving in all this plenty ; Ceres' demand
Feeds me with gall; stretching my doubtful thoughts
On many thousand racks : I would my dowry
Were all the gold of Tagus, or the ore
Of bright Pactolus' channel.   But, Urania,
'Tis hid : alas! I know not what it is.

SCENE VIII.

Before the Temple of Ceres.

Enter THESTYLIS, *with* URANIA *in the background,
dressed as a vestal.*[1]

My Thestylis, since first the sea-god's trident
Did rule the small three-pointed piece of earth
Of this our conquering soil, it has not been
A place of so much story as to-day :
So full of wonders.   O, 'twill serve (my Thestylis)
For our discourse, when we go fold our ewes :
Those shepherds, that another day shall keep
Their kids upon these mountains, shall for ever
Relate the miracle to their wondering nymphs.
O my Urania, it will fill their ears
With admiration.
   Thes.   Sir, Urania's here.
   Amyn. How, in this habit.   This (methinks) fits
    not
A lover, my Urania.
   Ura.   Yes, Amyntas,

---

[1] Old copies read simply, *Urania, Thestylis ;* but the former
does not come on at first.

This habit well befits a virgin's life.
For since my dowry never can be paid,
Thus for thy sake I'll live and die a maid.
    Amyn. O, is it just, so fair a one as you
Should vow virginity? must the sacred womb
Of my Urania, fit to have brought forth
A fruitful race of gods, be ever barren,
Never expect Lucina? shall this beauty
Live but one age? how cursed our posterity,
That shall have no Uranias! can one tomb
Contain all goodness? Ceres, rather blast
The corn thou gav'st us : let the earth grow barren :
These trees and flowers wither eternally :
Let our ploughs toil in vain, and let there be
No more a harvest! every loss is small,
Yea, though the Phœnix-self should burn to ashes,
And ne'er revive again. But let there be
Some more Uranias——

Enter PILUMNUS.

    Pil.   It is necessity,
We must obey.   *[Aside.*
    Amyn.   But yet, Urania,
I hope we may sometimes come pray together,
'Tis not profane, and midst our sacred orisons
Change a chaste kiss or two ; or shall I too
Turn virgin with thee. But I fool myself ;
The gods intend to cross us, and in vain
We strive (Urania) to cross them again.

URANIA *kneeling before the* OMPHA.

    Ura. Great Ceres, for thy daughter Proserpine's
      sake
(Ravish'd by Pluto from Sicilian plains
To reign with him Queen of Elysian shades),

Accept the sacrifice of a virgin ; for
It is thy pleasure—thine, by whom the earth
And everything grows fruitful, to have me
Be ever barren : thy impossible dowry
Makes me despair to be Amyntas' bride,
Therefore that cold chaste snow, that never should
Have melted but betwixt his amorous arms,
I vow unto thy cloister (awful goddess !)
Almighty Ceres, is not this life holy   *Echo. Folly.*
Better than live in an unhappy love ?
                              Echo. Happy love.
Be judge, ye woods, and let Amyntas speak.
                          Echo. Amyntas speak.
   Pil. The goddess is well pleas'd ; she deigns to
      answer
By gracious echoes.   Go, Amyntas speak.
   Amyn. Why, will she answer me before Urania ?
No, 'twas the music of her angel's voice,
Whose heavenly accents with such charming notes
Ravish'd the goddess' ears, she could not choose
But bear a part in that harmonious song—
Yet if she will after such melody
Endure to hear the harsh Amyntas speak.
                          Echo. Amyntas speak.
When wilt thou think my torments are enou' ?
                                 Echo. Now.
Alas, how is it possible I should hope it ?
                               Echo. Hope it.
How shall I pay the dowry, that you ask me ?
                              Echo. Ask me.
I ask a dowry to be made a husband.
                             Echo. A husband.
Answer directly to what I said last.
                        Echo. What I said last.
A husband, Ceres ?   Why, is that the guess ?
                                 Echo. Yes.
" That which I have not, may not, cannot have,"

I have not, may not, cannot have a husband.
'Tis true I am a man, nor would I change
My sex to be the empress of the world.
Urania, take thy dowry; 'tis myself—
A husband; take it.

   Ura. 'Tis the richest dowry
That e'er my most ambitious prayers could beg !
But I will bring a portion, my Amyntas,
Shall equal it, if it can equall'd be :
" That which I have not, may not, cannot have,"
Shall be thy portion : 'tis a wife, Amyntas.

   Amyn. Should greater queens woo me in all their
     pride,
And in their laps bring me the wealth of worlds,
I should prefer this portion for the best:
Thanks, Ceres, that hath made us both be blest.

                          Echo. Be blest.

   Cla. Pilumnus, let us now grow young again,
And like two trees, robb'd of their leafy boughs
By winter, age, and Boreas' keener breath,
Sprout forth and bud again.   This spring of joy
Cuts forty years away from the grey sum.
Once more in triumph let us walk the village.

   Pil. But first I will entreat this company
To deign to take part in this public joy.

PILUMNUS EPILOGISES.

——o——

All loves are happy ; none with us there be,
Now sick of coyness or inconstancy.
The wealthy sums of kisses do amount
To greater scores than curious art can count.
Each eye is fix'd upon his mistress' face,
And every arm is lock'd in some embrace ;
Each cheek is dimpled; every lip doth smile.
Such happiness I wish this blessed isle,
This little world of lovers; and, lest you
Should think this bliss no real joys nor true,
Would every lady in this orb might see
Their loves as happy as we say they be !
And for you gentle youths, whose tender hearts
Are not shot-proof 'gainst love and Cupid's darts,
These are my prayers (I would those prayers were
    charms)
That each had here his mistress in his arms.
True lovers (for 'tis truth gives love delight),
To you our Author only means to write.
If he have pleas'd (as yet he doubtful stands)
For his applause clap lips instead of hands.
He begs nor bays, nor ivy—only this,
Seal his wish'd plaudit with an amorous kiss.
                         [Exeunt Cantantes.